Integrated Security of India

Integrated Security of India

(Maritime Domain)

Series Editor

Adv. S N Desai

GYAN

Published, 2019

Published by

Gyan Publishing House
5, Ansari Road
Daryaganj, New Delhi-110002
Phone: 011-47034999, 9811692060
www.gyanbooks.com
E-mail: books@gyanbooks.com

Printed at: G. Print Process, Delhi.

Cataloging in Publication Data—DK
Courtesy: D.K. Agencies (P) Ltd. <docinfo@dkagencies.com>

SAGAR Discourse 1.0 Conference (2017 : Velha Goa, India)
Integrated Security of India / series editor, Adv. SN Desai.
pages cm
Papers presented in SAGAR Discourse 1.0 Conference held at Goa in October 2017, organized by Forum for Integrated National Security (FINS).
ISBN 9788121214940

1. Sea-power—India—Congresses. 2. National security—India—Congresses. 3. India—Relations—Indian Ocean Region—Congresses. 4. Indian Ocean Region—Relations—India—Congresses. 5. Indian Ocean Region—Strategic aspects—Congresses. 6. Marine resources—Government policy—Indian Ocean Region—Congresses. I. Desai, S. N., editor. II. Forum for Integrated National Security (Mumbai, India), organizer. III. Title.

LCC VA643.S24 2017 | DDC 359.00954 23

Contents

Preface

At times it is not only interesting, but also important to start with seemingly grand and outlandish propositions. For the forum for Integrated National Security (FINS), this report is more than a celebration driven by three propositions, In the first, it is a movement to bring likeminded people together in search of security growth for all in the region (SAGAR) apropos to the imperatives of our Honourable Prime Minister.

SAGAR Discourse 1.0 was aimed at the wellbeing and sustainable development of the present and future generations. The contributors – partitioners and thinkers alike deliberated on this theme in this volume. This time the search was in the expansive and abysmally deep ocean terrain.

Second proposition was the very scope of the conference itself. FINS' attempt was to bring all the stakeholders together on a common platform. The effort was to evolve policy recommendations for the implementers. Some of the highest decision makers attended the conference and listened to the expert presenters on the subject.

The third proposition was extending the range of attendees to include scholars, practitioners and policy makers from interested parts of world. Twenty three countries were represented. Three very senior ministers and veteran defence personnel marked their presence among many other dignitaries in the discourse. Many tanks were represented. The resolutions have been forwarded for considerations.

We live in an independent world today. Developments in other parts of the world have profound impact on the evolution of policies in any corner. The issues ranging from economy to ecology and security to sustainability are therefore our common agenda. The problems and prospects need to be explored in multi-disciplinary way. In this context SAGAR Discourse will continue as an annual feature.

Climate change, terrorism, technological change, religious fundamentalism, environmental degradation, economic pressures, and so on have increased the complexity of global and national governance and international organisations beyond the traditional boundaries. They include the

(1) Maritime space
(2) Air space
(3) outer space
(4) cyber space and
(5) genomic space

The volume deals with the maritime aspects. SAGAR Discourse 2.0 will focus on outer space.

FINS invites you to join this scholary odyssey for the betterment of all in the world.

Adv. S.N. Desai

Introduction

It is now 14 years, since we started as a small group of people discussing national security issues and national interests at large. From that humble beginning till now, it is a crucial journey as a think tank known to strategic circles beyond our national borders for its diverse capabilities.

In the last 14 years, FINS deliberated broad issues through various interactions, seminars, conventions and closed-door talks such as National Security convention, India-US Nuclear Deal (NCR & Mumbai), Development and Security of Bharatiya Island & Coast Line (Goa), Maritime & Coastal Security (Ratnagiri & Mumbai), National Seminar on Defense Manufacturing (Hyderabad) etc.

Strategic Network for India's Security

While mooting various National Security dimensions, FINS took up critical policy initiatives Agreement, Maritime Security, Self Reliance in Defence Manufacturing. This was made possible due to in-depth understanding of various aspects of National Security. I am thankful to scholars for their support and expertise in this journey.The professional diversity of thinkers and scholars has strengthened FINS and we continue to build upon that strength. Furthermore, our geographical diversity is a grate value addition for finding solutions on problems ravelled into geopolitics.

Future

FINS is undertaking following initiatives to nurture young thinkers and leaders.

- **School of Strategic Studies, Goa**
- Strategic Research Center At Mumbai, Delhi, Hyderabad & North East

Above establishment shall serve to further the cause of national in the long term. With your best wishes and support, FINS shall continue pursuing its core principle of deliberating, analysing national security concerns to find solutions, advocate initiatives which shall bolster national security.

Acknowledgements

The editor wishes to thank Ministry of External Affairs, India for their active support to the Sagar Discourse 1.0 Conference. We are greatful to State of Goa and Partner Country – Norwegian Embassy – Innovation for their support and co-operation. We also thank each and every contributor, speaker and participants whose keen insights into maritime issues provoked lively and constructive discussions. Finally, we wish to thanks FINS Members for making this Conference a huge success.

List of Contributors

Shri. M.J. Akbar

Shri M.J. Akbar is the Minister of State for External Affairs, India

Shri. Manohar Parrikar

Mr. Manohar Parrikar is Chief Minister of Goa since 14 March 2017. He also served as Defence Minister of India from 2014 to 2017

Shri. Nitin Gadkari

Mr. Nitin Gadkari is Minister for Road Transport & highways, Shipping and Water Resources, River Development & Ganga Rejuvenation in the Government of India

Shri. Sunil Lanba

Admiral Sunil Lanba, PVSM, AVSM, ADC is the current and the 23rd Chief of the Naval Staff of the Indian Navy. He assumed the office on 31 May 2016. He is also the Chairman of the chiefs of staff committee (CoSC)

Shri. Nils Ragnar Kamsvag

Mr. Nils Ragnar Kamsvag was appointed Norwegian ambassador to India in 2015. Mr.Kamsvag has served as ambassador to Serbia, Mecedonia, and Montenegro (2010-15),as Representative to the Palestinian Authority and as Ambassador, Middle East and north Africa, in the Ministry of Foreign Affairs.

Shri. Arun Prakash

Admiral Arun Prakash PVSM, AVSM, VrC, VSM, ADC is retired Four – Star Admiral who served as the Chief of the Naval Staff of the Indian Navy and Chairman, Chiefs of Staff Committee from 31 July 2004 to 31 October 2006. He is one of India's most decorated naval officers.

Shri. Jan Frederik Danielsen

Jan Frederik Danielsen graduated from University in Bodo with a master degree in business and administration in 1993. He worked in Norwegian

Ministry of Fisheries and Coastal Affaires from 1993 to 2008 in various positions. From 2008 to 2011, he worked as an economic analyst in the General Directorate for Maritime Policy and Fisheries (DG MARE) in the EU Commission in Brussels.

Shri. Ole Henaes

Ole Henaes is Regional Director Asia in Innovation Norway.

Shri.Barry Faure

Ambassador Barry Faure has been serving as the Secretary of State for the Ministry of Foreign Affairs, since his appointment by the President of the Republic of Seychelles in January 2013. Ambassador Faure was previously serving as Secretary of State in the President's Office, a role he assumed on 17th June 2010.

ASM Abdul Baten

Rear Admiral ASM Abdul Baten, BSP, NDC, PSC joined Bangladesh Navy in 1977 and was commissioned in the Engineering Branch. Presently he is serving as Vice Chancellor of Bangabandhu Sheikh Mujibur Rahman Maritime University, Bangladesh, the first specialized university on maritime field in Bangladesh.

Shri. Krishna B. Kotak

Mr. Krishna B. Kotak, is the Chairman of J. M.Baxi group of companies, a business house synonymous with the logistics industry in India.

Shri. Jayanth Colombage

Admiral (Dr.) Jayanth Colombage is a former chief of Sri Lanka navy who retired after an active service of 37 years as a four- star Admiral. He is also a member of the Advisory council of the 'Institute of National Security Studies Sri Lanka'. He is a Guest Professor at Sichuan University in China.

Shri. Zakariyya Mansoor

Brigadier General Mansoor joined the ranks of Maldives National Defence Force (MNDF) in 1984 and was appointed as the Director General, National Counter Terrorism Centre at the Ministry of Defence and National Security on 21st April 2016. Prior to this posting he was the Commander of MNDF Central Area.

Shri. Bimal Patel

Dr. Bimal Patel is a member of Law Commission of India, National Security Advisory Board and Financial Sector Regulatory Appointments

Search Committee. He is Director Gujrat National Law University since 2008.

Shri. R.K.Dhowan

Admiral R.K.Dhowan, PVSM, AVSM, YSM (Retd.) has commanded three frontline warships of the Western fleet – the missile corvette Khukri, the guided missile destroyer Ranjit and the indigenous guided missile destroyer Delhi. He also had the proud privilege of commanding the Eastern Fleet as Flag Officer Commanding Eastern Fleet.

Shri. Oded Gur Lavie

Rear Admiral (ret.) Oded Gur Lavie is a Research Fellow in the Haifa Research Centre for Maritime Strategy. He is the Chairman of the Dolphin Association of veteran submariners.

Shri. P.S. Goyal

Dr. Goel was Chairman, Spacecraft System Advisory Board for IRS – 1, Project engineer AOCS for APPLE and Associate Project Director, INSAT –II. He was Head Control System Division, Group Director AOCS, Deputy Director Mission and Control Area, Associate Director of ISRO Satellite Centre (ISAC) and was Director ISAC from 1997 to 2005. Dr. Goel was awarded Padma Shree in 2010. Currently, Dr. Goel is Dr. Raja Ramanna Chair Professor at NIAS, Honorary Distinguished Professor at ISRO HQ and is chairing technology Research Board (TRB) at Ministry of Earth Sciences. Research Council, NGRI / CSIR, member RC NAL/CSIR and Chairman RAC NIOT/ MoES.

Shri. Ravi Kumar

Mr. Ravi Kumar is the International Joint Co-ordinator of Hindu Swayamsewak Sangh and Sewa International. He is advisor of Chennai Center for Global Studies and Vishwa Adhyayan Kendra, Mumbai.

Ms. Sayedeh Hajar Hejazi

The first Iranian Researcher (woman) at the field of Maritime international law and security lecture atshahrekord law school. She is Scholar & Research Intern at Human Rights at Sea London, UK.

Shri. M Ravindran

Prof. M Ravindran was born on June 1, 1944. He received his Bachelor's of engineering degree at PSG College of Technology, Coimbatore in 1966, Master's of Technology in 1969, and Ph.D. in 1978 in the area of turbo machines at the Indian Institute of Technology (IIT) Madras.

Prof. Ravindran superannuated from the post Director, NIOT, on 30th May 2004.

Shri. Helge Tryti

Helge Tryti is the Commercial Counsellor and the Director of the Mumbai and New Delhi office.

Dr. Satish Shetye

Dr. Satish Shetye received MSc (Physics) from Indian Institute of Technology (IIT) Bombay, and Ph.D (physical oceanography) from University of Washington, Seattle, USA. He worked at National Institute of Oceanography (its director in 2004-12). He was Vice – Chancellor, Goa University in 2012-16.

Shri. Sarosh Zaiwalla

Sarosh Zaiwalla founded Zaiwalla & Co. Sclicitors in April 1982 with offices in Chancery Lane, London. He oversees all the activities relating to the firm which over the years has exported millions of ponds' worth of legal services.

Shri. Ram Thapaliya

Dr. Ram Thapaliya is faculty member of the Master's Programme in Conflict, Peace and Development Studies and Crisis Management Study at Tribhuvan University, Nepal. Currenly he holds the position of chairman at the institute of crisis / Disasters Management (TU) Masters in crisis and Disasters Management study programme.

Shri.Vo Xuan Vinh

Dr. Vo Xuan Vinh is the Deputy Director, Institute for South-east Asian Studies (ISEAS), Vietnam Academy of Social Sciences (VASS), Hanoi. He has undertaken research on politics, security and international relations in Southeast Asia, democratization in Myanmar, India's Look/ Act East Policy, and politics of Thailand and Myanmar.

Shri. Priyadarshi Dash

Dr. Priyadarshi Dash works as a Research Associate at RIS, New Delhi. His research interests broadly cover topics in foreign exchange reserves, macroeconomics, international trade and finance.

Shri. Bhujang Rao

Dr. V. Bhujang Rao is presently ISRO Chair Professor, NIAS. He was formerly distinguished Scientist & Director General of DRDO for Nava;

Systems and Material. He is a fellow of societies such as fellow of National Academy of engg., AP Academy of Sciences Etc.

Shri. D B Shekatkar

Lt Gen (Dr.) D B Shekatkar, PVSM, AVSM, VSM (Retd.) is the President, Forum for Integrated National Security (FINS). He has served Indian Army for four decades. His Army tenure includes important assignments such as Deputy Director General of Military operations. Additional Director General of Military operations and Director General of Perspective (Strategic) planning. He also serves as member of "Expert Group" dealing with boundary disputes and was member of drafting team of Peace and tranquility. Agreement signed during Prime Minister ship of Shri Narsimha Rao.

Shri. Prabhakaran Paleri

Dr. Prabhakaran Paleri is Vice President, Forum for Integrated National Security (FINS). He retired as the Director General of the Indian Coast Guard in August 2006 and thereafter continued as a research scholar and academician in India and abroad.

Shri. V.M.Patil

Lt.Gen V.M. Patil AVSM,VSM (Retd.) is Vice – President, Forum for Integrated National Security (FINS). He was the first defence Advisor in Indian Embassies in Vietnam, Laos and Cambodia from 1980 to 84. He was Commander of United Nation's Military observers Group in Iraq as part of UN Peace keeping force for Iraq and Iran during 1988 to 1990. Post retirement from Army in 1996, he served as Vice – President in Mukund Steels for twelve years. He is Chairman of Balaji Institute of Modern Management and President of Akhil Bhartiya Purva Sianik Seva Parishad.

Shri. Seshadri Chari

Mr. Seshadri Chari is Secretary General, Forum for Integrated National Security (FINS). Former Editor of English weekly ORGANISER, Mr. Chari was also Consultant on Governance to UNDP, South Sudan (2006-2009) He is presently Member, Governing Council, RIS (research and Information System for Developing Countries) He is also the Jt. Director (International Affairs) Institute for National Security Studies (INSS) and research Director, Chronicle Society of India for Education & Academic Research (CSIEAR) an institution engaged in promoting educational activities and conducting significant research in areas like

Pluralism and Democracy, Conflict Resolution, Role of religion in fostering communal harmony etc. He is also Director, Forum for Strategic & Security Studies, engaged in publishing reports on subjects of strategic importance for India and the region and publishing AGNI journal. He is Consulting Editor of HW News Network. Some of the publication: A New Era in Indian Polity, "Jananayak' a Pictorial Biography of the then Prime Minister Shri. A B Vajpayee. "Nepal – Emerging Republic: - 2008, Economic Federalism – issues before Smaller States, need to revisit India's Nuclear Doctrine, Anagharika Dharmapala – Dhamma Dharma Confluence, Azad Balochistan.

Shri. Bal Desai

Adv. Bal Desai is Secretary General, Forum for Integrated National Security (FINS). He is one of the founding members of FINS and is Prominent Bombay High Court Lawyer.

Shri. Atul Kulkarni

Mr. Atul is Independent Consultant & Adviser (International Projects), Indian Ports Association. He is National convener for Maritime Security Study group of Forum for Integrated National Security (FINS). And Vice President, Yachting association of India. He is Maharashtra State Co-ordinator for PIOCCI (People of Indian origin Chamber of Commerce & Industry). He loves travelling and Likes Music.

Capt. Sanjay Parashar

He is founder and Managing of VR Maritime Services Pvt. Ltd. And is co –convener of Maritime Security vertical of Forum for Integrated National Security (FINS). He has been speaker at various global meets of shipping summit. He has expertise in Technical Management of Ships, Indian Coastal shipping and Green ship Recycling. He sailed as Master Mariner on MOL ships, worked ashore for 14 years including 2 years stints as Head of operations of World's leading shipping company.

Presidential Address

India, the largest democracy of the world has always been conscious of her role as a responsible nation, poised to accept leadership role with the belief and philosophy of 'Vasudhaiva Kutumbakam', the entire globe as a family especially for co-existence and prosperity in Trade & Commerce. India, as arising economic power has always professed the ideology of working towards progress for everybody in the Indo-Pacific region.

India, Steering hands, for harmonious relationship with her neighbours and other parts of the globe, is conscious of her role in growth & security for all in the region. Bulk of the international trade & commerce is carried out thru' Sea routes. So safe and efficient Sea lines of communication are imperatives and in the interest of all. A step in this direction, we have tried to get different stakeholders on board for this SAGAR DISCOURCE 1.0.

This seminar is our contribution towards this cause. Scholars and experts from different walks of life have contributed by way of articles to reflect upon. From the fields as diverse as Ecology to economy, safety and security to Governance and theoretical construct, we have tried to include select erudite articles. We are thankful to the contributors.

Our patrons have helped us generously with advertisements. We are immensely greatful to them. Messages from dignitaries have graced this volume.

I am sure, this vast bandwidth of knowledge resonates our belief in mutual co-operation towards growth and security as destination.

This volume along with the discourse has queued up discussions on various dimensions of this co-operation. FINS soon wishes to release a white paper on "Principle of Coherence, Co-existence, growth & peace for all, in the Indo-Pacific region". This Journey is on, stay connected.

Warm Regards,

Lt. Gen. Dr. D.B. Shekatkar,

PVSM, AVSM, VSM (Retd.)

President- FINS

Key note Address

SHRI M. J. AKBAR: Hon. Chief Minister, eminent officers on the dais, this gathering of experts, stalwarts, and most important the true dignitaries of this evening, the children who lit their lamps and when I say the true dignitaries I do not mean this as an only affectation or as a sentimental track, if you are not discussing their future, then we are discussing nothing at all. Already the speakers before have given you the glimpse on more of the complexities of the issues that they face. Chief Minister was right, security itself of the oceans has many dimensions, one of the dimensions which I hope we will be able to protect given what I am seeing in the hall is saving the ocean from plastic for example security of oceans itself has many dimensions one of the dimension is saving ocean from plastic. It's an extremely if you see parts of the ocean, in parts of the spaces in shorelines, it's terrifying to see what is happening. Phrases and words have been used already which I hope that we will see the dimensions, the dimensions of, one way familiar reference has been made to a deep seated, belief of our Indian philosophy which is actually the whole world is affected, which actually sounds much better than it is. Alas, families are not free from conflict. See, first family according to the 'Bible' in the words 'Genesis', till King David. 'Mahabharata' is a family conflict, in 'Islam' the Shia's conflict is a family conflict, so family itself in this aue,us1 speech, an image or an metaphor for a larger growth is not complete without its consistencies or without problems which is why we are meeting here. When we use the word 'security', we have to understand the collateral security for whom, there was an age not too long ago when the only definition of security or security for needs or for ruling class between them, by them, for them. When majority of the people were bystanders, they accepted the victory and they got on life for more often or alas, got on with the consequences of war which is death. The first consequence of war is death; the second consequence of war is refugees. This world has changed extremely significantly, today security no longer needs a security of the needs, today security means security of the people of the masses and if you do not get the dimension, we will not be either addressing the problem or indeed knowing besides what to do. We are here in Goa, I just use a few lines and facts in order to try and build the pattern, Goa is also the first colony. Jeoga was actually the first Portuguese colony on top of Africa, the northern Antarctica of Africa and the Asians face and Goa was chosen as a first colony, not because of its importance, in the land system or in the land geographies of the world. It is a selected by the Portuguese and I think strictly very rightly so because of its importance as a hub of maritime country. So we have to take another look at many things, when you look at the map of India, they were almost automatically trapped in the land map of India, asking anyone of any age and the map of India comes like this triangle which is a land mass of our country but if you are discussing strategically and if you are discussing security you have to look at something much more that the land map of India and in fact I would suggest that the Land Map of India is far more secure than the Sea Map of 1ndia. Land Map of India in the north, large part of the north, if you remember whatever problems you might have that they remain, that is very important, but the sea map of India, in fact is indicate bigger than the land map of India. The Land map of India will illdicatc the signs of India, the sea map of India and India will indicate the reach of India and the rich of India is from Gulf right upto Malacca straits. I hope it doesn't come as a shock to you if you know that the Andaman's are less than the 100 kms and you will appreciate and that is the problem and this is the stage that they have to manage so when we try to understand which look familiar we have to begin today another look at the strategic dictionary and remember one thing that all through recorded and unrecorded, the earliest records of history through poetry through Sagar, through alien, through Mahabharata, etc., these are also days records and this records have actually remained imperishable in the memory of man precisely because they had the roots and something very significant and when we get to understand what they had the roots and something very significant to understand one thing that the meaning of peace, meaning of shanti, does not change, ever since the first consequence of the role in the human being. What changes continuously is the meaning of war. War is a thing that begins to define and redefine itself and each time it is challenged literally before every two or three generations. The challenge every two or three generations is to understand the latest manifestations of the problems or the evil of conflict and the evil of war and when we say that there will be a scene of conflict in perhaps with evil dimensions at this moment and this is what we have to look for and I don't know how much consciousness and that the last great terrorist attack in our country in Mumbai was the sear attack and yet I have not fully actually dipped it into consciousness, what implications or what consequences of that whole episode for where and are and will be. I actually began my preparations for this conference by seeing the whole list of statistics and facts including things like we have 7500 kms of the sea border and we have founded divers, then I picked it and I said everybody is sitting in this room and so I picked a little move on things and failures where we can incite imaginations and little bit into not by just thinking, but by great things. So, let me begin our attempt to understand our challenge today where I am asking a simple question. When did the 20th century begin? It's a very important question, because you cannot understand the 21st century unless you understand the answer to this question. A commonly understood by historians, is the 20th century which begins with the first world war, 1914 to 1919 and I suggest to you that this is true, but it is not true because of 1914, it is true because of 1919. Every birth has a back story, every birth has a pregnancy narrative, every birth has a room narrative where things can happen and these are consequences but the emergence of something new and the consequences thereof is what happened after World War. We live in the 100 years preceeding in the World War I through a various set of sequences and consequences ending up in this eclipse World War I. Something unprecedented happened, unprecedented, in the historical terms. Every single empire in the world which are controlled the geopolitics of the last political years have collapsed. You take a road map wherever east, west, centre, you know Japanese didn't have too much empire, but they too have one, Japanese, Chinese, Indian, Persian, Ottoman, etc., you can go upto the Spain, you can go upto Portuguese, you can go upto everywhere, every single empire for the last 50 years began to collapse and every world war collapsed also, what happens when there is a lapse, something has to fill the vacuum. The importance of 1919 is that the first time humanity, actually began to create political spaces not around the dynasty, you people must be still clinging on to dynasty with a democracy, but around the dynasty, but will be, otherwise you will have cheers of problems of the people will keep straining all the time, right now we are seeing that sometimes in all the time, right now we are seeing that in Spain. However as a Principal, this was truly, traumatically unprecedented. The political space would now be decided by demography and not by princes, kings and their various options and therefore this vacuum began to be filled with the idea of the nation State and having the idea of the nation State are in facts world sovereign and therefore we began to create a nation State, a sovereign State and this sovereign State means that today in century means that there are no big countries and there are no small countries. Every moment is a sovereign nation. Every country is a sovereign country. What we do have to recognize sovereignty is a different capacity but everyone doesn't have to say capacity, but these capacities now have to be inched into or carried back into the rights and indeed the obligations of sovereignty and this is one of integrity the problems is going to be the second boundaries, boundaries previously and actually even upto the second world war, boundaries where the extension of the military capability of rulings in it and typically so, conquest was not illegal, in fact conquest first began marginally, I am saying marginally because soon after the war, an act created by the US Government which nobody remembers, but it is all illegal, this was replaced by boundaries formed, fences formed round demography, spaces built upon continuous nationalisms or nationalities whatever we would like to say, but why I am saying 1919 is important because in the same year at the end of the world began to challenge with the hope that far of the State of the world 19l9 saw the rise of the challenge before 1919 everybody are making the reference of India, everybody thought, and in the quietists Indians thought, that the British empire would last for 400 years and then one man in the dhoti conduct and could not last for 40 years, but why they could not last for 40 years, personalities are very important in history we know that, but personalities by themselves come and go, personalities have to be backed by a tremendously powerful idea. Commitment, an idea that becomes an ideology and the miracle of Gandhi was not in my view that he made the first mass movement, the democratic mass movement of the people, the miracle of Gandhi lay in the time that he used an Indian idea in order to dischallenge and then destroy your colonial before that one day people said how could you defeat, even the Dutch in Indonesia or the Portuguese in Goa, I am delighted to say that Norway will be the only country which didn't interfere in this affair. Thank you. But it was the Indian idea called Satyagraha and Stayagraha is only non-violence, it is a power of truth and amazingly somebody who articulated something as philosophical not conventionally understandable to the mind. To digest a little, I always wondered why Gandhiji made the Salt march, such an important fact of the last portion, salt march because both in 1919 and in 1930 he was challenging the idea of loyalty. You know slavery comes from the same route as salt. Salary and salt and you were purchased by salary, in our language also means 'namak khaya' so there are deep resistances which are and achieved in 1919 he said in order to defeat to stop serving them, it happens suddenly. The point here is again that India was created not by the strength of an alternative army, not by geliler movement, not by military force and although India had its army. It was defeated by a mass movement inspired by a mass reality and motivated by the people and therefore India desperately became the first genuinely People s Republic movement and this too is important right ? The meaning of these changes actually begins to define the priorities as well as the compassionate opportunities of the State. So, you see the right of our nation State in the name of purple, basically a people's national or around the idea in India or rather not to be loyal to India or not to recast or not to a local tendency, this movement was known as against the 'Princes of India' right? And that yon will have to actually represent the power of people. The consequences of the rise of the nation's State finds immediately in its own lifetime a very interesting parallel there that somebody tries to create a nation State in the name of Islam and exactly in order to deflect the unity of the people, obviously this is found extremely useful by our colonial masters and it's a story by itself and by our own goodwill we went into it but what I will do it that is after the creation of the first Islamic State in the modern era, 70 years we can come to one conclusion that stability is the principle factor of the people's revolution, peaceful revolution and instability is the principle characteristic of a State, driven in the name of a particular faith and therefore what we have seen as a same time frame, the rise what I call a jelly state. What is a jelly state? Jelly is something that will never be stable. On the other hand, unlike butter it will not melt and disappear either, if it is melted and disappeared may be the problem would go, but it will not go. lt will remain and jelly will become more and more toxic, und when you add nuclear weapons to it then the toxicity becomes truly, potentially poisonous and the real conflict that we are facing today now, is the conflict between those who believed as faith, equality as principle, a constitutional principle and I have to say and I think almost everyone here in this room would belong to that irrespective or whatever system you may have and those who believe in faith supremacy, in faith, supremacy has the ruling aspect of the constitutional India and therefore others must be second class. You have seen this in Iraq, you have seen this everywhere, you have seen this in the treatment of the Christians there, how they are treating the Christians there. Moving fast forward, the 21st century and this I think you should be common everywhere, in the 21st century, the action was more in 9/ 11 and you can already with this attack and you can see that the nature of conflict has shifted very sharply. I will not dwell too much on what I would call the back stories or whom narrative, obviously you can link it back to Afghanistan in 1979 and so on, so forth but by the coming of age of terrorism as principle element or the principle threat to security you can see that 9/11 already represent a totally new kind of warfare. What is the warfare? Warfare is not based on using battle as a means to defeat the enemy. 9/11 may be defeat the enemy. 100 terrorist attacks everywhere have not defeated people. What it aims at and it is therefore much more complex thing what it aim is not simply defeat right now. What it aims at is destabilization. That if I can achieve destabilization then the purpose of that military assault is achieved and how do I achieve that destabilization not simply by the horror of defect itself but by living and sealing every mind with fear and fear becomes the most important weapon in this. Now, is it true, therefore that terrorism or terrorist are only seeking chaos for the sake of chaos. We have seen phases. I think in 1960 those of us who are unfortunate old enough to remember that would include the Chief Minister, I think, remember the 1960's, as an age when terrorism was used as chaos for the sake of chaos. It has no larger objective and therefore it could contain sort, managed took its share or took its price but eventually we got on. Europe was actually the center of that but it is not Europe alone. I studied in college 1967-70 Presidency College, Calcutta where in canteen everyday occurrence. Therefore canteen total leadership of Maoist movement, Naxalite movement was sitting in my canteen. Bengal had to go through a very difficult time but it's not Chaos. There are very serious political objectives. Number one, the contemporary terrorist our Prime Minister called them "existential threat" because they represent threat to two of the basic fundamental realities of the modern year. One, we all know that the stability even such as it is but the stability of the modern era has been built around the nation state and critical building block. You remove the nation state rights and wrongs what happens seventy years you can all look into but larger fact remains that nation states is now being directly and vitally accepted as the enterprise essentially of the stability. They challenge it because they do not believe in nations. They believe in religion based space and therefore Islamic space or some other space, in essence you really going back which supersedes the national reality and therefore you are really going back to the holy roman emperor empire in that sense. You really going back to ideas that lost their validity in the course of history, long while ago but have resurrected very sharply but the more important thing for me is that basically also they are challenging pluralism. They are challenging the harmony that nation, societies have created over history of long and many multiple experiences and come to the conclusion that citizen and human being can live as equal with their individual freedom and rights, being interfered with as human being without demanding individual or paranoid supremacy. This happen, this goes and this has consequences. All of you who come from Europe know it has electoral consequences and indeed those consequences are part of the objective but interesting the 21st century precisely because it is century which is controlled by popular will was politic is largely controlled by popular vision. The 21st century is also becoming the century in which they demand the freedom not only political freedom but freedom of thought, freedom of action, freedom of voice, freedom from hunger, freedom of aspirations, freedom to hope, to believe indeed if television has to be believed than freedom not only to talk sense but freedom to talk nonsense. These are part of this whole culture of freedom which are now increasingly becoming a dominant, important and inviolable reality because this is the century which belong not only to ruling elite, not to dynast but to the people and along with that freedom comes the economic aspirations. So this is the century which is going to demand economic aspirations as prevalent, central reality of evolution in the immediate future and those countries which do not enter the prosperity map of the world will find themselves in terrible state. So we have therefore the challenges as I think he briefly hinted at previously, you know man according to old Charles Darwin, the old man of the long beard according to him we actually emerged out of the sea. I don 't know if he is right or wrong but let us see assume for the purpose of this evening that he was right that we essentially some past age were sea creatures but we became land creature and then we become totally land centered. We look at everything in terms of land. Our industry is land based. Our agriculture is land based here. Broadly, we are 80-90% l and. Despite the fact that probably 60% of inside us is also water. Despite that the moon affects us because of the water inside but the land is getting exhausted. Even the water on land is getting visibly exhausted. It is happening in front of us. So, when land gets exhausted, when green has become brown, the option the mankind will have is to look at the blue and therefore the conflict area when the challenge for prosperity comes we will become more and more sea centered and I offer you the thought that the challenge of this century will be the S4 challenge, seas, skies, space and security. This is the four 'S' and the answer to this 4S problem is in S5 which is the idea of SAGAR, which is that you can actually use these realities to create harmony rather than conflicts but for that you need a mindset and afford. Therefore as I keep saying there is need for doctrine. Why do we need doctrine? Because all the five 'S' including the solution have one thing which is you may want seriously think about over this conference all these spaces, all these areas don't have boundaries. Sea doesn't have boundaries. Skies do not have boundaries. Cyber space does not have boundaries. Security no longer has boundary and with great difficulty we manage to find stability with help of boundaries. Now we will have to go through the most difficult task of finding stability and finding rational answers to existence in area without boundaries and world need to find as quickly as possible doctrine that will actually meet this overwhelming challenge, the experience of UNCLOS and similarly this has arose, doesn't necessarily augur well but if it is going to be something for survival then we simply have to get on and you know get going in the process and I am sure with so much wisdom assembled in this hall this will be an important contribution to the search for the future. I began by saying that if this conference is not about this smallest kid the one who actually lit two candles instead of one which also speaks of her aspirations if this conference is not about her and her future and what the world she will see 60 years later than this conference is really about nothing important but I am sure it will be for her. Thank you all for being here. Thank you from our Ministry. Thank you from our country. Thank you from Goa's prospective. He is already looking at multiple conferences that add into the future.

Thank you all for being here and thank you very much Norway for being a partner. Thank you.

Speeches

MR. MANOHAR PARRIKAR: Mr. M.J. Akbar and Lt. Gen. (Dr.) D.B. Shekatkar, Dr. Prabhakaran. Mr. Bal Desai and all of you who are here, who have especially come to Goa for Sagar Discourse 1.0. I think Goa is always a place where you can do both the things, you can work and you can enjoy or rather you can enjoy the work, as I do. I was working in Delhi also, I did not enjoy the work with the polluted atmosphere and with overall atmosphere, Goa is much better. I think you will enjoy it, so welcome to this nice State. It is good that FINS has selected Goa as a permanent place. So it will give some sort of satisfaction to Bal Desai who is the organizer. As we say that the Indian Philosophy probably came out of Sagar Manthan. So you can be very sure that by the end of this your manthan or the churning of the ocean will result into some outcome which will be beneficial but I can give you one good news that Goa Government can partner with FINS for this dialogue if it is an annual event in Goa. I think we can do that. So any way whatever support you require, I will give from my side, right from this Discourse itself. I will not talk about the agendas before you, I will just mention that ocean or sagar as we call it, it is as important aspect of humanity and when we talk about security in the ocean, normally everyone thinks that security means military security, for me when I was thinking about strategies on this, I realized that ocean has more problems than we think, particularly in the Indian Ocean and normally in the east side of Indian Ocean is most of the time disturbed Malacca Strait, China Sea, East China Sea and those conflict zones that are normally seen but more than 60% of the trade of the India fasces various threat which are constantly coming us world passes through Indian Ocean and equally important is the western coast if India opposite which there are various threats which are coming up and subsiding also. While it is a military, security aspect will be definitely taken into consideration and I think we should also look into the aspects of threat to the coastal cites due to the rise in the ocean level or Island states. There are few Island states which may not exist on the map. If the current climate change continues with the same rate, where the ocean is rising quite rapidly, so this is going to threaten the coast of the big countries as well as also threaten the islands itself. So this is one threat which probably we may not be able to directly come out with solution but we can defiantly push for a better climatic solutions across the room. There are other reasons with depleting coastal fish catch, fishing itself, resources searching food in the ocean will also be much more complex. There are threats from pirates. The trade which goes from the Indian Ocean as of now, it is quite safe because we have managed to get most of the Somalians and other pirates under control. There are no incidences which are recently reported but you cannot totally ignore the threat. The most important aspect that ocean can also become big economic boost in Asia. So it is important that strategies about oceans need to be properly evolved in co-relation with many other countries who have common interest in the ocean and the trade. This needs to be evolved over a period of time. There are times where few countries have like how Dr. Shekatkar mentioned thought about their sphere of influence, I think the world has indirectly proved if world stays together the various legal provisions also can be enforced or even the countries which are aggressive can be told that your economy also can be infected. In fact in my last visit Shangri – La city, I had mentioned the aspects very clearly that threatening an area can actually be a boomerang which can economically threaten the person who is trying to raise the flag. So with this will only say that next two days discussions will come out with good solution on the issue and let Sagar Discourse come out with a mythological 'sagar manthan' come out with a solution and finale come out with amrut, the best of the lot. Thank you very much.

SHRI NITIN GADKARI: All dignitaries on the dais, especially from the 22 countries the delegates who are here, first from the side of the Indian Government I welcome you all for this Conference. This is a very important situation for India because it has got a huge potential for development. The growth in this industry is creating more employment potential and growth rate for the country. The Indian Ocean covers at least one fifth of the world's total ocean area. It is really a huge potential, an area of 56 million 5 lakhs 68 thousand sq.kms. and a coast line of 66 thousand 526 kms. It provides trade routes when it connect east Africa and South Asia and Europe in the West. The Indian Ocean marks several types of global economy importance. The Indian Ocean itself is rich with energy reserves and more than 50 percent of the world's petroleum is produced in the Indian Ocean. About 18 percent of the oil and trade which originates in the Indian Ocean is extra ordinary in nature. The Ocean and sea surroundings represent the significant challenge and at the same time also represent development of its territories. Significant challenges are also very important because in the world we are all facing the problem of terrorism, terrorist organizations and one of the important thing is that the security of all the countries is very important. It is a million dollar question all over the world. As far as our Government is concerned, the new Government under the Prime Minister Narendra Modiji, we are giving highest priority for development. The Oceans Seas and waterways have potential to develop means for eco living in the region. Already we have taken decision in the Parliament, we have already passed a Bill by which we have already converted 111 rivers into waterways. These 20,000 kms of river length can be used for water transport. We have already started to work in Brahmaputra and just one month before we have started working on Godavari in Tamil Nadu. The most important things we are making 40 river coasts and 1680 kms of this we are making three major docks and already we have a system like air traffic control we have a river traffic control system which has already arrived. This will be the Game changer. Here the dignitaries present from Bangladesh from Varanasi or from Sagarganj it is lengthy mode of transport, the national highway, the waterways and the railway at the same place. From Saidarsh we can now take any material up to Myanmar as we take to Bangladesh. We have lot of plans, we have already signed agreement with Bangladesh Government on Brahmaputra and development like Ports area. While we can take all material from Saidarsh to the Ports in Bangaldesh which can easily be distributed to the North east and we can save the logistic cost. So that can be a good opportunity for business. At the same time we have started working in Brahmaputra, we are building 16 river Ports, we have 9 roads services and 8 rail services. In Brahmaputra we have ro- ro services and 9 ferry services which is very much useful for the public transport. At the same time we have started working in Barak so from Saidarsh we can connect up to river Manipur from Barak river also we can go to that area. So this is a Game changer. Regarding this availability of these 20,000 kms of river length it is a huge potential for the country. That is the reason the Ocean economy is very important. The ocean Economy or the Blue Economy is most important. As far as Indian law is concerned up to 12 nautical miles it is the right of the State to give the permission for the fishing. After 123 nautical miles it is the right of the Centre to permit. Presently, our fishermen are not in a position to go beyond 12 nautical miles. Now we have a problem, so we are now making a policy, just few days before I took this issue with the Prime Minister and he is ready to call a meeting and our idea is that this subject is having many Ministries, Fishing Ministry, agriculture Ministry, Sagarmala, so our plan is to give trawlers with development of good technology for the trawlers and we can only give it to the fishermen not for the traders or Industry persons. The idea is to give them 15 to 20 lakhs as subsidy, they will get loan, one crore of loan and only 10 to 15 lakhs goes for the trawler fishermen. They can get it, they can start it in partnership form and they will find earning. India got huge potential and this sophisticated trawlers which we have to develop in a way that we have to save the environment and at the same time going in deep sea our fish production will be increased by three to four times. There will be fish packaging and processing industries, we have 200 minor and private Ports and 12 major ports and now we are planning of making 6 major Ports. So I feel that there is huge potential available in the Blue economy also. The most coastal and highland countries are keen to indicate the idea of Ocean economy in the development policy. Lots of people from Norway and from the different parts of the world now they are interacting with the Korean companies, Russian companies for business. Unfortunately for last 60 years, the previous Governments, I don't know what was the reason but there was no priority for development in this field. I feel that this is the potential field and our Government want to use it for public transport, cattle carrier, hovercraft, harbour, cruise tourism huge potential is there. Lately in Mumbai we received 80 cruises and within five year in Mumbai we are expecting 950 cruises. There is huge potential available in cruise tourism internally and externally. Now the idea is taking tourist for Mumbai to Andaman Nicobar to Maldives. Huge potential is available. Goa is a destination where everyday 89 flights are coming to Goa. Now we are planning for a new International airport. So, by using this cruise in India and out of India, there will be a huge potential available for tourism. Even we can start transport from Mumbai to Goa, Mumbai to Cochin, Mumbai to Chennai, Mumbai to Srilanka, Mumbai to Bangladesh and there is lot of opportunities now we are making next to seven cruise terminal. In Mumbai we have already started a Cruise terminal, where the cost is 700 crores. So, I feel that this is the field there is huge potential available. Yesterday there was a meeting in my Office in Delhi, with Planning Commission Member Dr Saraswat and all players who are manufacturing the hinges particularly in this field from Mesilla and all and Mr. Kotak you should give priority for that, so that we should use Methenol as a fuel. Methanol is available for Rs.22/- per litre and it is a comparatively clean fuel, import substantive, cost effective and pollution free. In Sweden, a lot of companies were with me yesterday. The technology which they can make, they can supply the kit by which we can change our diesel engineering to methanol and we are getting methanol from coal and now we are Coal surplus. Even in India today the fertilizer companies are manufacturing methanol. Mumbai, the Deepak fertilizer, RCA, the Gujarat petroleum all got capacity of methanol and from methanol we can make DME and you can add DME the cost is very less in LPG by which we can reduce the 20% cost of the asset. So, here the coal is available now, the Volvo has got already the ten tyre bus motor engine is of 100% methanol. So I am trying to get an estimate for me to start the Volvo buses by using methanol. So my suggestion is because this is cost effective 22 rupees per litre. It is a huge thing and in Sweden one of the companies Stena, they are using their Cruise ship of 100 percent Methanol. When I was in Gautamgarh, they had hosted a dinner for me. I was seeing a Ship and the person with me was telling me that boat is on 100 percent Methanol. So my suggestion is that this can be looked by all of us to go for. The Ocean Development has to be sustainable and economical and lucrative. Innovation technology is knowledge and innovation of knowledge is the future of the country and this is the field where all the people from 22 countries having a lot of new innovation, new technology, cost effective technology and position to do it is very important. Our private people and the Government neglect this field and this is a very important field for our economy. The innovation, investment and infrastructure can help in an equitable benefit. Our Prime Minister Narendra Modiji has a strong aim of making Oceans, seas and river ways prospective to the people. The Oceans and seas can provide in achieving our goals. The Global manufacturing has undergone a major change and trade has also increased. The logistics cost plays an important role in determining the quality. The logistic cost in India is 18 percent and China it is 8 percent and in the European countries it is 12 percent. In support, I am the Minister it is not appropriate for me to say but we want to discourage the road traffic because the way our roads are there, 22 percent roadways every three years or may be one year that cost 80,000 crore to the country creating huge pollution. So we need public transport on electricity, we need water transport, our priority is to give water transport and public transport on electricity. The pollution we are facing is too much. We are breaking the roads. When I took charge it was 96 ooo kms NH, in the country we have 52 lakhs kms of road length out of which is only 2 percent as NH and 40 percent of the traffic of the country is on this 2 percent of the road. So now we have decided to make it 2 lakhs kms then 18 percent of the traffic of the country will be on NH. We are making it as an exercise, where the traffic is more than 10,000 we will make four lane roads, if it is more than 20,000 we will make six lane roads. We are making 12 Express Highways. On this Mumbai to Goa highway we are spending 18,000 crores. We are making four lane cement concrete roads, we have started Express highways. It is a big thing which is going to reduce 50 percent of pollution and traffic jam at places.

So water transport can be a good option for that. Now our Ports capacity has increased. We have three flag ship Organizations, Shipping Corporation of India, Dredging Corporation of India & Cochin Shipyard. Yesterday they received an order of 6000 crores from Bhutan and when I was in the Capital of ... it was 1650 crores Bhutan on that day I was in the Stock Exchange in Mumbai the index was reduced by 300 points and on that days when I want within half an hour of 1650 crores we received 1 lakhs 26 crores. 76 times more. So money is not the problem. The problem is we need the competitive people in the Government and in the private sector who can take the advantage of the situation. I always say that there are some people who can work problems into opportunities and there are some people who can work opportunities into a problem. I feel that there are some problems, that the capability of the sector, the capability of the people and the politicians and the bureaucracy if all of us work together it will be a great development of the country.

Globally manufacturing value addition is the highest around Ports, approximately 18 percent of India's population lives in the 17 coastal regions. Manufacturing in the hinterlands also depends on the Ports and waterways. There is a need to create more opportunities for our people to improve their living standards. An ambitious programme of Ports development is initiated by Sagarmala. It would be appropriate for somebody from our Department to present what is Sagarmala. Sagarmala is a huge and very big project, the first type in India. The holistic development of the maritime sector has been planned under the Sagarmala programme. Reduction in logistics cost and ease of doing business is the primary focus to boost our domestic trade. This programme is aimed to develop Ports, the 7500 kms of coastline of 111 waterways and its strategic locations of international maritime. A National Prospective Plan, (NPP) has been developed as a part of this programme. More than 100 projects are identified in the areas of Port modernisation mechanization and development of Ports. For Port-road connectivity, rail connectivity and all, today it is a great pleasure for me, out of 4 lakh crores projects of more than 1 lakhs 60 thousand already we have started. Now we have port-road connectivity cargo also. We don't have money we are taking 50 thousand crores dollar loan with two percent interest. The Railway Corporation Office in Mumbai, I am expecting the work of railways of one lakh crores. Then Ports more connectivity, we are making lot of roads in it. These projects are expected to mobilize more than 15 to 16 billion U.S. dollars infrastructure investment. More than 110 billion US dollars is invested in this. Implementation of the projects in Sagarmala will enable creation of 10 million new jobs. We are making Special Economic Zone in Mumbai, where we are creating employment potential for one lakh people.

There are Economic Zones, there are Coastal Zones where this employment potential is there in addition to this, 300 thousand construction jobs will also be created in the development of Infrastructure projects. We intend to increase the Indian Port capacity from 15 hundred MMTPA from 2015 to more than 33 thousand MNTPA in 2022. This will include 100 MNTPA by efficiency improvement which is already going on. Now everywhere we have decided to make parallel the International Port and our Port so that we can understand what we need. Today, capacity augmentation of the existing Ports is going on. Now development of six more Ports including the tranship hub in Kerala. In port connectivity more than 80 connectivity projects have been identified. Now LNG is very important. We are making more transport on LNG because for transport it is very important by which we can reduce the fuel cost. 14 Coastal Economic Zones, CEZs including 27 Port based Coastal Industrial Clusters have been proposed. 41 are Industrial Clusters of Energy, 7 in Steel sector, 13 in Manufacturing sector, these sectors are expected to boost India's merchandise exports by US dollars 110 million in the next decade. By our Sagarmala objective of coastal community development, fishermen and other communities are also been identified. We have also set up a Company, India Port Global Limited for Port Development outside the country. We are developing Chabahar Port, Mr Gupta is here and now that Chabahar Port is a new gate way, the distance between Mumbai to Delhi, the distance between Kerala to Chabahar is less than Mumbai to Delhi. From Chabahar you can go direct up to Afghanistan you don't have to go to Pakistan. So it is a new Gate way opened and gas is available in Iran so huge opportunities are there. So this is an important thing now that we are concentrating on the development of Ports.

As a part of Sagarmala's objective of Coastal development skill and other developmental projects are also been identified. The company which is a global company. Global Limited this company is doing Port Operation at the Jalan Port, we had discussions with Bangladesh also and Srilanka also. We have an Agreement signed with Bangladesh. We are constructing 250 crore buildings in Bangladesh. So by going by this route the Water ways it will really be a game changer. While the importance of shipping and global trade is well recognized, we have a huge potential to use the Oceans and seas for development purposes. I feel this is an important field. For the last three years I am discussing it, 15 days before I had a discussion with a Shipping Company, I also had discussions with some Korean companies saying you come to India. Cochin Shipyard is developing their dry dock. I said you go for Gujarat. You go from the east part of the country. They are starting manufacturing in Kolkata that Korean company. So I feel that these are the opportunities that are available and in Indian scenario a huge potential is available as far as this business is concerned and the people from abroad you are welcomed to start these cost lucrative technologies mini revolutions and we are prepared for that. At the same time I am confident that in tourist tourism there is a huge potential. Now our Transport Ministry we are planning for introduction of scrapping of vehicles we want to work on 15 years, we want to have an Automobile Zone and all this automobile Bangar which we use by recycling it can reduce the cost of spare parts for new cars and maybe we can hope for automobile manufacture. It is going to have a turnover of 4 lakhs 50 thousand crores. By making this scrapping policy which is already not in our project but by this we will develop an Economic cluster in different parts of the Ports which is going to create a new automobile hub. The manufacturing of automobile in India will be the cheapest. So a huge potential is available. I feel that it is a great opportunity for both our Indian people and the people from abroad, Sagarmala is our flagship programme, you are welcomed in all this, all types of new projects, new technologies, we expect no corruption, Zero tolerance against corruption, fast track decision making process and I know that there is red tapeism in the government that I will try to get rid from it. So I invite all of you to invest in India to take whatever the opportunities, support us and give us your valuable good suggestions with technologies and investment. I am giving thanks to the Organization FINS that has organized this, you are welcomed to all the opportunities in India and again I give my best wishes to all of you. This is a great opportunity for all of you to invest in India. From my side, the Government side and my Department side I am always transparent and open for good suggestions, anything if you have don't hesitate come directly to me either convince me or get convinced by me, we will take the decisions and we will go ahead. Thank you very much.

ADMIRAL SUNIL LANBA: Admiral Arun Prakash, Admiral R.K. Dhowan, formal Chief Naval Staff, General Shekatkar, President FINS, General Patil, Vice President of FINS, Shri Chari, Secretary General, distinguish delegates, participants of the inaugural session of SAGAR Discourse, a very good evening to all of you. It is indeed an honour to interact with this august gathering of scholars and policy makers at the valedictory session of SAGAR Discourse. At the outset I like to thank Forum for integrated national security for inviting me to deliver the valedictory address today. My compliment to the Ministry of External Affairs for having chosen me and associated to this event that promote meaningful meeting of minds on contemporary issue. FINS has shown commendable commitment in taking forward Government's vision of SAGAR by selecting a very apt subject for the maiden edition of SAGAR Discourse. The central team of integrated Ocean Governance is reflected on growing realization that a rule based order is essential for judicious management of the oceanic commerce. I am confident that the stated aim of this seminar that is examining the various policy facets of ocean governance has been adequately addressed. Personally I wish I could have spent last two days here observing the intellectual discourse of this very complimentary subject in enchanting time of Goa. Nevertheless now that I have opportunity to spend some time amongst this august gathering let me share my view on subject of Integrated Ocean Governance. Ladies and gentlemen, it is widely acknowledged that the fortune of a nation is determined to a great extent by its geography. For a maritime nation like ours we can only be grateful for our good fortune. The peninsula landmass jutting out into the vastest of the Indian Ocean offers us tremendous opportunity to harness the sea to our advantage. I don't need to dwell into the statistic related to our geographical dividend to this audience. Our long coastline, numerous islands, ports, proximity to important shipping lane and abundant ocean resources certainly provide us ample avenue of resources and trade. Equally important is the fact that the monsoon and climatic condition so critical to our agrarian art land are also influenced by our surrounding ocean. Suffice to say that sea stand to be the strongest enabler in our pursue of holistic national development. Speaking in a more commercially inclined outlook 11% of India's own hydrocarbon needs are being feed from our domestic offshore fields, while the balance is coming from sea route. In addition India's companies export refine petroleum product to international consumers and also invested heavily in oil and gas exploration in foreign waters. These asset forms important component of our energy security construct but it is not just India's energy security that dependent on the sea, several other economic aspects such as external trade, fisheries and many more are largely dependent on the sea. While this geographic and economic aspect of the Indian Ocean are important for India as resident geopolitical entity. We fully appreciate its importance for the other countries of the region also. Veteran of the Indian Ocean as well as the western pacific which are home to more than 60%

of the world's population are already emerged as a cradle of global manufacturing in service industries. The Oceanic trade route passing through our neigbourhood make up around 60% of global trade and more than 80% of this trade is extra regional. In fact the oil and gas produce in this region not only feeding the bout engine of Asia but also numerous consumers across the globe. It is not surprising that then there have been unprecedented amount of global wealth is being committed to this region. However, you all will agree with me that financial investment of such magnitude would not be forth coming unless there exist concurrent belief that an environment conducive for growth would prevail and the ocean would remain free and secure for legitimate use by every nation. This is where the security paradigm comes into prominence. Such is the confluence of geography, economic, security and many other related aspects in the maritime domain that dealing with enumerable subcomponents of all these aspect would entail involvement and crosslinking of multiple domestic as well as international agencies. While each agencies has a clear charter of its own every link of the change should be strong enough to be able to withstand the pull and pushed generated by these complex environment. It is equally important that we understand that the shared ownership cannot be loosely interpreted as unquestioned resource plundering. Preserving the fragile eco-system and ensuring its sustenance for the common good and respecting the territorial sovereignty or all literal is also collective responsibility that may be conveniently ignored by a few. Managing these various governance issues over the vast ocean bodies is certainly a challenging task not only it would require forthcoming participation from all stakeholders for policy formulation but it also demands high level of commitment for abiding by these regulation once the rules are framed. This is precisely the reason why integrated ocean governance is increasingly being deliberated amongst all international stakeholders in context of a rule base global warming. I am sure that the participant of this conference would have discussed this issue threadbare during the various subject specific sessions over the last two days. You would also appreciate that the effective role playing by the maritime military and law enforcement agencies would be essential for ensuring compliance of collective award rules. This would help accrue optimum benefit from the ocean. I would therefore now focus on how the Indian Navy making its contribution to Ocean Governance. Ladies and gentlemen for ensuring the security of the only ocean named after a nation the expectation from India and Indian Navy are naturally very high. The global reckoning of India emerging status has also let us to a sense of assurance that India would contribute to facilitating next security in maritime sphere of influence. In the same breath let me also admit, the range and scale of maritime challenges that we face today are significantly increased. This is true both in the traditional and non-traditional category. Since the traditional maritime security challenges essentially have a State verses State character, the solutions can only be arrived through established conflict resolution mechanism. How a narrow and over nationalistic attitude at times tend to undermine such mechanism as seen in part of south China sea or in Korean peninsula. This remains a cause of concern for aII of us. Dealing with such threat would preliminary be military diplomatic functions. Non-traditional threats on another hand are quite different. You are all aware of the recent case of apprehension of vessel just registered in Panama with an Indian crew carrying counter bells from Wada to India via Abu Dhabi as witnessed in this well publicized case, casing and prosecuting illegal activities at seas involved of several intelligent, law enforcement and judicial agencies from multiple countries. A sinister nexus is also appears to be emerging between various forms of maritime crime such as maritime terrorism and piracy, the drug smuggling and gunrunning, human trafficking. Large scale illegal, unreported and unregulated fishing has also caused severe ecological consequence. Especially in waters or countries who do not have the requisite capability to check such activities. That was impact of climate change on human security is also high relevant in context of maritime nation going to the high density of coastal population. When one analysis all these maritime challenges or commonality that stand out in there is that distinct hybrid and transnational character. Therefore tackling such challenges would require concurrent application of several Government tools which demand well regulated framework not just within the nation but most importantly amongst the nation. In order to obtain the desired output for such collaborated framework the Indian Navy is working concurrently at various levels including domestic, bilateral, multilateral and regional. Over the next few minutes let me elaborate on such an approach to maritime governance. Ladies and gentlemen, good work very much like charity begins at home. Therefore, I should first discuss the progress made on the domestic front prior venturing further. In the aftermath of the tragic terror attack in Mumbai, the Indian Navy was entrusted with the overall responsibility of maretime security including coastal and offshore security. The process of evolving of functional structure for coastal security was immediately kicked off and we are progressively been able to establish working protocol between fifteen different agencies functioning under six Ministries of Government of India looking after dialogues aspect of maritime laws enforcement and security in coastal zone. Setting up of chain of coastal radars and AIS stations and integrating them to the national command and control communication and information network that is now greatly improved our maritime security domain and the effectiveness of the coastal security construct.

Also our shores, across our shores we have constantly engaged with our neigbours through bilateral and multi-lateral structures. We can now all recall how these are being shaped in our own neighbourhood and under the marine law SAGAR our assistance to friendly nations for their own capacity building and capability enhancement is not only limited military hardware but also extend to training, hydrography and technical support. The expertise achieved in domestic model of coastal radar and AIS change is also being shared with several IOR nations. In the pursue of superior MDA is also being supported by white shipping information exchange agreement as also coordinate petrol and ease at surveillance of smaller island nation undertaken on their specific request. In order to facilitate interaction among regional Navies on wider canvas, Indian Navy pioneers the Indian Ocean Navy Symposium 2008 which is now grown to strength of 23 members and 9 observers. Those are subject specific working group on maritime security information sharing and incorporating as well as HAVRIONS has been delivering on this promise of involving a common understanding and cooperative solution in the maritime domain. Though I spoke on maritime governance for security prospective. I am sure the auditions would have realised the perils that exist in mechanism adopted and I am therefore eagerly looking forward to the suggestions that would be forthcoming post this conference. Ladies and gentlemen before I conclude I would like reiterate a belief that the ocean are universally shared resource, cooperative governance structure and voluntary compliance of international law is essential for deriving sustain benefit for this medium. A stable and secure maritime environment would always go in hand and hand to rule based global boarder. A pursuit of economic growth therefore needs to be adequately supported by cooperative measures to enhance maritime security. I once again compliment FINS for taking up such a worthy cause and wish the organization fair winds in all its endeavours. Prof. Chari has brought out about doctrine, Indian Navy come out with Maritime Security Doctrine way back in 2008 and we updated that into 2015 and it is available on Indian Navy website if anybody wants to access it, it is available. There is a possibility of National Doctrine on issues of Defence and Security, that is still work in order hopefully we produce them in good time. Thank you very much for your attention.

Jai Hind.

Sagar Discourse

Dr. Prabhakaran Paleri,
the Convener

The Forum for Integrated National Security (FINS) is an emerging non-governmental think tank of India engaged in studying and analysing integrated national security matters. The objective of FINS is to share information, based on research through its scholarly research programmes, with the governments and responsible organisations for the wellbeing of people in an environment of quality life and peaceful coexistence. The forum is proud to organise its first international conference on the subject this year. The theme is ocean based national security in the form of a discourse. Ocean is one of the terrains of national governance where the game of national security is played according to the challenges faced by the governments the world over today. Under the concept of national security the identified terrains are the land — the terra firma of the human system — ocean, air space, outer space, cyber space and genome or the genomic space in the order of emergence (Paleri, 2002). Closer to the term "terrain" and for explanation, I may like to quote the Japanese term *gemba* made popular by Taiichi Ohno (1912-1990), the master architect of the Toyota production system, meaning the "actual place." *Gemba* implies a location where the action takes place or value is created. In national security governance the terrain is more or less similar to *gemba* in micro or macro level appreciation, though much bigger in conception, and will depend upon the quantum of exertion of responsible governments in national security maximisation. The imperatives and challenges of national governance are vastly spread out in one or more of the six terrains of national security. For this purpose, national security is not mere physical or military security of a nation. It is much beyond that. The concept of national security ultimately percolates to the wellbeing of the people that can be measured and indexed at any given time. The sole purpose of national governance in any system of government is maximising national security through its dedicated and mutually inclusive elements over the six terrains mentioned. These elements as well as the terrains can increase or undergo transmutation in the future.

But they are not likely to diminish in their importance in national governance. When Sun Tzu in his *Art of War* or Kautilya, also called Chanakya, in his *Arthasasthra* propounded strategic thinking, their considerations fell over the then prevailed unitary terrain of the land from where the term itself evolved. The situation is different today and obviously will be different and more complex tomorrow. But the concept of national security underpinning the overall wellbeing of the citizens will remain unchanged under the law of invariance (Paleri, 2008). The governments, therefore, have to be exceedingly upfront in their vision statements to meet the demands of the future.

As mentioned, this year the FINS discourse is on the ocean based national security perception. This discourse is the first in the series of annual meetings planned by the forum for providing an opportunity of discourse and fruitful dialogue among likeminded partners across the world. The chosen terrain of this discourse is the unitary World Ocean from where it all began billions of years ago on this beautiful blue planet.

Sagar means ocean in Sanskrit, a classical and source language of India. This discourse is titled SAGAR to indicate not only the ocean, one of the terrains of national security from where life on Earth emerged, but also to highlight the concept enunciated by the prime minister of India, Narendra Modi, as Security and Growth for All in the Region (SAGAR) in a sincere effort to grow collectively with all in the region where the term region is a variable extendable to the entire world. FINS sincerely hope to convey this message to the world through all of you, fine people, gathered here. India, like other responsible countries, believes in growth of all around for the total wellbeing of the people involved. This will require not only cooperation of the people of a country in governance, but also the governments of other nations and their people. Such an ambition may sound idealistic but for the world that is evolving responsive to the citizens needs under visionary leaders in governance. Human wellbeing is an achievable target of governance however strenuous the path towards it may be.

As already mentioned, this year the FINS discourse is focused on Ocean. The ocean is one. It provides life to this planet. We in India believe in the richness of the ocean highlighted in our ancient scriptures. The world is aware of the benefits humans can accrue by governing it punctiliously. This is evident from the fact that every geopolitical entity in the world, including the landlocked or geographically disadvantaged, is a maritime entity and has rights over the ocean under international law. Every one of them is impacted by the changes in the ocean anywhere in the world. This calls for cooperation of the international community at all levels on ocean governance or, what I would like to emphasise, the ocean property maximisation based on my studies (2002) in macro level strategy of ocean governance. Ocean property ideates in the overall ocean benefits that a government or a people can accrue by maximising their returns from ocean advantage, ocean resources, marine environment and oceanic islands. Ocean property returns need to be integrated with the overall national security governance to maximise the wellbeing of the community.

Presently there are many issues related to ocean that need to be reviewed and assimilated with national and global governance. This address refers to some of them at random.

Mapping the rim countries, in the geostrategic concept, may need a different approach to include the landlocked countries across the ocean rim in the respective regions. This has to be based on a nation's geostrategic policy. According to this matrix many nations may fall within multiple ocean rims. Such oceanic rim mapping will help in strategic networking linking multirim domains.

Another point for consideration is the UNCLOS itself which is the first step in taming the ocean anarchy by humans in a civilised and responsible manner. But it needs a review to meet the demands of situational changes. A fresh look may be necessary in terms of the rule of international law related to suppression of serious unlawful activities such as piracy, trafficking, human rights of captive merchant marine personnel, sea level rise, etc. I may even go to the extent of recommending a review of the maritime zones to cover the entire ocean with fixed and variable zones still maintaining the status of the global commons. The issue of sea level rise is serious. The ever migrant human systems in search of another country may add on a different genre as displaced humans who will not fall in the region of refugees according to at least one verdict so far. Refugee influx has been a serious issue for nations the world over. The flow is ever continuing. The issues of displaced persons of low lying areas, sometimes an entire nation, lost under the rising floods can be more complex. The situation is relatively imminent. The world bodies need to think about it to avoid a human catastrophe never experienced so far in such a magnitude. It is important to know that the umbrella regime of UNCLOS has consumed 25 long years before concluding consensually. A review could be equally long. The clock has been ticking.

Governing the ocean resources is another challenge. In the times of hunter gatherers there was enough harmony and cooperation among them as they needed to find food over land, the only reachable commons. Today's hunter gatherers are the fishers all over the world barring a few exceptions over the land. Marine fisheries is the most accident prone activity. The hunter gatherers reap what they don't sow as a right. It is the law of nature that needs to be respected. Besides, they are supposed to be more cohesive than a gated community first originated in the world at the advent of the farm culture. The world needs to show special attention to the welfare and prosperity of the fishers. Besides fisheries resources, the ocean is a gilded mine of various other resources. This too needs to be highlighted for sustainable resource generation and exploitation.

Corporate social responsibility (CSR), the phenomenon of donour behaviour of human compassion, is slowly finding a place in the ocean too. Whether termed corporate social responsibility or exclusively as corporate ocean responsibility (COR) the humans should understand they are already late for appreciating the health of the ocean. It is declining faster than the beneficiaries think. The beneficiaries are the ocean stakeholders, which every human clasping the land is. We are all perched precariously over the rocks that looks floating around the vast area of water. More and more will cling on to them as the demographic density increases. We and our generations to come have to survive in this position. The ocean has to be healthy, regenerative and sustainable for this. This is a major concern.

I must add that this discourse does not trespass over the realms of military affairs related to the ocean. But the term ocean advantage also refers to using the ocean for military purposes. The best example is the stealthily silence the ocean can provide under water for tactical gain. Equally important, if not more, is ocean advantage for shipping and maximum trade. The entire world depends on ocean trade that needs to be facilitated by giant ships and ultra-modern port infrastructure including multiport complexes. One of the points I would like to highlight in this address is actually a call to landlocked nations to participate in shipping and shipping infrastructure. This could be done either by entering in the commercial shipping trade with the help of friendly partners and also encouraging citizens to take up shipping employment through indigenous maritme education and training. This is an area which the landlocked nations can engage in especially since most of them are members of International Maritime Organization (IMO) and performs maritime law and treaty obligations.

These are a few points I would like to submit to the learned audience. More interesting addresses, dialogues, pointers, suggestions and recommendations will follow in the discourse.

As mentioned earlier, this is a beginning. The SAGAR discourses will continue annually. The intention is to consolidate the ideas of national security for integration in a terrain specific manner. The concept for the next year is expected to be based on the issues related to outer space in national governance. India has already embraced ambitious space projects in support of its immediate and willing regional partners in its space programme. More is expected to follow.

Dr. Prabhakaran Paleri,
the Convener

Securing India's Maritime Interests; Role of Science & Technology

Introduction

Not too long ago, I represented an organization the - Indian Navy - upon which the nation depends for safe-guarding its maritime security and interests at sea. The term 'maritime security', in a nutshell, means ensuring good order at sea, protecting our sea- lanes and deterring inimical forces from impacting on our citizens. Speaking not only for the Navy, but also the Army and the Air Force, I must start by reminding the audience, as well as the eminent scientists present on the dais, that our Jawan can only do as much as his countrymen train and equip him to do. The wherewithal for our fighting-man has to come from the nation's defence technological and industrial base (DTIB). The solider will do his best with whatever the nation puts in his hands.

With those opening remarks, I thank FINS for having asked me to speak here on securing India's maritime interest and the role of Science and Technology.

Our Maritime Heritage

Let me start by reminding this audience that Indians are heirs to a grand maritime legacy with a tradition of shipbuilding, seafaring and ocean navigation, going back many millennia. Our bold and adventurous seafaring ancestors left their mark, visible even today, all over SE Asia and the Middle East. The decline of Indian seapower was the reason we could not repel foreign invasions and fell prey to colonialism; which condemned us to economic stagnation and industrial backwardness.

In contemporary times, our failure to acknowledge India's intimate linkage and dependence on the oceans can only be termed as 'sea-blindness'. While our navy had nurtured ambitions of becoming a blue water force, for many years, the decision-makers did not share this vision. Fortunately, a 'maritime awakening' has occurred in the country, over the past decade-

and-a-half; bringing home, the criticality of the oceanic environment, and the dire need to focus on maritime security.

This awakening has come not a day too soon, because India's fast-growing economy is dependent on energy supplies and international trade – both carried overwhelmingly by sea. The oceanic expanse, known as the 'global commons', offers all nations a network of sea-lanes for commerce, which enables participation in the global marketplace. The seas, also, promise to become a cornucopia of food, mineral resources and energy; as soon as the technologies for seabed exploitation become affordable.

India's Neglect of Technology

History shows that it was rare for Indian armies to stop or defeat foreign incursions outside our borders and we have always fought losing battles on our own soil. The same story was repeated on India's undefended sea-shores and led to four centuries of colonialism, based on control of the seas by Europeans. If a leadershipdeficit was the primary cause of India losing its independence, neglect of technology was a crucial contributory factor.

15th century Europe had seen spectacular breakthroughs in the fields of shipbuilding and navigation. Not had the vessels become larger and more seaworthy, they were equipped with sextants, compasses and charts for better navigation. While these inventions enabled safe long-distance voyages, it was the European superiority in weapon technology that tilted the balance in their favour. Thus, a few European warships carrying a battery of bronze canons could repulse massed attacks by ill-armed native *ghurabs* and *gallivats* in our waters.

It was against this backdrop, that India's post-independence naval leadership struggled to remind their countrymen that India's security as well as prosperity was dependent on the oceans surrounding our peninsula. Fortunately, the past two decades have witnessed a 'maritime awakening' amongst India's landoriented decisionmakers. A series of developments, including the phenomenon of globalization, the drama of rampant piracy, the traumatic 26/11 Mumbai terror attack, and the specter of a growing Chinese Navy have all served to bring sharp focus on maritime security.

Reliance on the Seas

Located astride vital shipping lanes, India occupies a dominant maritime position. Jutting a thousand kilometers into the ocean named after it, the Indian peninsula is rimmed with a 7500 km long coastline, containing many minor ports and has an exclusive economic zone of 2.5 million square km. India's economy is heavily dependent on foreign trade and energy imports; over 95% of which come via Indian Ocean sea lanes. The same sea-lanes are used by a 100,000 merchant ships, flying different flags carrying cargo worth a trillion dollars annually. The Indian Ocean sea-lanes are vulnerable to many threats and their safety is not only vital for India's economic well-being, but has also become an international commitment for us.

China, too, is heavily reliant on the seas for its economic growth and has crafted a grandstrategy, based on a powerful navy, to protect its seaborne trade and energy. In order to facilitate naval deployments, China has established a string of portfacilities in our neighbourhood and, commencing 2014 Chinese submarines have been regularly visiting the Indian Ocean. The Belt & Road initiative has many regional implications and we need to be wary of conflictpotential in the IOR

As a colony, India missed the intellectual renaissance as well as the industrial revolution that transformed Europe during the 17th and 18th centuries. Independent India has, thus, gone from the status of an 'agrarian economy' to become a 'service economy'; leapfrogging the industrial phase. Today, it is seen as a rising power on the basis of its size, population, growing economy and nuclear arsenal. However, we must recognize the anomaly of a nation seeking great-power status without attaining the requisite scientific and technological capabilities – so evident in the defence sector.

India's Defence Technological and Industrial Base

The essentials of India's DTIB are, undoubtedly, sound. We are fortunate in having, not only, a vast pool of world-class scientists, but also an extensive network of advanced defence laboratories, as well as production facilities for aircraft, ships, tanks, missiles, aero-engines and electronics; with the Indian armed forces as a huge captive market. Amongst India's major technological achievements in the military field are; nuclear weapons, a family of ballistic missiles and a nuclear-powered submarine. Our shipyards have delivered over a hundred modern warships, with many more, including an aircraft-carrier, under construction.

Given a functionally-oriented organization, visionary leadership and a user-friendly attitude there is no reason why this DTIB, over the past 70 years, should not have made our armed forces 75%-80% self-sufficient in weapon systems. Quite the contrary; India remains the world's largest arms importer, and our armed forces' inventories continue to be 75%-80%

of foreign origin. China, on the other hand, is not only self-sufficient in military hardware, but happens to be the fifth largest exporter of arms world-wide. Even Pakistan, with the comfort of Chinese support, has entered the arms-export market in a significant way.

Dangers of Foreign Reliance

Not many Indians realize the double-jeopardy this situation imposes on India's security. Firstly, every new weapon system imported from abroad creates a dangerous dependency for the life-time of the system on an unreliable foreign source. Secondly, such reliance takes away India's options to go undertake military action at a time of its choosing.

Our defence R&D has remained stalled in many vital areas and this has led to serious voids in national security. For example; our scientists have been struggling for decades to design and produce a jet fighter, a battle-tank and a jet engine. We have been unable to develop the technology for vital components with military applications, ranging from diesel engines and large guns to micro-processors, magnetrons and klystrons. Thus, at the heart of every ship, aircraft, tank, missile or electronic system, produced in India, are key items of foreign origin.

India's failure to attain a reasonable degree of self-sufficiency in weapon systems is rooted in three unpalatable realities which we have refused to face. Firstly; most of the military hardware that is claimed as 'indigenous' is actually produced under licence from foreign companies with few technological inputs by Indian scientists or industry. Secondly; our scientists have frequently over-estimated their technological capabilities and created a false sense of optimism. And lastly; we have failed to involve the private sector in defence production and to seek expertise and technology from external sources at the right time.

Mr. Modi's twin initiatives; 'make in India' and raising foreign investment in defence-production are indeed laudable, but both will have long gestation periods. Time is, however, not on our side. It is bad enough that India lags behind the world in defence technology and needs to import everything from rifles to bullet-proof jackets and night-vision devices. Far more serious is the fact that our neighbour and rival China is rapidly closing the gap with western nations and producing advanced weapon systems.

An Innovative Approach

In my opinion, a conventional, incremental approach will not address this problem. India's only hope lies in mobilizing its young innovators, many of whom have made their mark in Silicon Valley, NASA, CALTECH and the Indian Space Research Organization.

The world is in the midst of the third industrial revolution, enabled by developments in information and communications technology (ICT). India's 100-billion dollar IT industry and innovations like Aadhar, Flipkart and Snapdeal show that India has the talent and is on the right track.

The term 'revolution in military affairs', or RMA, was coined in the 1980s, when Soviet experts realized that radical technologies relating to computers, guided-weapons and surveillance emerging in the United States were going to become 'killer applications' on the battlefield. Today's galloping technology is providing enhanced capabilities to the military and another such revolution is underway. A few examples of such 'game-changing' or 'disruptive' technologies are:

- Additive or 3-D printing which will transform logistics by allowing military units to print specific parts from available materials.
- Autonomous or unmanned combat systems using robotics, artificial intelligence, software and wireless networks.
- Directed energy weapons using millimetric waves that have no flight time and huge offensive/defensive capability.
- Advanced cyber warfare capabilities.
- Nano technology which will permit nano-scale military devices with enormous capabilities.

The Navy's Requirements

The Indian Navy, which operates in all three dimensions of the maritime domain – surface, underwater and air – has many critical roles to discharge; both in peace and in war. For this, the navy requires the following:

- Sensors for detection, location and identification of targets at the earliest.
- Intelligent networks for control of forces at great distances.
- Long-range precision weapons for neutralization of the enemy before he can launch an attack.

The IN has been sharing its plans, perspectives and technology requirements with the DRDO for years, but congruence in aims, objectives and timelines between soldiers and scientists, remains to be achieved. The only way to meet time-critical operational needs is to import.

Let us remember that the only Indian Navy ship to have been lost in the 1971 war was INS *Khukri*; torpedoed by the Pakistani submarine *Hangor* with the loss of 194 lives. The reason was simple; the modern Pak submarine could find and attack the less sophisticated Indian ship before the latter came to know of its presence. Superior technology won the day.

The Lessons of History

I started my talk with a reminder of India's past and the weaknesses that resulted in domination by foreign powers. Regrettably, we have failed to learn the lessons of history. I say this for two reasons:

Firstly; the affliction of 'sea-blindness' amongst India's rulers, that enabled European maritime power to prevail over us, continues to persist. While we have created a strong, capable 'fighting navy', we have neglected to lay the true foundations of 'maritime power'. These lie in efficient ports & harbours, a modern shipbuilding industry, a dynamic merchant navy, an ocean-going fishing fleet and the ability to exploit seabed resources. Without all these, the edifice of India's maritime power will remain hollow.

Secondly; 70 years after independence, India as a nuclear weapon state and a leading military and economic power, suffers the ignominy of being the world's biggest importer of weapons. Till we can attain self-reliance in this domain, our national security will remain hostage, to foreigners and claims of 'strategic autonomy' remain hollow.

Conclusion

The fundamental reasons for India's dismal failure to attain self-reliance in defence are attributable to three glaring lacunae in the current system. Firstly the main stake-holders in defence research – the three armed forces HQs – are outside the Government's decision-making loop since they remain subservient to the Department of Defence of the MoD. Secondly; the DRDO having been given complete freedom to spend its budget; dedicates it largely to exploration of high technology, which may or may not have a bearing on badly needed defence capabilities. And thirdly; advice on scientific/technical matters with a crucial bearing on national security is delivered directly to the apex level by senior scientists. Therefore no instrumentality exists for a cross-check of overstated scientific claims, or failure to deliver weapon systems on time, cost and performance.

As far as the DPSUs are concerned, for far too long, have they claimed "transfer of technology" and "indigenization" when they have been engaged merely in assembling knocked-down kits imported from abroad using "screwdriver technology". In any self-respecting country heads would have rolled; but the inefficiency as well as consistent lack of ingenuity, initiative or innovation displayed by our DPSUs has remained shielded by the protective umbrella of the Department of Defence Production & Supply.

For all the criticism that is often, justly, heaped on DRDO and the DPSUs, the fact remains that, properly restructured, synergized with India's innovative private sector and made accountable to the armed forces, both these national institutions have the capability to rescue India from the unending arms-dependency trap.

That concludes my presentation.

Thank you.

Jai Hind!

1

"Marine Pollution, Eco-dynamics and Ocean management with collaborative mechanism framework"

—Admiral Jayanath Colombadge

Abstract

The Paper discusses sustainable management of unexplored dimensions of oceans in IOR. Pollution control, prevention and mitigation measures are dealt with. The impact of Sea level rise, eco-dynamics and future of small island nations is discussed. Man made pollution through plastic waste, contaminating the fish population, noise pollution and its impact on behavioural changes is explained.

Another dimension of ocean management being marine security. This also requires real time data on impact of maritime blindness. This requires collaborative mechanism like considering inclusion of Sri Lanka in Sagarmala Project, looking beyond UNCLOS, as its impact is not limited merely territorial in nature but even cohesive regulatory framework for dynamic ocean management with usage of advance technology is possible.

***Key-words** – Sea blindness, UNCLOS, Collaborative Ocean management framework.*

Article

The Ocean Management will be the theme of my topic and I use the quotation by US Senator State - John Kelly, he said, "protecting our Oceans is not an option, it is a necessity that contributes to our ocean economy, our climate and our way of life." Working together, we can change the current course and start to sustain the future. We all know that the Ocean is playing an important role in the sustenance of the planet earth and the human being like us to travel, explore and train and also the Ocean balance eco-system. Without Ocean, our survival would be threaten. We would inhale more carbon dioxide if there was no Ocean. Now we experience severe weather conditions in the 21st century. Whether it is cyclones, hurricanes, earthquakes, drought conditions and most of these are in fact attributed to be originating from the Ocean and we know, there are many opportunities and resources, 95 percent of the Ocean resources remain unexploited. So there is hidden wealth in this ocean and it also right now serves as the largest source of protein where three billion people depend on the ocean or fish protein supply. Also nearly 3 billion people depend on the coastal portion as their livelihood and the marine eco-system which we don't actually see are largest among the planet earth aquatic system, they include oceans, not only oceans but salt masses inter ecology, estuaries, lagoons, mangroves, and corals, this is a huge area we actually do not see. In the ocean there are may be more than 10 million species that we have not even explored. We only know the beauty of the coral and the fish but then there are others living deep in the Ocean more than 10,000 metres. The ocean is the major mode of transportation that we are aware of, 90 percent of the goods trade cross the waters of the oceans and therefore it is the life line of the world. No Shipping no shopping that's a very fundamental phenomena and then also ocean is an area for leisure, now the ocean unfortunate thing is this very beauty in the name of promoting tourism we tend to destroy that is a predicament and the Indian Ocean per se because our focus is Sagar and the Indian Ocean which is a very nourished Ocean because we have lot of rivers coming from the Himalayas, Yamuna, Ganga, Indus all these rivers definitely they bring pollutants to the ocean but at the same time they bring lot of nourishment to the oceans for thousands and thousands of years and they deposit so that is a huge source.

My focus is basically before I speak on management, is to share what I found out the threats to the ocean and I believe that the world oceans are under unprecedented level of pressure mainly from the human activities. It can be fisheries, shipping, marine culture, or aqua culture, extraction of minerals, natural gases and oil. Global warming is feared, few months ago we heard for the first time in our history a Russian ship crossed the northern sea route without ice breaker escort. Well it may sound good for the shipping companies they may reduce the number of days at sea, they can reduce fuel but what does it mean, it means that the global warming is real and the arctic ice is melting and that impacts the entire ocean system. It can impact the sea level rising and eco dynamics, changing in the ocean temperature and serenity, water quality, deterioration of the ocean, weather anomaly that does not augur well for our globe. Now when you look at the ten indicators of the warming world, most of them are associated with the ocean. Now we are not really able to find out the ocean temperature very accurately until recently but now we are able to measure the depth even up to 2000 mts. Now the scale used is the latest findings indicate that the temperature has grown by 13 percent more than the anticipated. So that is not the best news for the globe. Well human made pollution, 80 percent of the pollution changing place in the ocean originates on the land and mostly it is created by the humans and we assume ocean is vast, ocean is deep and therefore it can take everything but we are wrong and we have been polluting the ocean for centuries with impurities through industrialization through various activities may be through ignorance but it is time that we take stock of what we have been doing. Oil spills which are of great danger, dumping of toxic waste, everybody blames Somali for piracy but why what actually led to piracy dumping of toxic waste into those waters for may be one dollar a ton. That's the danger now they are not fishing so they have to go piracy. Plastic is the worst offender. Plastic do not de-generate completely, it breaks into smaller pieces and it absorbs the toxic into the ocean and it comes back to us because we eat the fish and it comes back to us. That may be the reason why we have diseases like Cancer unexplainable in higher percentage now. So plastic we have a chart and unfortunately most of the countries in the region are included, including Srilanka, one of the worst offenders of contributing plastic waste into the ocean. Vietnam, even India is not spared, Pakistan, even Burma is not spared. We all contribute large number of plastic to the ocean. There are plastic garbage patches and there is one near the equator in the Indian Ocean. Also we keep adding untreated sewage and that decompose system it does impact the marine eco-system in a relative way. So the pollutants can come from agriculture, it can come from Organizations, Industries, aqua culture and marine culture projects and oil from motor vehicles whatever we do on land finally end up in the ocean. And that impact, the reproduction cycle, behavioural changes of the species are finally causing the death and the extinction of the very species that we want to sustain our life. That is not the end, if I estimate nearly 40 percent of the world oceans are heavily affected by human activities including pollution, depleted fisheries and loss of coastal habitat. We have heard 80 percent of the world lives within 100 kms from the coast, you can imagine what an impact it is going to be. Another key pollution factor is the Noise pollution. We have done lot of noise to the ocean through our shipping, through our six feet survey guns and through our solar activities we create lot of noise in the ocean and this noise cannot be tolerated by various fish specially like whales and dolphins because they depend on the eco sounding method to travel food and mate and grow so this is the problem, difficulty raised the main stream has to be we are their protectors to swim in the ocean because we keep adding noise. Of course the good news is our shipping is becoming more silent with the increase of technology but still this acoustics breaching as we call it, is a major noise in the ocean.

We heard in the morning the potential of Blue economy. There are many more Industries coming into the Ocean. The population is rising, land resources are depleting and we have to look at the ocean. That means more players, more stake holders in the ocean that also means more pollution. So, we have to balance somewhere up. Then, of course Maritime Security is another part of the Ocean Management. Without security, you can't do it. You can't have any management without maritime security. We call it this is the sea blindness like we are blind, we don't see may be beyond 10 kms, we don't see may be more than 3-4 mts we don't know what is happening. 57 percent of merchant shipping does not report their time location accurately or the type of fishing taking place in the Indian Ocean is IUU fishing, they don't want us to see, so there is this type of maritime blindness. So all that will include many simplifications, so what we have to do is, we have to balance the sustainable exploitation of the resources and the economic growth and the ocean health with ocean security. Of course, how do we go about, we have been speaking about collaborative mechanism. I think the time has come to move into collaborative mechanism, which actually translates our thoughts into action in the ocean.

Now, I come to the last few slides of my presentation. The Ocean is considered as highly dynamic. The ocean does not stay one day throughout the channel it is a very dynamic ocean and therefore our ocean management should also be a dynamic process. There are many actors to the oceans and they all add complications to the ocean and the ocean needs to be managed. He heard yesterday if there is a requirement we have to revisit the UNCLOS because the UNCLOS is giving us the territorial waters, most of the ocean pollution takes place in the territorial waters but is it impacting only the country which is polluting, no it impacts the whole region, it impacts the whole region for the years to come so we may have to look beyond the UNCLOS, beyond the territorial waters beyond the exclusive economic zones. Even the Coastline Maritime issues, in the morning we heard about the fisheries issues between Bangladesh and Srilanka, Bangladesh and India, Srilanka and India, they are very economically sensitive they are very politically sensitive. We need to address these issues we can't keep our eyes close and allow the entire marine eco-systems to be destroyed in the name of economic development. Yes we can have a good GDP if we catch more fish we can have a better GDP if we cut all the trees but is that the world we want for those little girls we saw lighting the oil lamp yesterday? Certainly the answer is not. So, we need to be creating a regulatory frame work for this dynamic Ocean management of course by using technology and we saw how the Norwegian person told of the application of technology for the oceans and then of course we have the U.N. Sustainable development Goal, I will not go into details of that and also very briefly how do we manage by recommendation we can prevent and significantly reduce all kind of marine pollution. We keep adding into the ocean, we have to stop it and we have to manage sustainably and protect maritime eco-system. The coastal eco-system is the lifeline of 80 percent of the world population and minimize and address the impact of the ocean acidification, we keep adding chemicals we keep adding toxic, change the acidification or salinity of the water it is endangered, the fish are not where they are they are migrating to other places. It is effective to regulate harvesting and over fishing. We fish in many ways, bottom trawling was mentioned, I am a person who is against bottom trawling because they scrap the bottom, they destroy the corals, they destroy the marine habitat and they destroy the fish. They destroy the future fish we catch and then ban IUU fishing because what is happening in some parts especially in Europe, they are quite strict on this but I don't know people find ways to overcome that, they don't declare from where the catch came from properly. I have seen boxes of prawns in Europe saying Indian Ocean prawns. Well, it is not really this Indian Ocean but it came from Srilanka, we will argue about that later. So, we need to take very positive impacts on this, at least we have to have areas which are protected, we converse, we don't use it and then of course we can't say to the small countries like Maldives or Srilanka don't go to Seychelles go to sea and then we have to support them. Scientific knowledge is also necessary, we are scientifically blind, we don't know what is happening in the ocean. We also have to enhance the conservation and sustainable use of the ocean and Sagar I think is the way forward and I would sum up saying that we need a frame work, and I believe that FINS and Sagar can get together and come out with a proposal, come out with a legally binding mechanism for our Indian Ocean region, how do we manage this most vital Ocean for the sake of the human kind so there is hope and I don't think we have any time not to take action, time has gone we have to take action for the benefit of these little girls that we saw lighting the oil lamp.

2

Israel's Perspective of Sea for Strategic Depth

— Rear Admiral Oded Gur Lavie

Abstract

Development of maritime perspective in west Asia is explained through Israeli perspective. The paper includes issues like Suez canal, commercial aspect of ocean management, security dimension of Sagar and importance of small island states. For this purpose, Israel perceiving using sea as strategic depth.

Key-words: *Israel, ocean management, small island nation.*

Article

I know that many Israelis visit India after 3 years of servicing the idea of to leave it, for me it took 33 years and this is my first visit to India and I very much like it and I am sure it will not be the last one. I think this picture captures what we are speaking about and I am sure you will recognize Prime Minister Narendra Modi and Israel Prime Minister Benjamin Netanyahu, they were actually on the shore, not far away from I live. They were talking about special equipment and technology for distilling water. We will return to this later. I will like to present to you Haifa University maritime strategic centre and the goal on national security and issues of maritime domain that we have in Israel and then continue with some point of view and what I think, what the global challenges are that I think need to be dealt. Haifa University is a very nice university which is situated on the top of Carmel mountain not far from the sea above the Bay of Kaifa and it has more than 18,000 students there, a very diverse group, many Jewish and new immigrants, Arabs, a lot of different points of view brought into the classrooms. A lot of military and officers have their security studies there and finish their first degree and we have undergraduate and post graduate course of degrees. In the university we created the Haifa Research Centre for Maritime Policy and Strategy and it is a new strategy centre focused on creating awareness and closing the gap between what we understand most of the politicians and other people acting and taking decisions situations and have a lack of understanding of the maritime domain of the Israel and the global maritime domain and we see our purpose to do and to teach, educate and make sure to do and they can get good decisions based on good information. We give our annual report, publications and other things. A few reports on Israel, Israel is an over sea member with population of 18.5 Million, 76% Jews, 18% Muslims and there are others. GDP is sea and export and import, 62% of our GDP shipping and 99% from foreign trade is by sea of course. Israel is virtually an island but connected to other countries and we have 5 ports and an oil pipe line as well. So this is an infrastructure of 60-100 years. You see in the picture our first yoga master but actually this is our first visionary Prime Minister Benjamin Netanyahu as the expansion of the land and understood the strategic meaning of the sea of Israel because of our small country and this is a basic thing and one of the great visionaries and hoping to have more like him. Israel has been the link for centuries or millennium Suez Canal especially between three countries, so it was the cross roads between Europe, Asia and Africa. There a lot of empires tried to capture it and cross it. So it is a strategic area, since quite a few millennium. Abraham set there eventually and that is our home land today but after the Suez Canal, there have been many changes but still it is the important cross road in connection with Eastern and Western seas. I will talk about that but there are some problems with unresolved border and are creating challenges in that area, especially with Lebanon and we have good result with Cyprus, and also resolved the Greek, Cyprus and Egypt and the Lebanese is the possible friction and possibly not only an opportunity. The sea of Israel it may be small but 22,000 square kilometers close waters but for Israel the size of it greater than the length, so this is creating twice the size of Israel, you can see the tarnish of fisheries and the amount of ships and cargoes and we have 9 marine reserves, 46 identified habitats, 600 known archeological sites this is quite an area that needs to be secured and also needs to be exploited to best of our next generation and that is a great challenge these days. We talked about populations, Israel's population, 50% of it more than 4 million people are in 10 kilometers of the shore line. This is an extremely small area, you can see the sea area along the coast of Israel and most of the population is there. There are around most of the people in the area of Jerusalem, if you know and have been to Israel, it is just in the middle of the country. So this is another challenge for securing the population. The next thing is water. In the 60's when Syria tried to build the dam to close a river, the water going to Sea of Israel and dam, we had to attack it in order to make sure we get water. These days we are making more than 6 million cubic meters of water each year and there is plenty of water, there are no reason to worry, there is enough of water to give Jordan, and no shortage but water needs energy. In that aspect, the sea luckily now easily created that solution and found gas solutions in our areas. We are self-reliant on energy and we will be going for full energy from gas quickly. The region and gas issue is an opportunity but also bases for friction because an unresolved border is an easy to create friction and it might create friction and even the UN was on that border was agreed upon and now we are trying to open it again and see the possible situation for friction on those areas who possibly have gas and I say it again Cyrus and others and it is an good opportunity and a good corporation good for the entire region. Just to understand where we were 71% was coal, every little on gas we are going more than 50% on natural gas. All our industry is going that way as well. So this is a very big issue in Israel. The other thing in trade, as I was saying, it used to be trade going from Israel and now from Israel 99% of its trade by volume is by seas. Haifa port is also able to accommodate other countries of the region, if needed to bring goods through that and send it in the Mediterranean and another opportunity for corporation but all that is nice and we are still in the geo-strategic situation which are not simple. Israel virtually does not have any strategic depth as I was saying, 10 kilometers is the area where the population is and the depth when you see where the Palestinian authority is and if you see the very close where I live, it is a very small business and there is no strategic depth and obviously our first visionary Prime Minister said that our seas our strategic depth and we need to utilize it that way to our best capabilities. Some of the threats and these are not virtual threats they have more than hundred thousand rockets and I am not sure how many people here understand many of the countries don't have something close to it. It is in the hands of organizations and North of our order and they have been used. They have land wars and rockets and missiles from Hamas itself. Hamas the war of 2014, we were thinking distance by rocket time, I live 90 seconds rocket time from Gaza, my sister lives 30 seconds from Gaza, she has 30 seconds to run with her kids to the shelter that is kind of different way of thinking. So these are not virtually threats which I was saying. Neighbours threats also began to hit us. These missiles are being used and they are being put by Syria or Iran and they are pushing equipment from and capabilities into the hands to terror organizations which do make friction in the area and not a simple issue and it is some more complicated rush then there is a serious threat on the infrastructure of Israel. On the other things I will go quickly, as I think it is an opportunity to calm things down in the area. We have dependent from the sea from water, energy, trade, economy, population centers and the link you see from the red sea and the west Mediterranean sea and Haifa Port is the gate for landlock other countries, Jordan in a way and defence from terror attacks on these strategic issues and it is greatly improved and these are the first issues and the visit of Prime Ministers visit of India to Israel, the Forbes states that the both the countries quickly realized the shares interest in host of different ranging from counter terrorism, border security and everything in between. What he said is that we have confidence in each other and friendship with each other. I think it is a very important base to create a vision. So if looking at global challenges and I am looking from a point of view from another region and but then again global challenges are at height in our area can be very very quickly found in other areas. It is not easy to take lessons from one area to the other but I suggest to throw open at the start as it is growing broad in a strategy which can create, a lot of misunderstanding and it is better to reduce and that is my opinion. I think the security in the trade is the main and the first issue, there is an article, before the internet the communication was done by the sea. Letters were send by ships. We communicated across the oceans. So taking that back and then not only talking of trade, I think we all need our lines of communications open and again going to the value of openness and speaking and making sure that we understand so it has double meaning in my mind. To enhance security in the maritime domain and we have not talked about it yet but it is beginning to have an impact on the sea on different grounds but I think there will be enhanced Science and Security threats and we in Israel are already beginning the start the startup hubs to begin to create the startup hubs for the maritime security and for these issues as well. Control terror and piracy, it is extremely important, it cannot be done one side of one country, we need a corporation and it fell against the dues UNCLOS, the international laws and I stress before you, when you have a law which is good. The international laws we see in the news for different terror organizations making sure they use against the democratic countries that are abiding by the law and that is a very difficult situation, the interpretation of the international law and finally I presented my points of view and there are but I think the important thing is the common vision and may be Sagar Security and Growth for All in the Region is that vision.

3

An account of Indian Posture as Maritime Superpower

—*Admiral R. K. Dhowan*

Abstract

This paper takes a historical account of Indian maritime domain, over 70% of earth surface is covered by water and 80% of world's population stays near the ocean, 90% of world trade passes through ocean, Blue economy concept has developed as a new paradigm, Sagarmala project and comprehensive island development plan has been dealt with. The importance of ocean has been explained in various domains from tourism to security through trade. India's new posture as a maritime power is described.

Key-words: *Maritime power, Sagarmala, blue economy.*

Article

As a maritime nation, India has a glorious maritime heritage covering over 5000 years and the Indian sea borders have been the gate-way of the intense maritime activity over centuries. The Indus Valley civilization which existed in the western part of the country dates back to 3300 years BC, even today we have a dry dock at Lothal in Gujarat which dates to 2200 BC. It is from these small ports that ancient sea farers travelled to distant sea lands in Mesopotamia, Ancient Egypt and East Coast of Africa. On the East Coast of India, we had the sea faring kingdoms of Kalinga, the Chola's, Panday's and the Chera's who sailed to South East Asia to establish trade and cultural links and even today, we can see glimpses of India's rich cultural heritage in these countries. The British period was a period of extensive ship building in India. In commencing in 1753 over 144 merchant ships, 150 war ships including 84 gunships for royal navy was build in Bombay docks which is the exact same location of the naval dockyard at Mumbai today. Some of the most famous ships in the world were built during that period. HMS Kamoli is the oldest warship afloat in the world today. Its birth took place in U.K.

HMS Kamoli was built in Bombay dock in 1817, 200 years ago. The National actives of United States of America, the star spanker banner was written by Francis Kee in Baltimore on boarder ship HMS Milton and that ship HMS Milton ladies and gentlemen was built in India. The treaty of Hongkong. British was signed on board another warship HMS Cornwallis also built in Bombay docks. Regrettably even the transition took place from sail to sea. We got left behind because India was then not part of the Industrial revolution and the maritime abilities took place post independence in the later part of the 20th Century. Today India occupies a dominant position in the Indian Ocean and the country seeks to strive busy sea lines of communications which transits across the Indian Ocean over which 1000 ships transits every year. Carrying 66% of the world's oils, 50% of worlds train and traffic and 33% of the world's cargo traffic. Our blue planet, the earth has a dominance of the maritime domain with over 70% of the earth surface covered by water, nearly 80% of the world's population living within 200 nautical miles of the coast and 90% of the world's trade transiting by sea. As we have heard over the last 2 days oceans are central to life on earth. They are rich in oil and mineral resources. They are the suppliers of oxygen and absorbers of carbon dioxide. A virtual heat sink, rich in biodiversity. With depletion of resources of land, human kind has turned to seas for its resources and there is a misperception that the oceans are the unending resource base and infinite sink. Nothing could be further away from reality. Over the past few decades, we have witnessed indiscriminate pollutions of the oceans and contamination of the natural marine habitat resulting in a detrimental impact of climate change in the oceans. Studies have indicated that nearly 80% of all pollutants in the ocean and it is also mentioned by Admiral Colombage, emanate from land and the current rate of pollution continues in a few decades we will have more plastic in the ocean than fish. The concept of blue economy has emerged as new pyridine and I would like to define harnessing the blue economy as the economic development of our maritime interest by optimal utilization of resources with minimum impact on environment and ensuring sustained development of the oceans.India is essentially a maritime nation because of the natural outflows towards the seas. We have a long coast lying around 7515 kilometers and an exclusive economic zone of over 2 million square kilometers. Over 90% of our trade by volume, 72% by value transits by sea and this accounts to nearly 50% of the country's GDP. Our maritime interest have a vital relationship with the nation's economic growth and in recent years under the leadership of our Hon. Prime Minister Shri. Narendra Modiji, there have been series of initiatives development in the maritime domain including the transition from the policies.

These initiatives will act as catalysts to further strengthen India's growth at incredible maritime hub. Our maritime interest are also enablers of blue economy and I would like to highlight some of the maritime sectors which are likely to witness significant growth in the coming years and will also act as avenues for harnessing the blue economy and maritime corporation with the countries of the world. India has 12 major ports in all over 200 minor and intermediate ports. The cargo handling capacity which stands today at 15,000 Million metric tons per annum is likely to increase to 2500-3000 million metric tons per annum over the next 10 years. The Government has launched an ambitious Sagarmala project which is a port land development initiative based on 4 pillars of port modernization, connectivity, port land industrialization and coastal community development. Actually sagar mala comprises of 150 projects with investment of 60 Billion US Dollars. We will also see the aspect related to the 5th pillar which Captian Parashar spoke about which is the coastal shipping and the other aim is to ensure interconnectivity in the major and minor ports and the hinterland through road, rail network and development of inland water ways. India has over 15,000 kilometers of navigable inland water ways and the first phase over 4500 kilometers are being developed as five major national water ways because we know that travel and movement over sea and water is cheaper and saver as well as it is cleaner. These will open up avenues for green fee infrastructure development in the port development sector a stronger economy and also employment opportunities in the maritime sectors. India has a vibrant ship building industry with over 27 shipyards and recently the government has given major boost to the ship building industry by according a special infrastructure status and also permitting 100% foreign direct investment into ship building. In area, I would like to specifically mention is there about war ship building in India. For over 50 years now, our naval designers have designed our indigenous ship yards have build ships for the Indian Navy, resulting in our transformation from a buyers Navy to a builders Navy. The blue print for the future Indian Navy is firmly anchored on self realization and Indianisation and it is a matter of great pride that every Indian proud to learn that all the 40 ships and sub-marines which are under construction today being built in the Indian

Shipyards. It is our endeavour to progressively increase the indigenous content so that future warships can be 100% made in India. This would open up avenues for joint venture partnerships in the ship building sector and offer employment opportunities in ship building. India has a thriving fish industry with two hundred and fifty thousand boats, 4 million active fishermen, 14 million and above fishing community and our annual catch 10.05 million metric tons which earns us 5.5 Billion US Dollars exchange on account of fishing export.This is only scratching the surface because 90% of the fishing in the Indian waters is restricted to coastal areas, where we have an entire 200 nautical miles of the exclusive economic zone to be exploited. There is hardly any fishing in the deep Indian waters and it is said that fish in deep Indian waters are dying of old age. This provides a unique opportunity for deep sea fishing projects which will also result in coastal community development and provide employment in the fishing sector. India has about thirteen hundred islands and islets as far as Andaman and Nicobar Island groups in the Bay of Bengal and the Lakshadweep group in the Arabian Sea. The Government has prepared a comprehensive island development plan, taking into account the aspects of security, economic sustenance, the environment preservations, social and cultural sustenance. The aim is to develop green field infrastructural projects and also control eco-tourism. This would open up host of economic opportunities in marine tourism, in development of marinas and cruise tourism in India. The other sectors which are likely to witness growth include are offshore oil and gas, deep sea mining, renewable sources of energy such as wave energy, tidal energy and ocean thermal energy conservation. It can therefore be seen that we have ocean of opportunities for economic development of our maritime interest. The challenge however is to ensure that these are green field projects with zero carbon footprints. So we therefore need to outline a comprehensive way ahead for harnessing our blue economy and sustained development with the oceans. The Indian Ocean had emerged as the world's centre of gravity in the world's maritime domain. It is the third largest water body spanning an area of 68.5 Million square kilometers and countries on the rim of Indian Ocean are home to nearly one third of humanity. The threads and challenges on the waters of Indian Oceans are as wide and varied as it comes. Who could have imagined that in the 21st century, we would be once again grabbling with fire or the major threat in the maritime domain could be from ace metric warfare in maritime terrorism but that is the reality today, the other challenges include arms trafficking, drugs smuggling, human trafficking and porting. Another threat on the waters of Indian Ocean is that nearly 70% of all extreme climate conditions turn into national disasters and our coast guards have to be ready to provide humanitarian assistance and disaster relief. The instabilities and turbulences on land on some parts of Indian Oceans region have the potential to spill over in the maritime domain and the situation can be best be described as fragile. Consequently over 120 warships over 20 Navies are always present in the Indian Ocean to safeguard their maritime domain. India has vast maritime interest and responsibility of protecting this interest falls squarely on the shoulders of men in white uniform because it is the responsibility of the Navy and the coast guard to ensure that our maritime interest which have a vital relationship with the nation's economic growth are allowed to develop un-hindered at all times. The Indian Navy has emerged as multi-dimensional network force which is ready to take any challenge in the maritime domain in the Indian Ocean. To meet the role of the Indian Navy and to ensure coastal and off-shore security in coordination with the coast guards in recent years we have leverage technology to enchase the maritime domain affairs. The ships of Indian Navy are continuously deployed in the gulf in the anti- piracy patrols in the 2008, we also deployed our ships and aircrafts for ease and patrols and co-ordinate patrols in the waters of some of our literal neighbours in co-ordination with the maritime agencies of these countries to meet the diplomatic role, the Indian Navy has expanded its role of operational foot prints across the Indian Ocean and beyond to interact and to carry out exercises with Navies of the world. We also carry out capacity building and capability enhancement initiated and information exchanged to enhance maritime domain awareness. The aim to stake a favourable maritime environment in the Indian Ocean region. In 2008, the Indian Navy launched a unique initiative, the Indian Ocean Naval Symposium and a maritime construct to promote corporation among navies of the Indian Ocean. The Indian Ocean rim association is another forum which is a forum to manage the maritime affairs of the countries of the IOR. To further promote corporation among the navies of the world, the Indian Navy conducted the International flee at Vishakhapatnam last year where 50 Navies of the world came together to strengthen bridges of friendship. The theme of the interview was that we may be separated by geography but we certainly united through oceans. Speaking at the conference, the Hon. Prime Minister of India Shri. Narendra Modi outlined his vision for blue economy and he also linked with the blue chakra or the wheel on our National Flag with the potential of our blue economy. He later spoke at the maritime summit and articulated the vision for maritime India. The recent initiatives by India in the maritime domain are pointers to indicate that India has once again turned towards the seas and it is destined to emerge as a certain maritime nation in the 21st century. In conclusion, I would like to highlight 6 major take aways. The United Nations documents transforming our world's agenda in India 2030 and the SGD 14, provide a template for conservations of the oceans, seas and resources. We now need to outline a perspective plan for sustained development and growth for different avenues in the maritime sector. As a maritime nation, India has considerable potential to harness the blue economy. We need to chart a comprehensive part ahead to draft a national maritime policy on the blue economy for sustained development in the oceans. There is also a need for good level organization to coordinate and integrate the planning process of different stake holders in the maritime domain for the economic development of our maritime interest to emerge as a certain maritime nation. The Indian Ocean Association Naval Symposium and the Indian Ocean Rivers Association are two maritime constructs for managing the maritime affairs. There is a need for a greater interaction between the two agencies and organizations so as to provide synergy for maritime corporation among Navies and countries of the Indian Ocean region. To fully implement the Hon. Prime Minister vision of Sagar which is Security and Growth in All the Region we need to draft a detailed maritime corporation with road map. With a whole Government approach for promoting corporation among the nations and also with the aim to shape a favourable and positive environment in the Indian Ocean region and finally the Hon. Prime Minister has started a movement of Swachchha India. Today, I would like to recommend that we have a movement for Swachchha Sagar which is clean oceans. Actually Sagar Discourse 1.0 should be the beginning of such a movement which rely on the power of one, it should be the peoples movement when every individual not only in India but across the world should take· a pledge to come out with an action plan to make our coast lines and oceans clean once again. The seas around us are getting importance as each day goes by and I have no doubt that the current century is the century of the seas. I am sure that the deliberations during this conference will throw up some suggestions for harnessing the blue economy as well as for promoting cooperation among the nations of the world across the global converse.

4

India – Maldives co-operation – a case in Ocean Resource Management and Security

— Brig. Zakariyya Mansoor, Maldives

Abstract

The paper discusses various maritime security threats including unconventional threat. A case study of Maldives – exploitation of ocean resources and lack of enforcement capacity is addressed. The recourse would be co-operation with friendly neighbouring country for surveillance is proposed. Sustainable habitat is emphasized on. The required co-operation needs to be on the basis of mutual trust and respect. The initiative between India – Maldives - Sri Lanka coastguards – Dosti is cited on an example of this.

Key Words: *India – Maldives, ocean management.*

Article

So when I think of the Sagar my colleague from Bangladesh has said it's a similar ocean or sea. Sagar means but I think when I think of SAGAR it comes as a very beautiful Hindi song to me; Saagar kinare, dil ye pukare, words and words so if you call it to be, I will start with the song so I can wake up some of you also but let me not do it.

Let us look at the scope Indian Ocean Region domain, maritime threats, what is Paradigm and also the area of Paradigm. These are some of the issues I think we cannot simply neglect. The effects are always very important bedrock of the issues that we live in. So Indian Ocean region has 20% of global water bodies. It also has a population of 8 billion, 37 of littoral states, 80% of global Maritime Trade and Commerce, and 60% of trade. So from the east to the west of the Indian Ocean, these are itself challengers to commerce, to business to literal states has huge population of the world and a huge water mass. Now yesterday we heard that even in fact my colleague from Bangladesh, Admiral had the expression that or some other presenters who presented said that land is exhausted, there is too much exploitation but yet when we look at the ocean also we have some problems. We have conflict zones, we have unreported fishing, illegal fishing, drug trafficking, using ocean and chokepoints as strategic locations, maritime security related. Main chokepoints of the world to this region to the Indian Ocean and Pacific are real. So definitely Indian Ocean Security matters are very much important in many ways. Let's talk of them, disastrous in 2004 Tsunami, Maritime Terrorism, needless to mention it is still a threat, an opportunity threat. Yesterday we heard about the Mumbai attack, seaborne used long line of sea passing through undetected yet attacked to a very important part of India, Mumbai. Climate change, over and over again we have discussed about it. In detail, the looming threats what world could be after 20 years, I 0 years, silver rise, islands like Maldives, I do not where to go perhaps to India or anywhere else but these are the real threats that our region is facing and they are real national security threats to those countries and the consequences are high; total loss of people's livelihood and their economy.

Drugs and arms trafficking, IUU Fishing are in various parts. With these topics it relates to Ocean Governance. We have so many commissions in the Indian Ocean, Tuna Commission. We have other regulatory policies in the regions to get control, fishing control, fishing licensing and so and so forth. Who will give the exclusive economic zone to other countries and many other questions arise in this aspect. Yet these are the challenges in every country's mind that speaks very loudly. For example, Maldives has a very robust economy, 60% to which 80% depends on tourism which is again it's a Maritime Tourism. Every island, Maldives Resorts are comprised mostly of one island one resort concept. Each island is a resort itself. There is no local population on those islands so those are the environmental issues that we have. Even in fact they are security issues that islands itself it has to be secured, guarded, well monitored from treats of incursion, tourism and so on and so forth. Drugs and arms trafficking, piracy we have seen that in the Indian Ocean region, many, many times coming and going, yet our countries are able to control before it really comes a real threat. Human trafficking, human smuggling, and Maritime Piracy; if you look at one of these topics is the Tsunami. During the Tsunami, Maldives was destroyed up to 60% of its economy and was very difficult actually for Maldives of the effects of Tsunami. If you look at the total impact of Tsunami in Maldives, we lost around 82 people but yet about 5 to 6 islands were totally submerged. Those are the real issues that we went through and when we talk about Maritime Terrorism, I always want to remind the people about the 1988 armed attack Maldives had from the LTTE group and we are very glad that the terrorist network of LTIE had been totally destroyed from our region. As well as there is not a threat of Maritime Terrorism at least at the moment in our region. The illegal and unregulated and unreported fishing has been one of the main sources of damage to and translate the Maldives. We are dependent on the fish stock available within our exclusive economic zone, incidences of resource exploitation by resources from within and outside the region are of a big concern. Maldives has an abundance of marine resource within its exclusive economic zone which have been exploited by foreigners for years due to our lack of enforcement capacity but today, with assistance of friendly foreign countries such as India, continued surveillance of the Maldives waters are maintained. This is the one area we collaborate very much from the very beginning. Every month or every 2 months, Indian government sends either an Indian naval aircraft with surface patrol crafts, naval vessels jointly patrol our exclusive economic zone and our waters. As a result of growing and existing conflicts and lack of enforcement capabilities, Indian Ocean again is thriving drugs in illegal arms market. Both maybe interconnected to the other as some part is found, some part is fund or arms from narco-traffic while growth of narco-terrorism is also a threat in this aspect. Reliable, effective, and timely intelligence sharing and information sharing among the state is crucial in curbing these threats. As I mentioned, it was similar to the human trafficking as well. Yet Maldives has not experienced any form of human trafficking or smuggling at sea. We may not be located at a transit for the crime or may not be given for the criminals but what I say is a set up efficient labour tools to deal with human trafficking through other models as with other crimes. Regional and global cooperation is an·important tool in suppressing this crime jointly.

The national security of Maldives is considered as a mixture of curvy thoughts that have been shared. We established regional collaboration between partners related to a non-offensive, defencive, and collaborative security. This can be related through search and rescue assistance provided by Indian Naval or coast guard visits in the Maldives and HADR assistance provided by the friendly foreign forces during 2014 water crisis in the Maldives and in 2004, Tsunami.

I just want a little bit to elaborate on the 2014 water crisis. Male, the capital of Maldives is a city that has nearly 100,000 people on about 4 sq.

km the full size of Male the capital is about 4 krn2 and it has more than 100,000 people. Per square feet is the populous city in the world if you look at the reports. The whole water supply system on, but there was a huge problem, the system failed. The system caught fire, the engines broke down, the pumps did not work, and therefore the whole city was without water. Is this an environmental problem or manmade problem but these are the issues that we are going to face. There is no water anywhere but the regional collaboration assisted in our drinking water as well as for other necessities but when you look at the impact of it, a city of 100 plus 1000 people without water for a couple of days is unthinkable. This city is vertical. It has 10 storeys, 15 storeys buildings and there is nowhere that you can pump any water up so the elderly, the sick, the children, everybody was suffering and in that respect we received generous assistance from regional countries; India, Sri Lanka, Pakistan, Bangladesh, and the SAARC regional countries as well as other assisted regional countries. For a small island national city as the Maldives, the assurance to the security of smaller communities would be through collaborative, collective, and strong information and intelligence mechanism. Furthermore, due to a tremendous interdependence among countries in the region as well as far out in the global community, a small national city as the Maldives, to sustain our aspirations to the dear point of harmonious society, and to elevate the expressions of economic growth should be encouraged by the supplementation through multiple facets. This is one area that I would like to just highlight that we have understood very well and we have learnt very well through various presentations that the numerous challenges in our region. If we want to have integrated security mechanism, where we have to collaborate, with whom we should collaborate, obviously collaboration within our society, within our friends, and similarly our regional cooperation has to be much stronger than the extra regional cooperation. Neighbours to neighbor, the understanding between our neighboring states and countries, the difficulties the countries face; India and Sri Lanka, Bangladesh and-India, India and Maldives, Maldives and Sri Lanka, Sri Lanka and Nepal or Bhutan whatever country maritime or not but in this respect we believe that it has to be well encouraged through the collaboration. The respect for sovereignty and seeking equal respect; it is also vital for the countries to adopt a diplomatic strategy which will not waive our security arrangements by giving in to any other regional and extra regional powers. The Maldives and trading diplomatically is a nation which respects the sovereignty of other nations while seeking mutual respect to its own sovereignty. We were told that it does not matter whether small or large, it's a sovereign independent state so regardless of the challenges and diversity in the region peaceful co-existence among the nations have been a prime goal. The resolutions of underlying in Bangladesh Maritime boundary dispute is a good example of this as well as we the undertaking of dispute of fishing grounds of India and Sri Lanka fisherman. Good governance by means of mutually bound multi-lateral agreements as longstanding disputes and challenges are important in the securing the peace of the Indian Ocean. Today, we are so glad that these disputes are being resolved through peaceful means. No country went to war, there is no fight but peacefully the government of Sri Lanka, the government of India, the government of Bangladesh has peacefully resolved these longstanding issues in Maritime Security.

Their main factor is supplement resilience through collaborative mechanisms. An example may be the trilateral Maritime Security Agreement between Maldives, Sri Lanka, and India. We also included the Sri Lankan coast guard in this. So now it has become a trilateral initiative. The initiative of IONS, Indian ocean, national security, Indian ocean which was achieved by then Indian Navy commander, Admiral Arun Prakash, I had the privilege to attend the first ION meeting in Delhi.

The next important factor is filling capacity gaps through capacity built-in projects such as providing training opportunities or acquisition of enforcement equipment. However, we talk about the law of the sea unclose and so and so forth about the regulations and rules in Ocean Governance. I think the capacity of nation itself encountering illegal activities in their maritime zones is vital. They must have their capacity in leading and attending these issues.

To conclude I would like to emphasize the fact that this region walks on a vulnerable path of security over an ocean of challenges, fortunately we are not in continuous disputes as we are seeing like in South China Sea nor we are perfect. It is imperative to praise the efforts set by India to secure the peace and prosperity of this ocean which is the efficiency of these efforts which will keep at bay the brain extra regional powers as well culturally and historically mutual cooperative security mechanism in the Indian Ocean. Which I have spoken already about the nations, good governance, mutual respect, understanding between the leaders, leadership of the countries.

We have 350,000 people of population from North to South it is like 874 km, it' s a maritime country, one million sq. km. of exclusive economic zone and we speak the same language, it is called Dhivehi . It is very similar to all the languages in the region. It is very similar to Hindi, Tamil, Urdu, Pakistani and Bangladeshi language and I think it is somewhat a mixture of everything. So you should not hesitate to come to Maldives because you can still survive the language and we have one religion. We have the one religion. Islam is the sacred religion. Our language is Dhivehi. The ethnic city is the same. We do not have any different races. All belong to one race. So I think you all have sent a mixture of people from various countries and states to Maldives to be a little bit peaceful country without those issues. But yet we have problems, believe me, though we are all Muslims, all belong to Shafi Madhhab yet they have a lot of issues among themselves. This is one of the issues that I am dealing right now after the Maritime Security problems of my naval background. Now I am dealing with counter terrorism and counter radicalization and if you see that for this security and growth for all in the region, that is well included, very, very included. So though they are one religion, one language, one national city still yet the population, the people will find some issues to dispute.

5

India's Advances in Science and Technology in the domain of Maritime Security

— *Dr V Bhujanga Rao*

Abstract

India, with vast maritime domain to protect, systematically built the S&T capability over the last three decades to counter any challenge of maritime security. Today S&T systems needed in maritime security have to be designed to counter challenges borne out of threats like coastal security, port security, piracy, cyber security, coastal terrorism, unlawful acts like drug smuggling, stowaways etc. India is fully geared up with many advanced indigenous S&T systems to secure not only India's maritime domain but of many friendly neighbouring countries. My presentation will briefly lay emphasis on S&T strength of India in this domain.

Key-words *– Maritime Domain, Security, International co-operation, AIS, Marine Radars.*

Article

To begin with, I feel very happy to note that the subject of maritime security has drawn the attention of FINS Discourse. When we talk of maritime security, we have to visualize threats coming from sea, above sea surface and below sea surface (underwater). The security scenario could be in the nature of threats to coastal security, port security, cyber security, or issues like coastal terrorism, piracy, unlawful acts like drug smuggling, stowaways or any activity against our nation's interest. This calls for S&T systems which can monitor 24 by 7 at 360 degrees with wide area coverage so as to cover all scenarios of threats and detect & identify any suspiciously moored or moving sea going vessels of size as smaller as 30 ft. length perceived to be working against our national interest. Though I am not going to discuss in depth what this instrumentation is, in this forum, I will briefly explain how these systems can be used to neutralize or to counter any kind of security threat.

There are varieties of static surveillance radar systems developed indigenously over the years and fitted across the coast line with AIS receivers, to monitor and manage vessel traffic at coastal area. These surveillance systems provide active information on ship traffic in the vicinity of 25 to 30 Km and this information will be fed into MDA(Maritime Domain Awareness). When it comes to dynamic surveillance we have well equipped organizations like the Indian Navy and/or Coast Guards and/or even coastal maritime police in multiple layers from coastal lines to deep into sea. Besides systems like Long Range Maritime Reconnaissance aircrafts, Standard patrol vessels, one can use UAVs(Unmanned Air Vehicles), micro UAVs, ROVs(Remotely Operated Vehicles), AUVs(Autonomous Underwater Vehicles), AVSSs(Autonomous Sea Surface Vehicles) etc. with network centric management support, based on data fusion and data correlation techniques. Automatic Identification System (AIS) is used to help track vessels of suspect and make the sea borders impervious to enemy vessel penetration.

For detecting underwater threats like underwater intruders, underwater vehicles etc, there are well developed systems like intruder alarms, underwater sonars, sea bed sensor detectors, magnetic anomaly detectors etc. These acoustic/ magnetic systems compliment land based systems effectively. There are ocean data buoys, underwater gliders to collect oceanographic data required to interpret information of sonar detection ranges. These data buoys are also used to detect tsunamis in advance as part of disaster management strategy.

With the launch and availability of GSAT-7 satellite, maritime command, control and communication power (MC3) of India has gone up multifold. Similarly airborne early warning aircraft net worked with sea based systems can provide impervious firewalls to the enemy at sea. Well-developed geographical information and satellite position fixing systems give force multiplier capability in precision engagement of weapons during maritime operations. A number of indigenous communication satellite programmes are on hand for maritime domain applications in India today.

Like radars, India's capability to design world class sonars for detecting underwater objects is well known. Today India has the capability to design submarine sonars, ship mounted sonars, towed sonars, and helicopter operated dunking sonars etc to detect very small objects to the size of submarines at considerable distance which enhances India's capability to counter underwater threats.

I really do not mean a nation's maritime strength solely lies on S&T prowess of that country. As we all know, we have other areas such as cultural, social, scientific cooperation to focus to strengthen relations between nations. In this vein, our PM Narendra Modi's offer to all Indian Ocean rim countries to enhance ties and share maritime security information with each other leading to a broader cover of security in the region is worthy to emulate. As part of scientific cooperation, India will be willing to give a helping hand to all friendly countries with latest technology. Thank you.

6

"Need for review of legal issues in ocean management – 21st Century challenge."

— Dr Bimal Patel

Abstract

"The Paper deals with legal issues in ocean governance. Critical analysis of UNCLOS is done. CFP has included narrative principles including precautionary principle and eco-system based approach. The governance structure, stakeholders' involvement in fishing regulation, rights based system is called for. Outcome based management is proposed. Coastal geography and demographic approach like sea level rise and its impact of littoral states requires detailed study. New neighbouring states coordinating mechanism to effectively implement new legal regime is required. Underwater cultural heritage has impact on overall governance of sea. For this purpose, separate underwater wing of Archeological survey is proposed by the author, which is imperative for ratification of UNCLOS 2001 Convention. India needs to develop framework for technical cooperation for addressing recovery criteria and procedures to prevent illicit recovery and export of UCH in maritime domain. The Author also critically analyses civil disobedience at sea including shared authority, overlapping jurisdiction and functional governance divided between flag and coastal states. UNCLOS doesn't adequately address marine bio-diversity issues. The Paper states possible use of genetic science in this legal framework."

Key-words *– UNCLOS- inadequate legal framework, ocean governance, jurisdiction of flag states, civil disobedience.*

Article

SHRI BIMAL PATEL: I have chosen to bring here the legal issues to define the future of the law of the sea and since discussing, yesterday the legal issues. It is a privilege for me to Chair the session.

As Chair of the Session on Issues and Challenges for Governance at Sea which will have presentation on suppression of unlawful activities at sea, law of sea - issues and future trends, maritime border dispute resolution. Among contemporary big regime of laws, the law of the sea remains very relevant as the issues and challenges are continuously evolving giving rise to variation in state practice. UNCLOS has been in force for last 23 years and remains perhaps the most important instrument in the ocean governance for 167 Stages and the European Union. What are the major issues which will bear crucial importance for the future of the law of the sea? Let me enlist them with brief remarks. The EU, which perhaps is the largest consumer of fish and other products, has adopted CFP and it has been reviewed at regular intervals. CFP has incorporated the new normative principles including the eco-systems based approach and the precautionary principle. However, the European CFP based on traditional approach has not been successful and 88% of EU fish stocks had been fished beyond 2009 maximum sustainable yield and according to Prof. Long the European common fishery policy remains most controversial one. Despite its controversy, few elements of the EU CFP are adoptable, namely, the governance structures, stakeholders involvement in fishery regulation and right-based fishery management system as a means to allocate individual fishing rights to fishermen, fishing vessels, enterprises, cooperatives or fishing communities. Furthermore, EU has focused on involving the industry more closely responsibilities and rights. Industry can be given more responsibility through self-managment. Results based management of fisheries could be a move in this direction, instead of establishing rules about how to fish, the rules focus on the outcome and the more detailed implementation decisions would be left to the industry. The result based management would relieve both the industry and policy-makers of part of the burden of detailed management of technical issues and I think in Indian condition, this can really work well. The second issue is a climate change. We all know the land dominates the sea remains one of the fundamental norms and understanding. Coastlines now form the key objective circumstance for generation of rights of states to maritime zones. With variable and shrinking coastlines that are being affected by global climate change, however, profound re-examination of international law is required to recast such concepts as the legitimacy of existing territorial claims and even basis notions of human rights. Coastal geography due to its perceived stability serves as the objective circumstance on the basis of which the rights of states to maritime zones are determined and maritime delimitation disputes resolved. In fact a defined territory is indeed a constituent criterion of statehood under the international law. In the not- too-distant future, important questions may arise about the sustainability of those aspects of international law and changes may likely require a profound re-examination of various currently accepted paradigms of international law. Analyzing from the contents of UNCLOS provisions negotiated in 1960 and 70s that negotiators could have hardly foreseen substantial changes in coastal geography caused by a major natural phenomenon such as sea-level rise. With rising sea levels, the baselines from which the breadth of the territorial sea is measured will move landward affecting the outer limits of various maritime zones. The purpose as we know the current rules of international law of the sea is to maintain certainty. The effect of the consequences of the sea level rise will be to introduce uncertainty and increasingly exacerbate it. A possible consequence of projected sea level rise - reversing predictable and relatively stable characteristics attributed to coastal geography, so as to become a less stable factor and ultimately practically meaningless will be the potential of major destabilization in international and I would say even intra-state relations such as country like India. The fundamental purpose of the law for maritime delimitation is to facilitate expectations of certainty, or predictability hence of stability. The consequence of climate change and sea level rise could seriously undermine this objective law of meditation. Changes affecting the basic criteria of statehood such as territory, population and government, separately or together, do not aquatically affect the existence of a state unless territory and/or population disappears. The criterion of territory will no longer be met and the claim to statehood will fail. The very foundations of the current legal system and its current parameters need re-evaluation. Certain cornerstone concepts of the law of the sea architecture, like the rules pertaining to baselines and the consequent determination of the maritime zones, may have to undergo thorough scrutiny and be supplemented by new rules and with new coordinating mechanisms to enable their implementation. Underwater Cultural Heritage Convention 2001 : Another important issue is the Underwater Cultural Heritage, a subject though remains in margins of important forums but critically important as it have past, present and future importance in the overall governance of the law of the sea. India is yet to sign and then ratify 2001 underwater cultural heritage convention of the UNESCO. Although the reasons may be not completely known, one could expect that maritime jurisdiction and issues of sunken ships in and around Indian waters maybe one of the important factors for non-membership of the Convention. India can develop both administrative and legal arrangements to respond to changing international and national environments concerned with the UCH. As India has maritime boundaries with 7 States, it needs to initiate cooperation to prevent future conflicts over UCH. In fact none of the 7 states having maritime boundary with India has signed or ratified the Convention. Out of 21 member States of IORA, only three States Iran, Madagascar, South Africa and two dialogue partners, namely Egypt, France have ratified the Convention. Although India has not ratified the Convention, can it enact a legislation of preventive - nature like South Korea to ensure protection of UCH? India has very rich underwater cultural heritage, however, in the absence of domestic laws and also lack of ratification of UNESCO 2001 Convention, the country can start preparing its views as to how to deal with concepts of warships and other government ships and military aircraft found underwater, the scope of temporal limits and ownership of and jurisdiction for UCH. In my view, such a preventive legislation will supplement missions of the Underwater Archaeological Wing in the Archaeological Survey of India as well as supplement the existing laws on the Ancient Monuments and Archaeological Sites and Remains Act, 1958, and also the Antiquities and Art Treasures Act, 1972. I also like to take this opportunity to advocate that India should take a lead for technical cooperation at least among maritime neighbours which can develop standardization of recovery criteria and the specification of procedures and measures to prevent illicit recovery or export of UCH. There is also another issue of whether marine archaeology is considered as marine scientific research during the negotiations? While pure research does not simply direct economic revenue, applied research is primarily focused on future and foreseeable commercial activities. The information gathered by modem underwater technology, when directed at an archaeological target, a shipwreck, e.g. is likely not characterized as pure marine scientific research. This has significant impact as to how we implement the UNCLOS. Activities directed at UCH in the EEZ or on the continental shelf may then be subject to the coastal state's direction, depending on the nature and purpose of that activity. UNCLOS AND UNESCO conventions are by products of their respective epochs. UNCLOS was negotiated when underwater technology was not as advanced or relatively available for deep water exploitation and UCH was an exotic subject of interest. The UNESCO convention arrived when seas and oceans already were spaces where integral policies are to be developed, when technology is unveiling information unimaginable just a few decades ago and where thanks to evolving scientific methods, underwater remains are indispensable to understanding our common history. Maritime security threats reports 2008 UN Secretary-General Report has identified 7 specific maritime security threats like piracy, terrorism, illicit trafficking in arms and weapons of mass destruction, narcotic drugs, smuggling and trafficking in persons, IUU fishing and damage to the marine environment. My analysis of the threats and state practice mainly focusing on the legislative framework among the ORA countries have shown that there exists absolutely a low level of critical awareness among policy-makers about the scope and size of each of the maritime security challenges. The development of legal and juridical framework ranges from a very robust system to weak system in some parts of Africa. The IORA states also need to identify and systematically assess the impact of each of these threats on their varied level of political and economic development including the future growth potential. The Civil disobedience in the maritime domain although piracy may have receded, there are other threats or challenges such as how to address aggressive civil disobedience about appropriate boundaries between two bodies of international law that is international human rights norms that reflects the rights of all people to exercise free expression and the principles of good order, safety and security at sea embodied in the international law of the sea. The laws which govern protest on land and protest at sea are different. In last 10 years, the Mox Plant, Arctic Sunrise case and Whaling case are all too vivid reminders as to how the NGOs and like-minded institutions could pose challenge yet also offer certain opportunities to state institutions to reconcile the conflicting interests. Civil disobedience at sea occurs under conditions and geographical areas of shared authority, overlapping jurisdiction, and functional governance divided between flag states and coastal states. If a ship is entering or leaving port, then port authorities may also come into play. Green activists are driven to direct action to push the envelope of safe and acceptable behaviour in order to promote social causes that they deem ineffectively addressed by society or Government. Legal environment at sea is more complex than on land. Rather than having to consider only the competing laws and divergent public policies within a single polity, incidents of maritime protest typically fall within the jurisdiction for several states. Protesters at sea may be from one or more states, and they may not share nationality, either with the people that are protesting or law enforcement authorities on scene. The time has arrived therefore for countries to start preparing code of conduct. For example, the Japanese code of conduct resolutions adopted by the Japanese Diet that condemns dangerous actions at sea including collisions or ships by non-state activities. The code is the only instrument that explicitly balances the rights of free expression at sea with the imperative for navigational safety. As India has embarked upon Ocean Economy in its search to emerge as a maritime nation, attain goals of sustainable development, become net security providers, it will face maritime protest of different size, scale and actors. Therefore, it is imperative that India develops urgently code of conduct to prevent, reduce and control maritime protests. The final issue is Private Maritime Security Companies. The (PMSCs) employment has now become quite an established norm but they raise questions on liability for wrongful acts 5y PMSC on board ships, such as use of force with regard to corporate civil liability for wrongful acts. PMSCs have been successful in suppressing piracy in the western Indian Ocean and are used in the Gulf of Guinea but they have their fair share of controversy. Flag state, coastal and port state jurisdiction are all in play against a background of and often in tension with basic UNCLOS provisions and a set of larger international law concepts. Moreover, even when carrying weapons on board and where the use of force is authorized by international law and guidelines, there remains the difficulty in harmonizing human rights standards and penal regimes. Can victims of wrongful action seek both criminal and civil penalties? Therefore States should strive to achieve legal harmonization on the use of force by PMSCs and aimed personnel, as well as the treatment under national law of human rights abuses or violations, namely through the enactment of legislation on liability of PMSCs and armed personnel on board. Meaningful cooperation between states judicial and judiciary bodies on the enforcement of common standards is indispensable to avoiding a permissive environment for wrongful acts by companies of all kinds without adequate sanctioning and reparation. The rendering of military and security services by PMSCs and the presence of armed personnel on board ships shall continue to be key element of maritime security as a result of their impressive levels of efficiency, taken together with the fact that the overwhelming majority of the world's trade will continue to depend on maritime transportation. Likewise, the profitable and complex business that is criminality at sea makes it highly difficult for states to tackle comprehensively the different root causes. Another major issue is the Marine Biodiversity. The environmental issues in UNCLOS are not as well focused or fully defined as some are numerous other issues. At UNCLOS negotiations, genetic technology was only in its very initial phase and the authors did not foresee the importance of possible exploitation of genetic resources on the area. The irony is that genetic resources beyond national jurisdictions, which could possibly soon be exploited and become much more profitable than mineral resources, lack specific provisions UNCLOS. Unfortunately States disagree as do some specialist scholars over whether such resources may be addressed within the regime of high seas freedoms or whether they might fall under the regime of seabed mining part XI. G77, India, China argued that marine genetic resources should be regarded as a common heritage of mankind, much like mineral resources in the area, and they sought to get agreement on sharing of benefits, even successful exploitation of genetic resources should take 15 years from discovery to production. On the other hand, USA, Russia, and Japan resisted including marine resources within part XI. They assert that the freedom of high seas regime for living resources applies to living resources in the area and should preclude a restrictive new regulatory regime. The main priority for developing countries is protection of their interests in marine genetic resources, whereas developed states give their priority to the development of marine protected areas and environmental impact assessment. Law of the sea like almost all other faculty of international law has remained Eurocentric or Euro/North American-centric. The above issues which are critical are also emanating from the state practice of these two regions and obviously therefore, their state practice and, views would prevail over other region and other states too. Therefore, in the larger interest of the universal norms of the law of the sea that developing states shall play a more meaningful role. The time has come whereby the notion of the common heritage, the traditional legal framework and technique could adapt to encompass the coastal states' claims to exclusive rights over broad areas of the sea and combine these claims with the needs of international community and with those of intensified and more institutionalized cooperation for the exploitation of common resources and the protection of marine environment which characterize the law of the sea.

Friends, I have tried to identify only the major critical issues but if we look deep into the functioning of the UNCLOS and IMO instruments which govern the oceans, you will find myriad of issues each competing for eariier solutions, preventive measures amidst of competitive claims by the 12 major interest groups which put together is what we know is the constitution of the ocean mainly the UNCLOS.

7

Effect of Sea level Rise and Displaced Population

— *Dr Prabhakaran Paleri*

Abstract

This paper is effect of sea level rise and displaced population. An overview has been taken of research agenda for modelling the same. A specific case of Kiribati has been discussed to explain the hardships of low lying states.

Key-words: *Sea level rise, Kiribati, displaced population.*

Article

The Forum for Integrated National Security (FINS) is an emerging non- governmental think tank of India engaged in studying and analyzing integrated national security matters. The Forum is proud to organize its first International conference on the subject this year in the form of a discourse conference. The theme is ocean based national security. Ocean is one of the terrains of national governance where the game of national security is played according to the challenges faced by the Governments the world over today. Under the concept of national security the identified terrains are the land - the terra firma of the human system - ocean, air space, outer space, cyber space and genome or the genomic space in the order of emergency. Closer to the term "terrain" and for explanation, I may like to quote the Japanese term gemba made popular by Taiichi Ohno, the master architect of the Toyota production system, meaning the "actual place".

Gemba implies a location where the action takes place or value is created. In national security governance the terrain is more or less similar to Gemba in micro or macro level appreciation, through much enhance in conception and will depend upon the quantum of exertion of responsible

Governments in national security maximization. The imperatives and challenges of national Governance are vastly spread out in one or more of the six terrains of national security. For this purpose, national security is not mere physical or military security of a nation. It is much beyond that. The concept of national security ultimately percolates to the wellbeing of the people that can be measured and indexed at any given time. The sole purpose of national governance in any system of governance in any system of government is maximizing national security through its dedicated and mutually inclusive elements over the six terrains mentioned. These elements as well as the terrains can increase or undergo transmutation in the future. But they are not likely to diminish in their importance in national governance. When Sun Tzu in his Art of War or Kautilya, also called Chanakya, in his Arthasasthra propounded strategic thinking, their considerations fell over the then prevailed unitary terrain of the land from where the term itself evolved. The situation is different today and obviously will be different and more complex tomorrow. But the concept of national security underpinning the overall wellbeing of the citizens will remain unchanged under the law of invariance. The Governments, therefore, have to be exceedingly upfront in their vision statements to meet the demands of the future.

This discourse is the first in the series of annual meetings planned by the forum for providing an opportunity of discourse among likeminded partners across the world. Sagar means ocean in Sanskrit, a classical language and source language of India. This discourse is also titled SAGAR to not only the ocean but also to highlight the concept enunciated by the Prime Minister of India, Shri. Narendra Modi, as Security and Growth for All in the Region (SAGAR) in a sincere efforts to grow collectively with all in the region where the term region is extendable to the entire world. FINS sincerely hope to convey this message to the world through all of you, fine people, gathered here. India, like other responsible countries, believes in growth of all around the world. This will require not only cooperation of the people of a country in governance, but also the governments of other nations and their people. Such an ambition may sound idealistic but for the world that is evolving responsive to the citizens needs under visionary leaders in governance. Human wellbeing is an achievable target of governance however strenuous or conflict laden the path towards it may be. We in India believe in the richness of the ocean highlighted in our ancient scriptures. The world which is aware of the benefits of human can accrue by governing it's punctiliously. This is evident from the fact that every geo-political entity in the world, including the landlocked or geographically disadvantaged, is a maritime entity and has rights over the ocean under international law. Every one of them is impacted by the changes in the ocean anywhere in the world. This calls for cooperation of the international community at all levels on ocean governance or, what I would like to emphasis, the ocean property maximization based on my studies in macro level strategy of ocean governance. Ocean property ideates in the overall ocean benefits that a government or a people can accrue by maximizing their returns from its four components, ocean advantage, ocean resources, marine environment and oceanic islands. The return of ocean property regime needs to be integrated with the overall national security governance to maximize the wellbeing of the community.

There are many issues this address refers to some of them at random. Mapping the rim countries, in the geostrategic concept, may need a different approach to include the landlocked countries across the ocean rim in the respective regions. For example Lesotho in South Africa can be a rim country. This has to be based on a nation's geostrategic policy. According to this matrix many nations, landlock or otherwise may fall within multiple ocean rims. Such oceanic rim mapping will help in strategic networking linking multirim domains.

Another point for consideration is the UNCLOS itself which is the first step in taming the ocean anarchy in responsible world. But it needs a review to meet the demands of situational changes. A fresh look may be necessary in terms of the rule of international law related to suppression of serious unlawful activities such as piracy, trafficking, human rights of captive merchant marine personnel, sea level rise and demographic displacements, etc. I may even go to the extent of recommending a review of the maritime zones to cover the entire ocean with fixed and variable zones still maintaining the status of global commons. The issue of sea level rise is serious. The ever migrant human systems in search of another country may add on a different genre as displaced human who will not fall in the region of refugees according to at least one quote verdict so far. Refugee influx has been a serious issue for nations the world over, India is included. The flow is ever continuing. The issues of displaced persons of low lying areas, sometimes an entire nation, lost under the rising flood s can be more complex. The situation is relatively imminent. The world bodies need to think about it to avoid a human catastrophe never experienced so far in such a magnitude. The world country should not suffer. It is important to know that the umbrella regime of UNCLOS has consumed 25 long years before concluding consensually. A review could be equally long. The clock has been ticking.

Governing the ocean resources is another challenge. In the times of hunter gatherers there was enough harmony and cooperation among them as they needed to find food over land, the only reachable commons. Today's hunter gatherers are the fishers all over the world barring a few exceptions over the land. The hunter gatherers reap what they don't sow as a right. It is the law of nature that needs to be respected. Besides, they are supposed to be more cohesive than a gated community first originated in the world at the advent of the farm culture. The world needs to show special attention to the welfare and prosperity of the fishers. Besides fisheries resources, the ocean is a guarded mine of various other resources, this too needs to be highlighted for sustainable resource generation and exploitation. Corporate social responsibility (CSR), the phenomenon is slowly finding a place in the ocean too. Whether term corporate social responsibility or exclusively as corporate ocean responsibility (COR) the humans should understand they are already late for appreciating the health of the ocean. It is declining faster than the beneficiaries think. The beneficiaries are the ocean stakeholders, which every human is. We are all perched precariously over the rocks that looks floating around the vast area of water. More and more people will cling on to these rocks as the demographic density increases. We and our generations to come will have to survive in this position. For this the ocean has to be healthy, regenerative and sustainable. This is a major concern.

The term ocean advantage is one of the component of ocean property also refers to using the ocean for military purposes. Here I must add that this discourse does not trespass over the realms of military affairs. Ocean advantage also involves maritime shipping, navigation and maximum trade. The entire world depends on ocean trade that needs to be facilitated by giant ships and ultra-modern port infrastructure including multiport complexes. One of the points I would like to highlight in this address is actually a call to landlocked nations to participate in shipping and shipping infrastructure. This could be done either by entering in the commercial shipping trade with the help of friendly partners and also encouraging citizens to take up shipping employment through indigenous maritime education and training. This is an area which the landlocked nations can engage in especially since most of them are members of International Maritime Organization (IMO) and performs maritime law and treaty obligations.

As mentioned earlier, this is a beginning. The SAGAR discourses is expected to continue annually. The intention is to consolidate the ideas of national security for integration in a terrain specific manner. The concept for the next year is expected to be based on outer space in national governance. India has already embraced ambitious space projects in support of its immediate and willing regional painters. More is expected to follow.

8

"Ocean Research – its use and management in (Indian Ocean Region) IOR for sustainable development."

— ***Dr Priyadarshi Dash***

Abstract

Paper deals with Trade and Investment in Maritime Domain and Regional Co-operation in IOR. The need to activate resources in IOR, its sustenance and replenishment in accordance with biological necessities. This calls for study in ocean research, its management, its uses and Government mechanism in relation to Coastal development. The Paper also deals with the efforts made to quantify Blue Economy, Ocean Research and management and issues related to governance. Thus Blue economy be considered as Policy Component which also deals with inter-ministerial co-ordination issues. Each Country needs to identify target sectors of Blue Economy for its sustainable development.

Key - Words*: Ocean Resources, Coastal development, Blue Economy, target Sectors.*

Article

I will try to link the subject to the economic part the opportunities that are there in Trade and investment.

The Indian Ocean countries are interested in investing in each other rather than investing with other continents. It has a list of members which are the developed country members. The Indian Ocean Countries Association which is a representative grouping for Indian Ocean region. Before I go to the economic sector, I want to tell you here is that why do we emphasize the contribution of the economic potential of the Ocean resources to the growth and development. We have already consumed the maximum land base resources. We need to activate the resources in the Indian Ocean region to its optimum use and then ensuring the sustainability of those resources, their replenishment in accordance with the biological part of the species like fishes and the ocean habitats, all these things we have to take into account when we talk of the Ocean resources. So, economy is the terminology which captures all the different aspects of Ocean resources, its management, its uses, the Government mechanism for that, to ensure that these resources cooperate with the human development in relation to the coastal development.

We have done a couple of papers at RIS, I will give you a sense of that how these sectors are inter linked and what type of potential it offers to mankind. You must be wondering that human civilization has depended on all Oceans for centuries. What we have to discuss is to create a frame work which does not destroy the resources, replenishment of the resources, so that the faster use is compensated by the process of restructuring of the resources as well. 90 percent of our fish is already consumed. So, over fishing is already done so you don't have to bother whether there is any fish to catch or not. In fact in certain areas the biological stock has gone down significantly so it is a danger to the sustainability of that resource because so many people have taken fisheries for livelihood.

Is Blue Economy a significant component of the economy? It is. If you find some indicative figures here that Blue economy output constitutes to disproportionate GDP you can see somewhere it is accounted for 15 percent like that 4 percent somewhere it is 2 percent like that. There is no system in the account of the Blue economy. These numbers indicate that and we need to seriously take it into account the pollution existing in the Blue economy sectors.

What is so contentious about the Blue economy. Blue economy is being discussed everywhere in the regional forums and world forums but nobody knows how to get it and ·that is precisely the point. The problem is that we do not know what constitutes the Blue economy activities. So, we have started in RIS categorizing these sectors into traditional emergency sectors and then clubbing them to the activities as per the statistical processes available. So that some sort of foundation can be given to estimate this economy. How to plan for the investment so that estimate of the economy is important.

But if you ask the small island countries, they say we depend on the Oceans for everything, for livelihood, for achieving high growth, for everything. How to go for those issues? There is a need for a proper accounting system. That accounting system could be based on anything. People have written on papers about National accounting system etc. None of these systems are contingency and complete to account for all the changes and dynamics in Ocean Resources Use and Management. Besides this, accounting problems, there are several other problems relating to the governance, suppose there is a case of a boat is seen in the high seas who governs that? What is the role of the flag state, how much jurisdiction does the Regional Management Fishing or the Organisations have over that? So Management and governance issues also need to be properly examined.

So, main stream of the Blue Economy means sensitizing the Government and other stake holders that Blue economy has to be considered as a policy component. So far Fisheries is dealt by the Minister of Fisheries, Shipping dealt by the Minister of Shipping, there is very little inter relation and co-ordination from the point of the Government. There is co-ordination but not to the point of prospective Blue economy betterment. So, there is a need for sensitizing the policy makers that these are the opportunities and these are the challenges. In each sector we find problems, fisheries legal and illegal fishing is happening, aqua culture, lot of proportion with farm, tourism if you say slowly hotels will come in the coastal cities it will get to see its pollution, plastic in the sea water itself. It has already started.

Another sector would be what is not there in the ocean. How to regulate, once you decide how to mainstream it there should be a target sector approach.It would vary from country to country. Fisheries some small countries like Mauritius, Maldives they can focus on fisheries. Each country has to find out which are the sectors to begin with, which may be called the target sectors of the Blue economy. So this should essentially be the Blue economy approach to the Ocean Resources Management. There are issues between the Security and the Ocean Resource Management. Unless there is a frame work on the coastal issues there will be conflicts to use the resources especially the migratory species. Migratory species they move in the sea. Today they are in the Thailand waters tomorrow they will be in Bangladesh waters. So- if we plan we can catch those fish. That is not the solution to the issue we are talking about. So the Trade and Investment part of the Coastal economy has lot to do with the management of the Blue economy. Investment and the working mechanism something like regional fisheries mechanism, the same could be for other sectors, so that the Ocean economy that we are talking about will address a lot of issues and then all the sustainable development goals and other things can be achieved.

9

Science and Technology in Maritime Domain and its Security Related Issues

—Dr Ravindran. M

Abstract

The paper covers highlights of science and technology related activities in maritime domain in IOR. The contributions are on food security, energy security and industrial progress coupled with hazard mitigation within ocean domain. Benefits are immense. Seismic studies for resource estimation and technologies for resource exploitation will contribute to economic security of our country. These and activities in the IOR have to be protected against security related issues. and commercial advantages.

***Key-words**: Security of Marine resources, Food security, energy security, industrial and economic security.*

Article

1. Marine Resources and EEZ

The IOR has enormous resources, when harvested, could provide food security, energy security and industrial security for the people of the region and contribute to the economic growth of the entire region and beyond. The marine resources consist of food, energy and minerals .Deep sea fishing, harvesting of rare beach minerals from shallow waters, collection of deep sea nodules containing Cobalt, Nickel and Copper and exploitation of Gas hydrates will add to the growth of economical activities in the entire region. The long shipping lanes in the IOR have to be protected to provide lifelines for the development. But at the same time, the people living in the region are exposed to natural hazards from the oceans like cyclones, storms and tsunamis. Extensive science and technology related activities are going on in the region to survey the marine resources in the shallow water and deep sea regions and to develop technologies to harvest the resources without damaging the ocean environment. Furthur, we have to understand the air – sea interactions and its impact on monsoons and climate. Global warming and associated sea level rise is threatening the life of people in the islands. All these S&T activities in the large IOR have to be protected in the interest of economic security of the entire region. I am not going to talk about S&T activities related to Defence needs. Dr. V. Bhujang Rao is here to address those issues.

The marine sources lying within a 200 nautical miles boundary from the landmass, known as Exclusive Economic Zone ,belong to that country. Indian EEZ boundry is shown by the dotted lines(Ref fig) and the hatched area is the additional area claimed by the country in the International Seabed Authority under the conditions of UNCLOS. This means that India will have exclusive rights over marine resources lying in an area of about 3 million sq. km, almost equal to our landmass. So, ·have we surveyed the ocean area of 3 million sq. km.to identify all the resources?. Not completely. We have to survey the total area, first to locate and estimate the resource and then develop the technologies to harvest these resources for benefit of people.. First is food security. Our present fish catch is around about 9 million tonnes,mostly in shallow water regions. We want to raise it to about 16-17 million tonnes from our own EZZ. We don't have deep water fishing boats . We have to develop the deep sea infrastructure and ports for deep sea fishing.. Presently, we are having technology demonstaration activities to have additional fish protein from sea farming using cage culture. We are using the experience of Norway in this respect.. We have deployed something like twenty such cages in Andhra Pradesh, Rameshwaram area and Andamans .These cages are of 10 meter diameter and we are growing exotic species, commercially valuable fishes like sea bosses. We are able to give economical support to the coastal fishermen communities and this is to be expanded. Once we have the deep sea infrastructures like deep sea ports, deep sea trawlers, then there is no limit to the economical benefit on the food front. So these activities are to be protected so that they could go on unhindered.

2. Energy Resources

Secondly, we have a variety of energy sources from the sea. First and well known resource is the offshore oil. Out of 17 billion barrels of hydrocarbon production, more than 50% comes from off shore areas like, Bombay High, Kaveri basin, Godavari basin . We are moving from shallow water of 100 meter water depth to deeper water of 2000 meters moving away from shore. When we move far away from land, these platforms and these operations have to be protected. Another important and new energy source for the future is gas hydrates.This is nothing but frozen methane gas which is lying at the depth of about 100 meter below the ocean bed where the ocean bed itself is at about 1000 to 2000 meter water depth. So the area as you can see here (ref Fig) on east coast region, with red dots, have something like 1000 Trillion cubic meter of gas potential for the future. So, we have to conduct seismic surveys and also drill boreholes to provide seatruths to identify the depth and thickness of the gas hydrates layer. A technology problem here is that gas hydrate changes directly from the solid phase to gas. 1 kg of hydrate produces about 400 m^3 of gas. Therefore, if slight heat is generated, then it will explode. So, we have to develop a safe technology for exploiting gas hydrates .First ,for providing sea truths NIOT is developing an autonomous coring system. This is lower from a ship to ocean bed by a cable.. It has an Automatic Coring System.

The hydrocarbon based energy sources are not renewable. The renewable energy sources from the ocean are offshore wind energy, ocean thermal energy, wave and tidal energy. NITI Ayog has recently estimated the total wind energy resource as 350 Gega Watts and the sum of other ocean renewable of tidal, wave and ocean thermal energy sources to be about 90 GegaWatts. The slide shows a wave plant installed at Vizinjam harbbour in Kerala ,which was the longest surviving wavey plant in the world.In this experimental plant we developed different types of turbines, generators, control systems etc. over a period of 25 years. This concrete caisson based system will be very useful as a multipurpose system where these concrete modules will form a breakwater for a harbour construction in addition to capturing wave energy and provide an economical option.

In ocean thermal energy, the surface sea water and deep sea water at 1000m depth have temperature difference of about 20 degree Celcius. Using this temperature difference, we can run a Rankinecycle that is like a reverse of a refrigerator i.e. converting thermal energy into electrical energy. We can have floating OTEC plants or land based OTEC plants depending on the distance from land where the 1000 metre depth is available. Floating plants would be able to move wherever we have offshore islands or where deep sea mining plants are working ,where multiple 100 Megawatt power is required. OTEC is the only power source for such installations.

3. Mineral Resources

There are different types of valuable mineral resources in the ocean . One must have heard about the beach minerals or heavy minerals in Kerala, Odisha and also Tamil Nadu which consist of illmenite, sillimanite, garnet and similar heavy minerals. India has about 320 million tonnes of these minerals. The rivers bring these minerals to the ocean and and waves push them up on the beaches. W could collect them from the beach. The second set of mineral resource is Phosphorites from tidal flats where energy is very low. The deep sea water bring these minerals to the tidal flats where they setlle down.

Then, we have certain locations where the water depth is around 5000 meters ,where we find Polymetallic nodules. Central picture (ref. fig) shows the Polymetallic nodules which are lying on the surface of the deep ocean bed. We don't have to dig into the bed to collect the nodules. The nodules contain cobalt, nickel and copper which are not available in terrestrial mines in our country. Therefore, to provide for these very important metals in the future ,we have to develop this technology for deep sea mining. NIOT has been working from last almost two decades on this technology development. IMMT Bhubaneswar has developed technologies to extract the actual metals from the nodules.

In the ocean ,we also have Hydrothermal Sulphides which are spewed out during the volcanic eruptions in deep sea. The magma flows over the chimneys and they settle down and solidify. These are the Polymetallic crusts which contain Cobalt and Nickel on hard surfaces. Sometimes, some of these volcanic crust are softer and one could suck them up or use hardcutting tools to remove the cobalt crust.

Beach minerals are very close on beach, within our region but you can see that the Polymetallic nodule site is in the central Indian Ocean basin which is about 15 degree south. (ref fig). Two main elements in the nodules are iron and manganese but the most important elements are cobalt, nickel and copper which together constitute only about 2% (The estimated potentials are given in the figure).

Just south of Sri Lanka we have the site for the cobalt crusts. Further down below the Polymetallic site is located . (fig). Furthur south, we have the Hydrothermal site .That mean it is 3000 nautical miles away from Kanyakumari,the southernmost tip of India. Thus, we have activities now which are far away from EEZ and these activities have to be protected. We are well advanced in the Polymetallic nodule mining technology. For

Hydrothermal sites and Cobalt Crust sites,we have to survey more areas with the permission from the International Sea Bed Authority.

On the polymetallic nodules, NIOT is working on a flexible riser system (ref fig) One can see the crawler on the sea bed which is designed for 6000 m depth. This crawler collects nodules, crushes them and pumps along with sea water using a displacement pump through a flexible riser and delivers to the ship deck. This Crawler, one can see in the central picture, has rubber tracks. The ambient pressure is 600 bar. Temperature is around zero degree Celcius. The seabed on which the crawler has to move is very soft with less than $1/10^{th}$ of the bearing strength of a normal floor. So we have to provide buoyancy on this machine so that it doesn't sink itself when it is trying to collect these nodules. Power is supplied through the 6000 meter long cable .NIOT is using special ship ORV Sagar Nidhi for this technology development.

4. Fresh water

An important resource needed by the islands and island nations in the region is fresh water. NIOT has developed a very simple and reliable desolation process to convert sea water into fresh water at locations where steep slope is available on the shore, reaching about 600 m water depth within 1 km from shore. This process uses warm surface water and cold deep sea water at around 10 degree Celcius. Three such plants are already operating in 3 islands of Lakshadweep group for more than 10 years, operated by the local people. NIOT would be glad to assist other island nations in this regard.

5. Ocean Information system

In order to understand the air - sea interaction, monitoring of cyclones, storms and Tsunamic warnings, Ministry of Earth Sciences, Govt of India has established an Ocean Information System with NIOT, Chennai and INCOIS, Hyderabad as major participating institutions. Under this programme, NIOT has deployed about 15 morred Ocean Data buoys in the bay of Bengal and Arabian sea collecting ocean and meteorological data like, wave heights, wave period, current speed, sea water temperature profiles, wind speed and directions, atmospheric pressure etc continuously and transmit them via satellites to NIOT at a three hour intervals. These data are shared with India Met dept, INCOIS, all ports, naval establishments etc on a continuous basis. NIOT thanks our Norway friends who gave us 15 data buoys twenty years ago under the NORAD assistance scheme.

We have indegenised the buoy systems now and celebrated the twentieth anniversary of the implementation of the programme a few months back. These data from the buoys are available to everybody on a continuous basis. Now,NIOT has developed Tsunami Waining Systems after the 2004 tsunami. In this system, sea bed pressure sensors detects the Tsunami signals and convey to the floating data buoys which send it to the shore stations through satellite communication. This information is made available to all countries in the region.

For understanding the long term variations in the vertical current and temperature profile at critical locations in the sea, Mooring Systems are installed. Mooring System stay at a fixed location continuously for one or two years recording currents and temperature profiles at various depths. The stored data is analysed on recovery of the mooring system at the end of the required period.Such mooring systems need protection in the international waters much beyond our EEZ.

To protect the islands and other island nations from sea level rise, we have located 24 stations in the region which are monitored by us regularly.

To understand the spatial variation of sea surface temperatures and air pressures above the sea surface many drifting buoys have been deployed in the oceans around us. We throw drafting buoys on the sea surface from ships and they go around carried by the currents .They have GPS and measure the surface temperature and pressure at that location at that time which are received through satellite links.

We have the ARGO buoys which are measuring the vertical profiles of temperature and salinity which are very important to study the ocean characteristics and has direct impact on underwater communication. These floats are simply thrown into the sea from ships. They have buoyancy varying systems, by which they move up and down the ocean depths measuring the temperature and salinity profiles. They move around with ocean currents in the sea and when they pop up, they transmit their data to shore via satellite. These are very useful buoys and they save costly ship time for such profile measurements. ARGO floats are deployed under international cooperative programmes and the data are shared. In IOR region, as you can see in fig, that there are multiple hundred ARGO floats floating around collecting data.

In addition, thousands of Bathy thermographs are shot into sea from ships which collect the temperature profiles at the site and transmit the same to the ship. The straight lines in fig indicate that bathy thermo graphic measurement locations from All these data add to the valuable Ocean Information system.

As could be seen from the current discussions, one realizes the importance of Ocean going research vessels to undertake the variety of scientific and technology related activities. India has about 10 ocean going research vessels and more are being acquired. These ships ply continuously in various parts of IOR upto Antartic. These ships need also protection from pirates and other intruders in the high seas.

The other important thing which is very important to Ocean security is the free movement of ships at the few choke points located in the critical sea routes. Some critical choke points in the region are the straights of Malacca, Hormuz and the Suez canal. It is of great importance for the countries of the region to keep these choke points free from blockades at the time of a crisis. You can see that China US are having their bases near these choke points.

6. Concluding Remarks

India has developed tremendous scientific, technological and defence capabilities to take up S&T activities which boost our economy and also to protect these activities. India is also located geographically in an advantageous position in the region to take the lead. At the same time, India should be alert and not loose the initiative to strengthen our security in the region by cooperation and participation with countries in the region.

I am Sayedeh Hajar Hejazi, research internat the human rights at sea (HRAS) in London

I feel to be honour and privilege to be speaking at this gathering today. I would like to take this opportunity to thank Professor, Mr Parli for the invitation and I would like to express my appreciation to the FINS conference organizers for their support and technical assistance

Today I am presenting my topic about seafarer's abandonment

Shipping is one of the fastest-growing and most dynamic industries in the world today. It makes a significant contribution to the prosperity and wealth of nations. It has been said that, without ships, half of the world would freeze and the other half would starve.

Approximately 1.5 million seafarers serve daily on a worldwide fleet of over 100,000 ships that transport over 90% of world trade – manufactured goods, fuel, foodstuffs and commodities, that we all relay on but which we generally take for granted.

In terms of legal protection, under international law, seafarers are classified as labour or workers.

- in fact, they are regarded as belonging to a special category of workers because they are subject to different national jurisdictions, That's why, the possibility of abuse is not remote.
- Their lives involve Physical abuse such as Beatings and sexual assault and mental abuse arises from isolation that seafarers suffer.
- Non-payment and delays in wages and in entitlements, which very much affects the seafarer's families, are additional aspect of abuses in seafarer's abandonment.

In my point of view, seafarer's abandonment is a case of mental and physical abuse and a type of torture to seafarers. The crews can go for many months, sometimes years, with no pay and little hope of repatriation.

Paradoxically, Seafarers have plenty of rights and plenty of resources to obtain their rights: seafarers are entitled to receive

- human rights, Labour and Welfare rights
- Right to life
- Right to have equal protection of law
- Right to wages
- Right to have reasonable working hours and holidays
- Right to receive medical treatment for sickness and injury, for instance.

The ILO 164 convention gives rights to health protection and medical care to seafarers. This obliges all State Parties to ensure facilities are available, such as:

- The right of to visit a doctor without delay and free of charge, also
- To have Medical advice by radio or satellite communication at sea
- Ship owners are required to insure seafarers under a compulsory sickness insurance scheme.

Abandonment at sea occurs for a number of reasons.

- It is often a calculated economic decision by a ship owner facing bankruptcy or insolvency

- or it can be due to the arrest of the vessel by creditors
- In many cases, vessels are abandoned after they are deemed unseaworthy by inspectors.
- In abandonment, the ship owner fails to meet financial and social obligations.
- when the ship owner fails to cover the cost of the seafarers repatriation or if the ship owner sets sail leaving seafarers behind their ship or
- He has left them on board the ship without the necessary maintenance and support. This might be filer to provide adequate food, water, accommodation or unpaid wages for at least two months.

At the very least; abandoned seafarers are often subject to cruel, inhuman and degrading treatment and at the worst, they may find themselves in life threading conditions with no means of sustenance available.

I would like to give an account of a specific case of abandonment: Last July, the HRAS received a report about the seafarers of the oil tanker IBA abandoned in Dubai. The Seafarers were from India, Sri Lanka and Pakistan. The report concerned the detention of seafarers on board a shipwreck, without necessary maintenance which was off the coast of the UAE.

The Alco shipping services, the ship owner had left the seafarers on board shipwreck, and he had failed to provide food, water and essential fuel to seafarers.

During the abandonment, Food and water had to be provided by the Indian consulate (as the national country of one the crews) in Dubai.The ship owner refused to organized the crew document, for example the crew's passports had been taken on their sign on date, and had not been returned on signing off date despite repeated requests.

All of their correspondence with the ship owner on these points had been ignored.

The crewmembers of the ship have begun to encounter a multitude of emotional and legal problems,

- They were long way from their homes and families
- The crew were facing serious health problems.
- they were suffering from an undiagnosed
- They had not been paid for almost 6 months

Being Detained on board the shipwreck for almost 5 months and being unpaid for almost 6 months is classified as detention and a type of mental torture of the seafarers and their families. A very stressful situation was created during the period on board ship, which was compounded by extreme boredom, worry, and fear with the crew also suffering from skin diseases.When the crew raised the safety concern with Alco shipping, they were threatened with criminal proceedings if they were to reported their concern to a local authority.

Moreover, I must also mention that the port state and the flag state of the ship also, refused to facilitate medical treatments for the crew.

They did not cooperate with the crew but the crew did received Advocacy and investigative support from by the Human rights at sea organization.

It is the legal obligation of the ship owner as the first responder to provide the crew with financial and social security of in such case. In this case the ship owner had refused his responsivity.

The second responder is the flag state of ship, the UAE and then the port state UAE, here, the UAE failed to meet the obligations.

In this case, many provisions related to seafarers' rights had been expressly violated:

For instance: united nation declaration of Human rights, the maritime labour convention, The amendment of 2014 on MLC and the regulation 930.(22) of IMO.

When difficulties arise, the seafarers have various avenues they can pursue to obtain help:

The first and foremost resources of seafarers rights is (a) Seafarers contract of employment,

An individual contract employment between seafarer and employer, which sets out rights and obligations. The Ship-owner as the employer of seafarers is defined as the owner of the ship who has assumed the responsibility for the ship and the seafarers.The Ship-owner has to meet financial and social security obligations.

(b)The second resource is: the flag state of the ship: The ship has the nationality of the flag that it flies.

Under international law: the law of a flag state applies to a ship regardless of the location of the ship and regardless of the nationality of the seafarers.

(c) The Port state one of the important resources of seafarer's is the port state, it is important in terms of the security and safety of seafarers in the hosting port,

When the ship enters a port, that port state can exercise powers over the ship while it is in port.

In general, a port state does not intervene in the internal affairs of a ship unless there is a dispute, which concerns the peace and good order of the port. However, in many jurisdictions, if seafarers have a legal claim, for example, for unpaid wages, they will be able to start a legal action through the legal authorities of the port state.

(d) Seafarers home state law: Seafarers will be able to rely on their home state law if that law governs the seafarer's contract of employment.The Seafarers home country should provide support and assistance through its consulate offices wherever seafarers need support.

(f) The last resource of seafarer's rights is: International law and the international legal framework. International laws are made at the highest level between states, United Nations through the international laobur organization (ILO) and IMO has set international labour standards for all seafarers. Specifically has set standards for seafarers in more than 65 conventions and recommendations, which were updated and consolidated in the maritime labour convention, 2006 that is known as MLC 2006.

What has been done to prevent abandonment?

On a closer evaluation of the legal aspects of the seafarer's abandonment:

ILO have ratified MLC as a financial security system to prevent incident of seafarer abandonment.This is a compulsory provision to state parties which have ratified the MLC 2006 and Ship owners (of the countries who has ratified the MLC) shall ensure that requirements are in place in ships flying of the signatory states:

- MLC is a financial security system, which provides direct and sufficient access to cover payment of the outstanding wages and entitlements, limited to four months.
- MLC provides necessary maintenance and support, including food, accommodation, drinking water, essential fuel for survivors on board ship
- MLC provides the necessary medical care
- It covers the costs of their repatriation

Under MLC, seafarers have maritime lien. (maritime lien is the right to obtain and order to prevent the ship owner to removing his ship from port or, depending on the circumstances and national law, to arrest the sister ship or other asset of the owner, in place of the ship which seafarers worked. By maritime lien, seafarers can sell the ship and cover their claim for wages (The assets seized by court order can be of any type of bank accounts, insurance proceeds and ships)

Under MLC: If the ship owner fails to meet the cost of the reparation, the ship flag state must arrange for the seafarers repatriation. if it fails to do so, the country to which seafarers are to be repatriated or the country of which they are nationals

- May arrange their repatriation and recover the cost from the flag state of the ship.

When the ship is not subject to MLC: If seafarers could not obtain their rights through MLC, In this circumstance there is a Seafarers Emergency Fund ('SEF'), which may provide seafarers with accommodation, food, water and medical assistance and the costs of their repatriation.

In addition, seafarers should consider the additional rights that they might have under the national laws of the country in which they have been abandoned.

In regard to the IBA case, seafarers were entitle to receive rights from the UAE, according to article 1 of the constitution of the UAE. The UAE government was obliges by its own law to force the ship owner to follow the UAE national law.

The MLC 2006 mandates that commercially operated ships if they operate on international voyages, be required to carry, two specific documents:

- MLC, which is the maritime labour certificate
- DMLC, the declaration of maritime lobour compliance which is evidence that the ship is in compliance with the requirements of the convention.

These two certificates will be subject to inspection when ships enter the ports of other countries that have ratified the convention.

Moreover, ships flying the flag of countries that have not ratified the convention will also be subject to inspection with respect to working and living conditions for seafarers when they enter ports of countries in which is in force

However, MLC applies to a wide range of ship operations on international and national domestic voyage and is compulsory to all state parties as I said that have ratified the convention.

10

Norway – India co-operation in Maritime Technology - A Case Study

— Shri Helge Tryti

Abstract

The paper elaborates Norway's application of Ocean space technology, not only in security but in various other spheres like, vigilance, environment, energy and blue gardening. Ocean farming has seen a lot of application of the technology used in Norway and therefore India – Norway co-operation in maritime technology domain is proposed.

Key-words: *Norway, ocean technology, blue gardening.*

Article

I am going to say a few words of how we follow-up with the security and monitoring of the Indian oceans and parts of that used internationally and I am going to go through how we organize the Maritime area within Norway and then go through some of the areas where I think that India and Norway can do business and some of them you are already in business in. So 70% of the earth is covered by ocean and 90% of the world's productive mass is ocean so this is huge and the growth in population is enormous so we have 9.6 billion people in 2050 and we need food, some say its 2 and some say its 4% of the food that is coming from the ocean today, it is not that much, it has to increase a lot.

On the South pole, where fishing in Norway is very active and there is enough biomass on the south .pole to feed the whole global population many times over and we make omega-3, etc. Population in this region is very big. South Asia 1.6 billion people, within 20-years will be close to 2 billion people and in the region you find also some of the most populated areas and that means that there will be a lot of sea traffic as most of the goods are currently being transported by ships. The transport along the Indian Coast has had difficulties for example earlier from Bangladesh to India and you had to go via Singapore or Colombo. Now there is a new agreement so that makes it much easier for the transportation and that is why I think the coaching transportation along India will increase in the years to come.

I think the region should look at ports and means of transportation all the way down to Singapore and the fight for the oceans space has started. We all know about China and the South China sea and we also know that there are a number of countries that are already claiming space in the oceans, for example south of Madagascar. China has claimed the rights and that is in the Indian Ocean.

So ocean space technology is the space programme of our century. This is where it is going to happen and there are a number of elements that goes into this and Norway will be working basically in all of these. We have the biomass part with the fisheries, aquaculture, and algae production that you can use for biogas. You have the organic oil and gas minerals and metals and you have energy potential with the ocean wind and waves and sea titles, etc. And then you have a lot of transport and logistics in a number of areas like short sea shipping, coastal shipping, deep sea shipping and you also have a lot of in land waterways and then as also mentioned earlier today about cruise and tourism and that there is a lot of equipment that goes into this without building the ships etc., it is also surveillance that needs to take place.

So in Norway, we have created a number of clusters, competence areas related to the Maritime sector. We have made an ocean space Centre so that all the different industries can work closely together because you need all the different components to make this work so it is not only the ship owners and the legal classification and the education etc., for the ships itself, but we need banking and the finance. We see the development in Arctic is coming up more and more as mentioning of this Russian ship that had gone in Arctic route to Asia without being an icebreaker that is coming. Currently there is not much traffic there but it might be in the future. And to take care of the whole area Norway we have started up something we call the balance watch, established in 2011 and it is 25 different partner organizations in Norway that are involved in this work; 4 of them are ministries and then we have a lot of different organizations with interest in this space. So it is everything from you know taking care of the environment to rules and regulations, fisheries, aquaculture, shipping, oil and gas, all these elements are represented and we need to have a good overview of what is happening in our oceans and we in Norway would like to have very good transparency. So in this organization with the balance watch there are number of things we can go in to look at. This is open on the net, very transparent. What we see here, every dot is an aquaculture site and the sea lives is an issue and any one can go in and look at any particular week of the year, you can how many cages of these have had the lanes and you can how many who did not and you can zoom in a specific company or you can zoom in to see where are the sites with the lanes The escaped salmon which is not good so we do not want it into our rivers and the red dots that are the aquaculture site with too many lanes. And then you can zoom all the way to nonspecific aquaculture site and you can see the number of lanes and all the details, the temperature in the water, etc, so very detailed and very open for everyone. The same thing with the ports, we have 238 ports in Norway. They are all registered here and you have your inland waterways, you have ports in many, many places and with this system you can tell what kind of ports it is, what kind of draft you can you go with etc, so very much in detail. And what kind of industry can set the oil products is it dry bulk, is it containers, etc. and then of course we have the overview of the ship traffic again this is a system that you can use globally. It is based on AIS, on GPS, via satellite, etc., and you can get very detailed the traffic information. You can choose what you want to see just the cargo vessels, tankers, or what kind of vessels you want. If you want to look at the fishing vessels you can choose that and then you can zoom on a particular ship. So this is the blue dot in the middle there and it says what kind of ship it is, it says what kind of draft it has, it says what kind of speed it has, etc. And this you can do on every single dot throughout the world and then we can also further zoom on the ship to get more details. The other changes in the ocean space are we have the traditional areas and then emerging ocean industries has renewal LNG when entitled off shore aquaculture we have been talking about earlier today. Subsea mining is coming up as a very important area, ocean bio-prospective and carbon capture is one element. So in all, we have the six largest maritime fleet in the world and that is of course being developed in a number of areas and we look for newer solutions for the sea, autonomous container ships where you have a longer ship that can go into small harbours or into the inland waterways for example.

LNG was mentioned earlier today. Norway is very good on LNG in the whole value chain, about 70 LNG ships in the world, 70 out of 90 there is no mention, we have all sorts. So when you are looking for clean and green shipping, LNG is a very good alternative and we have 40 ports along the

Norwegian coast that can handle LNG and one suggestion would be when you look at the LNG travel for example in the Cochin which is running at 10% capacity instead of waiting for the pipelines and the...to be solved, you could actually transport with the small LNG vessels as an alternative. Tourism has been mentioned. Goa is being on tourism about from ship owner's perspective mostly right out of Florida and I think there is a big potential also in the regions of India.

Ocean farming. We have talked about that, that is a potential in India which is not kept and we just have an agreement between Eika Group and West Coast Group in India to join forces to make aquaculture systems that will fit for the Indian needs. So I hope that will materialize in a good way. We do a lot of research and investment in aquaculture as it is such a large and important industry for Norway and as a part of that we do a lot of the hatching and the first period for the salmon. We have actually the longer they can stay on land, the better they grow and that is a big potential of course in India you have a large fish farming industry but it is primarily or almost only land based and here we have food circulation systems so you have to clean the water and use the waste for biogas and fertilizer etc so it is a good system.

We can harvest from the Blue Garden a number of things, sea weed for example they grow it on the sea. In the sea, it is 10 times faster than it is on land so you could use this for making bio fuel instead of sugarcanes for example. A lot of research goes into this. We have done some research also in India when it comes to vaccines for shrimps. Then of course we work fairly good at the DC oil and gas, I mean that is our main industry coming on the deep sea and now we are opening on sector 98/2 on the east coast where I think Norway has a lot to offer. Fishing vessels and inventions and you see one factory ship and the green one is actually an electrical fishing vessel. We make a lot of electrical vehicles like electrical fairy and if you go down to the left there that is actually a factor for cleaning sewage that can be put on a ship for example outside Mumbai, take the sewage onboard, get clean water, get biogas and fertilizer, so it is a win-win.

11

"India – Bangladesh Maritime Co-operation – Sub-regional and bi-lateral Issues"

— ***Shri Hussain***

Abstract

"This Paper deals with India-Bangladesh Maritime relation in terms of aspirations for prosperity, climate change, tourism development and to ensure confidence building measures in place. Also non- governmental channels are activated. The five Pillars of Indo-Bangladesh relationship being – security and border management, trade & investment, water resource management, people to people contact and development co-operation. India & Bangladesh also support each other in multi-lateral issues, Physical connectivity, link territories & communities – helping peace, prosperity & stability across the region. The Paper analyses the importance of Protocols, inland water transport & line of credit for infrastructure development. The Author expressed confidence that development of inland/inter country water transport will regionally build confidence and trust between the communities."

***Key- Words**: Sub regional Maritime Co-operation, Protocol and inland water transport, confidence building and community development.*

Article

I will give a quick snapshot of the issues of Bangladesh. Since I took up the issue on day-to-day basis and since I had bilateral cooperation and connectivity that we have with India and all the other countries in the region. We know there were ups and downs in the 70s and 80s in the relationship but some amount of relation and cooperation has been gained in the last one decade. It all depends on the amount of trust. I think there was lack of trust or a kind of deficit in trust but currently the trust is fulfilled and we are expecting the trust to suffice.

We believe that trust can make us go forward in our relationship.

There are some dynamic commodities. There are some challenges and aspirations. The Hon. Prime Minister of India, Mr Narendra Modi he said in India I speak Hindi very well saath- saath, pass -pass. So they are common aspirations for the share of prosperity and there are challenges like terrorism and the climate change that we have seen since 2009. Our Hon. Prime Minister, Sheikh Hasina is in the South east, for the second time in Bangladesh, there a lot of initiatives have been undertaken between the two countries, to restore the confidence based on which we are taking forward the relationship between Bangladesh and India. On the extent of co-operation I have stated there has been a fresh beginning on the political level, there have been some high level political meetings, our Prime Minister Mr Modi visited Bangladesh and our Prime Minister this year came to Delhi and a lot of things happened after that and before that. There were two tricky issues I would say, the land mark which was set after 68 years and thanks to all the Parties in the Indian Parliament and the dynamic role of the India Prime Minister, the land mark issues are now settled. The people are now feeling happy and safe. We have also peacefully negotiated on the Maritime issues. With one Clause we have made it at the arbitration Tribunal and both the countries are happy with that.One issue which I would like to highlight other than the Government, our Civil society or Non-Governmental Organizations they were also interacting on various occasion in the last two years. So you can see here the extent of relation between Bangladesh and India.

There are deep rooted fixed commonalities. The culture, history, linguistic, ethics and other things so since it is deep rooted, these two act as the pioneer of the building and the foundation . As you all know in 1971, we were liberated from the occupation of Pakistan and the people and the Government of India under the leadership of the then Prime Minister, supported to the cause of Bangladesh's liberation. Number of people took refuge in the neighbouring States of India and also a few thousand soldiers of the Indian army died for the cause of Bangladesh. This very important happening and also the ties between the leadership makes the foundation of that building. In the building there are some pillars, I call it as the five pillars of Bangladesh-India relationship, these are security and border management, trade and investment, water resources management, our Minister is also at the helm of the portfolio . People to people contact and the 5th one is the development part. So, these are the five pillars of co-operation. How do we approach the Bangladesh-India relationship? I said it is at the bilateral level, as I already mentioned Government to Government, there a lot of mechanisms through which we engage on various sector wise issues. Another approach is sub-regional which is actually taking prominence these days. Sub-regional means Bangladesh - India, north east Nepal Bhutan and also the coastal states like Srilanka, Maldives and this kind of relationship and the multi-lateral talks also Bangladesh and India discussed with each other, they consult and take interest in each other's aspects and support each other's candidatures at various multi-lateral forums. Now, if you ask me where is the roof? A building without roof, I say that way since sky is the limit I did not put any roof on this relationship yet so it can be let see what can be the size of the skyscraper.

Now the connectivity for trade facilitation can significantly enhance inter regional trade by reducing transportation and trade cost. We have been told here that it is a huge amount of cost involved when we carry things through roads and rails so connectivity through shipping and maritime sector reduces the cost and according to the statistics, Transportation by shipping and maritime reduces the cost by three times. I quote our Prime Minister Shaikh Hasina saying physical connectivity is important in ensuring peace, progress and stability across South Asia, physical connectivity links territories and communities. Bangladesh's approach towards connectivity is in that line of context.

Connectivity with Bhutan and Nepal through Indian territories and our connectivity with North eastern Indian states, we have direct bus services from Dhaka to Calcutta, Agartala to Dhaka. We are also constructing railway from Agartala to Bangladesh. We have also signed a coastal shipping agreement between Bangladesh and India.

For the shipping connectivity we have a co-lateral agreement we call it protocol on Inland water transporting trade. There is an MOU signed between Bangladesh and India in 2015 for the uses of Chetak and Bangla Port, we are still working on that for a detailed agreement and how do we use this Port. The Indian Government is also helping us in building infrastructure along the Inland water ways and there new Port House, new warehouses are built by the Indian support. So what connectivity does and how it helps us. As I said it is the people to people contact and trade facilitation. Bangladesh and India have already signed a MOU on that on the Inland water routes and the coastal routes. The Indian Government has extended the line of credit, in the first one it was one million, second two million and third one extended this year is 4.5 million. All the lines of credit are mostly on the infrastructure development.

For Sustainable Development what we can do. We have to device and look forward keeping that in mind we can develop the roads, Rules and Regulations. But what can be ensured and most of the countries in the region will see that non securitization of the routes. By non-securitization I mean the safety of the navigation. We look forward for the inter country connection like Bangladesh- India- Srilanka- Maldives but we would like to see the Crisscross connection from India's west to east so that the Indian goods· can be carried from their west to the eastern side at less cost and less time. So this could be an idea and this could be a thought and what would be the package. How we are thinking about the goods transport. We can think about the connectivity of the maritime logistics. We can think about the passenger and cruise vessels. We can think about the across region. Nepal and Nepal Government we can support them to bring their things by road. Bhutan from the Indian territory to Bangladesh and then use the Bangladesh's inland water and perhaps the Ports. Support is also given to India's North eastern States to use our Ports and from there to use the multimedia ways and connectivity to take things to the north eastern States.

So what we can do now we have to create an atmosphere that everybody is attracted to these new ideas, so that it can be implemented but for implementation you have to think about certain principles. There are some challenges, there are some capacity constraints in this country and since we are behind the developed countries we need a comprehensive co-operation and as I stated the mutual respect and the negotiation has to be done in such a way that all the countries get the benefit. So, with the amount of movement that has been generated in the last one decade not only between Bangladesh and India, I think few of the regions and sub-regions also, I am confident that the connectivity will be taken forward for the mutual prosperity and for the shared prosperity of our region, of course with certain shared responsibilities.

12

India's cultural and commercial linkage in IOR – A historical account

— Shri Ravi Kumar

Abstract

The paper is about maritime linkage of India within the region, cultural and commercial exchanges have strengthened India's relations with other maritime powers and this has added on to India's soft power, here is a historical accord of India's maritime ventures and development of maritime industry.

Key-words: *Maritime cultural linkage, India's maritime industry.*

Article

First to my sister from Iran, in India there was a queen, Abbakka Devi, she raised a naval force and fought against the Portuguese and the Jews and Zoroastrians came to India straight from Israel and Iran when they were persecuted there. In the morning people were saying about piracy, they said we should educate the pirates but I was wondering when you start teaching them A, B, C, they learn A, they learn B, but when they come to the letter C, they are all at sea. They don't see anything more than the sea and we are in Goa and before coming here many of us came via Mumbai, another port city and I'll say something about. We understand who is this Antonio Costa, anyone knows that? I am asking the Indian people here and Leo Varadkar, they had something to do with Goa and they are the prime ministers of different countries. Does anyone know which country" Antonio Costa is presently the Prime Minister of Portugal and his father studied in Goa. Then, is the first person who wrote a book on Indian Medicine on medicinal plants in a European language. He was here in the 1530s and 1540s and he was one of the victims of Goa inquisition. Even after he died his body was removed and then it was burnt. And one more port city I just want to mention is Haifa where the Britishers had also gone there and they feared that they will lose heavily cash so they retaliated but the soldiers sent by Mysore and Jodhpur Maharaja said in our dictionary we are not Shakti and there is no word called retreat so we have to fight, no matter what happens. These areas were having only swords and spears. The enemy were the Austrians, Germans, and the Ottoman Empire i.e. Turks, they were having canons and machine guns and yet this war was won by the Indians and a new country, the modern India was formed on that day. It was September 23, 1980. So this is the only war in the world history where swords and spears defeated the cannons. Can you guess this, in the year 1883, three ships were sailing three different directions, one a 21 years-old boy, a 23-years-old gun person, and a 30-years-old person.

I will lose half of my time.So there are temples inher name in Thailand. She is regarded as Devi Marianman. The second one is Dev, how did he cross the Brahmaputra river. He stayed in India for 13 years, collected a lot of manuscripts, very rare books and then he was going he came to Qalandar. The principal in Nanda said crossing the Brahmaputra is very, very dangerous so I will send four of my best students with you. These 4 students went with him. While they were crossing Brahmaputra which is the only river which is called Putra rest are all feminine, because it is a huge one, there ship got caught in the current so the captain on the ship said we have to unload some of these luggages and he kept Joao in a room locked him and said throw all his books into the sea. So all that Joao heard was four loads of books were thrown into the sea. Finally when he crossed the Brahmaputra and reached the Chinese part of land, he saw all his books all were there and he asked the captain how did you unload. He said do you see the four students who went with you, they are all missing because they jumped into the sea to save the books. That is why the Chinese historian Hu Shi says that for generations China will remain indebted to India. They say that India conquered China for more than 2000 years without sending a single soldier.

Then in the year 1990, he says how to save the sea animals. So thousands of whale sharks they come to Gujarat for breeding so they lay their eggs, so many people would catch those eggs, catch those sharks so Moraj Babu went to Gujarat the tortoise and various other animals they come. In India there is a practice that when a lady is pregnant for her first birth, she will go to her mother's house. Same way all these creatures are coming to Gujarat because they think that Gujarat and Bharat is their motherland. So when they are coming to their house how can you kill their children. 50,000 fishermen they pledged that they would not kill these creatures. So these are the common sayings in India.

Now various countries, if you see the initial chapters of those countries they were all created by various sailors from India. Many of the things that I am telling is part of history. Now in the period 550 BC Sri Lanka talks of Prince Vijaya sailing from Orissa and Bengal that is how their states are in Mahamotsav. Same way we have the Funan country. Funan is a region of Vietnam and Cambodia. The great excavator and archeologist John De Sales has written on this, the book is called the Indian Association of Southeast Asia and he collects all this information from Chinese and other proofers. The history of Indonesia in the year 130 CD also started with day 1 with a trader from India who goes and marries an Indonesian lady and then establishes the first empire in Indonesia. Similarly in Singapore, Rajendra Chola went there in the year 1025. The Chinese went there to prevent Rajendra Chola from attacking China. Rajendra Chola said "there need not be a war I can come as a friend also." So the friendship treaty between China and India was signed in Singapore and Singapore government takes the pride in saying that we were the helping agent of this peace. In the year 1299 the first kingdom of Singapore was also started by a person called Tripurvanath. So you can see the very first chapters of various countries. I have not mentioned about Korea. They say that a princess of Ayodhya in the year 42 AD or CD, she sailed from Ayodhya to Korea and then the Korean history starts. Similarly in Japan from 5th century, most of the words in Japanese language did not have Chinese content. Chinese content started after 5th century. Before that they were all Tamil and Sanskrit and our first speaker here has already referred about the history how it started in the Puranas and the Vedas so I will skip this and I will just say that he travelled the ocean. Now Gautam is also known to most of you as the first title, we will skip many of these. We have the many years compasses more than that we also use the stars and the bold stars. India was far advanced than any other country as far as the western countries that we know of which was more advanced in astronomy and in calendar Panchanga. Our Panchana also tells when the sun will rise, when the sun will set, what will be the seasons and direction of the wind, etc was all known to our navigators. This is the first story of Sri Lanka. Similarly I will skip Indonesia and Cambodia story, island Philippines, we have Baliatha. A bell is found from Tamil Nadu with Tamil inscriptions. It is of the 14th century and found in New Zealand. Then the ship of Vasco Da Gamma was towed by an Indian navigator. In the 16th century, the richest man, he was the port manakas, his chief was an Indian which is Maratha Devan, then there was the Battle of Trafalgar. Britishers with less number of ships where fighting in the enemy territory that is in Spain and still they won because the ships were made in India are of Indian timber, Indian of America, 'Star- Spangled Banner.' Similarly another ship, Cornwallis built in Mumbai is saved for 144 years and created the history of Hong Kong because the theory of handing over Hong Kong to the Britishers in the year 1800 something was signed on this ship. Now, the Britishers were searching for Netaji. They knew that he was going from Germany to Japan or maybe one of the Japanese territories. So they had laid their ships all along the sea route and yet they could not capture him because he went by a submarine. Then India got freedom because of what? They asked actually the Prime Minister. He said the navy mutiny which was inspired again by Azad Hind Fauz was the main reason in 1946 in Mumbai the naval forces, they revolted against the British bosses and that spread a wide fire all over India and so the Britishers knew now it is high time to leave India. Same way another history is in May 1971 War, when the Seventh Fleet came, our Vice Admiral N. Krishanan immediately told them if it enters our Indian water borders, our suicide bombers are ready to destroy your ship and Nixon was phoning again and again, "have you bombed India, have you bombed India?" and they were helpless. Same way PNS Ghazi which was given by the Britishers was sunk near Visakhapatnam, these are all landmarks. Similarly you can see this Mahendra Nath Mulla Captain who sank with the ship INS Khukri.

13

Challenges of Maritime Governance for Humanity

— Shri ASM Abdul Baten

Abstract

The author states, that maritime governance is multi-disciplinary in nature. The author refers to China – Philippines issue in SCS in light of UNCLOS. Rocks & reefs in SCS being a part of EEZ in continental shelves is also analyzed. Author suggests that maritime data needs to be shared and made publicly accessible. Further the data base about illegal migration needs to be developed. In Bangladesh, the author states needs more maritime lawyer and law enforcing agents, including for inland river marine courts are required. The mission therefore would be to identify more resource persons including multi-disciplinary persons is highlighted. Also, idea exchanges would lead to more areas of co-operation.

Key Words: *Maritime cooperation, South China Sea, Bangladesh, Maritime education.*

Article

It has been already expressed that at this time of the day it is quite challenging if you listen on a subject which matters about law, FVS, and governance issues.

The initiative taken by SAGAR, the Sagar Maritime Summit took place last year. I had the opportunity to come here to sign the MOU in the Indian Maritime University as the first Vice Chancellor of the Bangabandhu Sheikh Mujibur Rahman Maritime University in Bangladesh. I like the words Sagar because it relates to in Bengali my mother tongue language is Shagur also same as sea. And it has beautiful abbreviation of security and growth for all in the region, I mean region, not any particular country or number of countries but when we talk about sea, I personally say the opportunity and economy for all. Why I call security is because it guarantees the security of our life.

If we consider the ocean as the source of water and in my mother tongue, I can say pani is jeeven then water is life. So that is all, security of our life lies in the oceans or sea and the economy, every conflict whatever we see around or within the states, between the states, regions, and across the world, there is some point of interest for the economy that is why I think the whole subject is quite interesting and here the aim of the intention of my talk to this August gathering is to discuss some of the issues actually of Maritime Governance which I just randomly picked up to make a broad brush imaginary painting having titled *Challenges of Maritime Governance For Humanity.*

You know, I come from Bangladesh and it was actually independent in December 16, 1971before that, I think as a citizen of that place, our nation was totally sea blind sort of things, not much of importance given. It was actually opened by the Father of the Nation by whose name has been also from by enacting a law on maritime zone and act in 1974. But again the country was sort of in hibernation and the present government under the leadership of the current Prime Minister. She has taken the bold step and opened the first Maritime University in Bangladesh. Why I am telling this is because I consider in our region, our Maritime University has something different than other Maritime Universities.

I am going to say a few words on what I mean Maritime because generally speaking you know, when I talk about seas when I was in my childhood, we used to hear stories from my grandmother or others of the prince looking for the princess across the 7 seas and 13 rivers, so the topic of getting on this is seeing governance and since I am actually working with academic students at time we also had to discuss on some of the meaningful thoughts of some words and other things. So to me, it is still uncertain that how this 7 sea was actually named. Some literature says that it was in the great literature, it was transformed through English literature. In the Medieval period they used to think about their own agency and the seas around them but during the Midieval the name again changed and after Europe discovered it with America, the name of the sea again changed.

Now, there may be as many as 50 seas and 5 oceans. So when I talk about Maritime Governance so I try to give my own way of defining things just you may differ so as my University is Maritime so as a citizen of maritime nation I think it starts right from the land because the brays are within the land and from the coast, the bay, across the seas, deep seas, and oceans, even Antartic everything can be covered under the maritime area.

It would have been better as Mr. Arthur Charles Clarke who was actually an efficient writer in British who passed in 2008, he actually wondered whether it could be also named as ocean probably then the thought of out sea blindness would have gone away. I do not want to give much of the statistics which already we know about it.

The second part because you know, the governance is important not only for land it is important for sea or ocean or maritime at ease. So any regime or government's ability to make or enforce rules to deliver services regarding of whether that government is democratic or not this is actually 1% _ of mind, Mr. Fukuyama and the governance of maritime and marine space is the management of stakeholder activities of these areas or spaces.

Broadly speaking, the issues or maritime governance are intensely complex, overlapping, and diverse. It involves different stakeholders who may be locals, nations or internationals. So the other certain fundamental elements of governance like the rule of law when we talk about it, participate in transparency, consensus based decision making, accountability, equitable, inclusive, responsive, and coherent. Coherency is very much important so things should not just stop after the wash of a seminar, we have to implement it. We have to engage with things, we have to pursue things to happen. I just wanted to draw my own way of framing a consensual framework for Maritime Governance. You can see the parties like national, local, regional, and international and the challenges are mentioned, the weak framework, then climate change, and others we have talked about it, who are the responsible parties, and then the stakeholders and their opportunities. The problem of Maritime Governance is inter-related and needed to be considered as a whole where all nations should go in it and Maritime Governance is multi-disciplinary in nature. They should look for balance of economic activity, social equity, environmental equality, sustainability, maritime safety and security. If we talk about the legal aspects in every field that we talk like from a social, environmental, economic perspectives, technological, and security perspectives, they laid down procedures like the UNCLOS already discussed about it but it has its own limitations. The 1982 UNCLOS forms the basis of the model legal framework for ocean governance. A vast majority of the world's nations have signed on UNCLOS which is known as the constitution of the world proportion . The treaty provides guidelines for how nations use the world's oceans, seas, and their natural resources. UNCLOS has already resolved a number of vital age old issues though some states have not become parts so far. The convention has changed the political and geographical world. There are still threats during party order at sea, first the issue of continued proliferation of excessive maritime tents mostly at resource based for example at the China sea is a well-known case between the Philippines and China. Several unilateral claims show lack of respect for UNCLOS as they are starting ones for other claims on exclusive economic zone and continental shelf claims. Another problem is claims over unsustainable rocks or reefs in South China Sea or does the China sea generates their own EEZ in continental shelfs. The most controversial aspect of the convention was the regime for deep sea bed mining contained in part 11 and NS3. Some of the industrialized states have rightly rejected it and the convention has been gratified by 168 parties though.

The next point is Maritime Security is a crucial national as well as human security and terrorists often use the established sea routes of vulnerable illegal migrants of adjoining to their destination to circum their border controls. They blocked or as you can say see that the parties to it are the local, state, and the international organizations and the most important part is the awareness and the education and which comes there to training part of it. Then comes the policy and strategy and the actions operations which we need to do. Out of these several issues for the security aspect is one of them is the piracy. It's a whole issue and its presence could not be stopped over the years.

Piracy total number has decreased very recently but you cannot guarantee that. It is continuous process like most of the statistics say that in the East Africa and Indian Ocean there were very much prone to piracy. Maritime environment, I think the previous takers have about it. Environment is something which we have to give maximum attention. Then the sea level rise for which we are very much worried about it most particularly the low lying countries and island countries. These are given say from 1880 to 2017, the amount of sea level rise is just shown .So what should be done for Maritime Governance? We should adopt a holistic approach to all marine and maritime issues, the integrated Maritime policy, policy for maritime special planning by the states and the regions. Put in place a whole set of mandatory environmental rules to ensure maritime use maritime resources sustainable wherever required. The total level strategy to boost unsustainable includes the Blue Growth including Blue Economy standard policies as regards to national resources, energy, trade development, and security. Put in place national and local strategies to address common challenges and opportunities collaborating closely with distant countries and stakeholders from all relevant sectors. Develop fund for high education and research for marine and maritime irrigation improving cooperation and information sharing and making Maritime Data publicly accessible. Engaging international and cross sector forums to address the common challenges of ensuring safe, secure, clean and productive sea and ocean worldwide. Focus on well-being and safety of human for peaceful existence on planet. This is the humanitarian aspect of it I think this area is much overlooked. On the opening day the chief guest he carefully mentioned and he actually laid down a big canvas with huge upper and lower limit. Right from the common masses up to those who had the older things, we have to look into their matters. The humanitarian aspect just for an example, if we take the case of recent eviction or killing of citizens by Myanmar due their own purpose, the way they have actually driven them out almost more than half a million people they have no space to go. They are either going to the water, some of them may already have lost their lives, some actually given shelter by our present government and it is honourable to say it is a great humanitarian job they have done but you have to consider that if we not able to reason then how it can actually address the future this ocean on the region. It could be a security threat, it could be anything, health security, economy security, all these subjects will be affected by these people. Security of education is also a problem. There has to be clear understanding of the specific areas of interest, natural process and dynamics of marine and coastal system and the decision taken considering future implications and effect, people around the target maritime zone they must be addressed and participation by all stakeholders including local, administrative polls. Use of appropriate instruments to save research, education, technical solution, legal basis, economy support. Human capacity at all levels improved through comprehensive Maritime Education multi-disciplinary training is so much important that when I started working for this Maritime University, the first department opened at post graduate level was Maritime Law. It was very difficult to really get maritime lawyers but there are so much of maritime issues. Only inland river marine court they have more than 15,000 cases pending but not proper maritime lawyer. So we felt that urgency and the mission here is one of them is also looking for opportunities to share ideas and look for the resource persons. Although I have already connected you with 10 world Maritime Universities and including many other countries also from this region. So education and training, they have no alternative. Conflict resolution mechanism and public policy making is another area.

We must address these things and maybe we can have joint workshops to training our people how to address these issues. Any regime who won successful governance would have to acquire some guidance like political will to govern all control.Rule of law, set standard or principle in possession of Maritime policy for all efforts of the nation at sea. Some sort of military commander of the sea and regulatory proceedings when requested. So finally I just would conclude like challenges for maritime and Ocean Governance are numerous and each one is important.

In order to govern activities at sea, we need to set certain standards. We need to establish rule of law to govern activities by providing broad orders and create obligation and responsibility. This will aim to establish security, stability, order, peace, and minimize injustice. Health of UNCLOS and other legal framework is important but there are areas of uncertainties and challenges to some particular elements of international law which need to be resolved. The best means to resolve issues over resources and their use are more and more interactions and negotiations. We must develop the skill of the negotiation or the art of negotiation among our future leaders. Arbitration and cooperation between stakeholders, having enough understanding agreements and engagements between the security practitioners and services are also important to build confidence. Maritime higher education and research are important to develop skilled human resources as a lead for the different professions through well designed educational policies. Here the Journal and International Cooperation will be required to share our resources and information to boost the activities at sea. With that I would just want to finish it here just a few glimpses of the pictures that how the country can just evict their citizens and they are just helpless, many of them probably under water now.

14

Rationale and Importance of Sagarmala Project

—*Shri Atul Kulkarni*

Abstract

This takes an account of Sagarmala project of India. Rationale of Sagarmala being multimodal transportation. Multiple agencies are involved in this project and therefore their co-operation become an important factor. The project is aimed at improving the infrastructure as ports and in the hinder land, Maritime facilities at eastern and western shores of India are unbalanced. This project seeks to harness the potential of both. Coastal eco-system and small island development are also made a mention here.

Key-words: *Coastal eco-system, Sagarmala.*

Article

I will present the Sagarmala programme that the Government of India has launched. I think it is important for all of the people to understand what is Sagarmala is all about and when we go back we have clear understanding of how we are going to go ahead with this. Our coastal areas can be channels for global trade, we all know and everybody has talked about it, even the landlocked countries realized that it is the sea connectivity which is important for them to get engaged with the rest of the world. Hon. Minister said and I will quote "Maritime infrastructure and shipping will be an equitable role in India with economic engagement with the rest of the world. India is blessed with the longest coast line in the most strategic global trade to harnessing to generate rich economic dividends to the country. This is what he said when we launched the Sagarmala programme. Some of this has been spoken already but to put the entire Sagarmala project in the perspective I would like to repeat few things here. More than 7500 kilometer long coast line, 18% of the Indians population lives in the coastal states, 60% of the country's GDP is contributed by the maritime States, the 9 maritime states, 60% contribution to the National GDP. 12 major ports, 200 non-major ports, 95% trade by volume, 70% by value again the figures which were mentioned by many of the speakers. About 1500 million metric tonnes cargos handled and we are expecting to handle about 2500 million metric tonnes by 2025. What is the rational for Sagarmala programme? We have seen this over the last 60-70 years of our independence that the maritime sector lacks the cohesive institutional agreement, we have multiple agencies, when we started the discussion of Sagarmala, we have realized that there are about 10 Ministries of Government of India and about 16 departments under the 10 ministries which has something to do with this maritime sector and therefore each one of them works in this silo and therefore we are not seeing the real impact of this initiative and therefore this Sagarmala Programme is supposed to bring all this under one roof and have a very cohesive institution arrangement and then decide about the activities we do along the coast line. Of course the infrastructure is weak as we discussed it yesterday and our Hon. Minister spoke about it, therefore this programme is aimed at improving at infrastructure at ports and in the hinterland. Limited economic benefits, of course there are economic benefits arising out of the weak infrastructure and no great linkages between the coast line and vast hinterland we have. We have seen a consideration where, the birth maritime in the eastern and western part of the country are totally unbalanced, we are seen an activity where forcing the goods produced in the far east like the states like Assam and Bengal, to travel up to Mumbai Mundra Port on the west coast on the western world and European destination. Why this is happening and this is leading to huge logistics cost and which is leading to almost 13% of the GDP and managing for economy of trillion dollar economy. 30% of the GDP is on logistic costs. Small saving in the couple of percentages and we will see magnifying effect of that to our economy this why the Sagarmala is launched. People mentioned about pillars, port modernization, port connectivity and port led industrialization and coastal community development, these are the four pillars of the Sagarmala Programme. Everything that we will do in the Sagarmala Projects will be on these 4 verticals. Each one of them is described in detailed here. Port modernization and it will lead to port capacities, port connectivity will improve the efficiency and port land will give the economic benefits and give the economy a scale and the advantage to draw from that and the coastal community development talks about the sustainability and sustainable development goals which we have all adapted. Reduction in logistics cost is the primary vision of Sagarmala Programme and the 13% of the GDP what we spend on our logistics cost, everybody talked about it yesterday in the session. The land transportation cost from Delhi Ferrera Park to Mumbai which is thousand and plus kilometers more than the sea rate which we pay for a container which has to be shifted from Mundra to Europe. In order to bring down the cost, this the reason for the entire effort, therefore reducing the cost of domestic cargo movement and optimizing the modern means, we have water, railways, we have shipping and all of would be utilized to bring down the total logistics cost and also reducing the existing transaction cost in order to make our exports competitive. If we have to see, Make in India for the globe or Make in India to make the manufacturing hub for the globe all of that would become reality only if we are able to address these issues and this is what Sagarmala is going to focus on. If you see the infrastructure development, it will unfold at 1500 million metric tonnes and how we are going to achieve 3000 million metric tonnes, we will see huge augmentation of capacity through the new ports coming and there will be more ports coming up they say and this new ports that the government has announced including some of the non-major ports they would add to some 4066 million metric tonnes of capacity and then the other elements would be upgradation of equipments and upgradation of connectivity and then efficiency parameters would add to some capacities. How are we going to increase our connectivity infrastructure, there are massive programmes and all are the part of Sagar mala and the other initiative that the government has launched. You will see here number of connectivity programmes. We have the eastern dedicated way corridors and western way dedicated corridors, the rail line and the access control road ways, all is to enhance the speed on ground and also to increase the economic value to the population around this. You have all these programmes and you have currently going on at the moment and so it is not the infrastructure development on the coastal areas or at the ports but it is also the hinterland connectivity programmes which are the part of sagarmala initiative. Then the development of coastal economic zones and remote range western investors and we have a coast line of 7500 kilometers which is divided into 14 coastal economic zones. These 14 economic coastal zones are been identified based on the resources available, based on skill sets available of the people living in that area and also what is going to be India's strength nationally and internationally, so this clusters would have the infrastructure the regularity mechanism and also the eco-system which will promote and support the initiative under this 14 coastal economic zone. Some of them are gas based, some of them are petroleum, electronic depending on the raw material and the strengths of the region around. The most important thing and relevant for this conference is that Sagar is sustainable development of the coastal areas. So it is not just the infrastructure or quick and modem but also the sustainable development part of the coastal areas which is the part of the Sagarmala initiative, while this infrastructure is going to be the gateway for the economic engagement of the world, it is also important that we harness our unique natural eco-system, we unique preserve our natural eco-system and also improve the quality of life for our communities living in our coastal areas. So all of this is important and finally we move on to 3 specific initiative under sustainable development and initiatives of sagarmala. Somebody mentioned in their speech, the entire investment under sagarmala is over 16 billion dollars and we want to see the annual saving in logistics costs to the tune of 6 million dollars per annum. So that is the kind of impact we will have on our economy, it will have a very- very significant impact on our coastal community. About 4 million new jobs will be created. About 6 million additional indirect jobs will be created, through this initiative and about 110 million dollar boast to export. So this is in that sense, mother of all programmes that the current government has launched. Nurturing community and skill development, livelihood generation for the people around whether it is the fishermen community, whether these people who are working in this port or the infrastructure projects that will come in the coastal economic zones so a huge emphasis is done on building the skills and providing livelihood for the communities around. Marine fishermen development, the Minister spoke yesterday, somebody mentioned about it during the day also, about the deep sea fishing, providing them trawlers getting them in a system where you have better reums for the efforts that we make. Coastal tourism is a great opportunity for India. Admiral mentioned about 150 islands and islets fraternity which is totally unexplored around the beautiful sea and the ocean that we have. The corals and the coastal areas of the Lakshadweep and Adman and Nicobar islands are also the part of the Sagarmala Development Programme. So coastal tourism, the Minister spoke about it yesterday, the cruise tourism whether it is Lakshadweep and Adman and Nicobar islands, Malay, Mauritius or Seychelles. Therefore it is an idea to convert India into home port and the close circuits to be developed along the region. Vibrant natural environment, of course the focus is on greener energy and the Minister mentioned in his speech yesterday, we are looking at various initiatives wherein bring down the consumption and bring down the carbon footprint and also the importance of inland water ways to make sure that we don't pollute our environment more when we are adding to the capacities and looking at increasing additional values for our economic benefits.

15

Ocean Governance and Low Lying states – A Case Study of Seychelles

— *Shri Barry Faure*

Abstract

This paper is about Seychelles perspective on ocean eco-system as resource, Majority of world population stays near ocean. Seychelles depend for wealth, food, health water supply, energy on sea. But ocean governance is under threat. So is ocean health. In ocean conference at Malta, a lot of commitments about ocean governance have come through, especially about pollution control. Difficulties which low lying states world face due to sea level rise in also explain in this paper. This requires marine special planning as a structured participatory and evidence based decision making tool and collaborative efforts for eco-system management.

Key-words: *Marine governance, Seychelles – India Blue economy.*

Article

This is an opportunity to remind the shipping industry that annual news that piracy is very much active and we all need to maintain vigilance. This was the key message that the annual primary session of the Conduct group on pirates of Sumerian which was co-hosted by Seychelles in the Indian Ocean Commission in Mauritius last July. India and Seychelles enjoy excellent diplomatic, friendly relationships which is dates from pre-independence days. Our corporation expands a wide spectrum of sectors including the Blue Economy and Maritime Security. Since piracy hit the Seychelles in the 2009, India has increased its co-operation in the maritime sector, Foreign Secretary Dr. Subrahmanyam Jaishankar was in Seychelles in October, 2017 to have bi-lateral talks with the new President and Minister for Foreign Affairs. In 2015, the Prime Minister Modi made a historic visit in Seychelles, last year retired Admiral Arun Prakash and then the Chief of the Naval staff of the Indian Navy was in Seychelles of handing over of the Naval vessel gifted by India. Our two countries share the same ocean space and work hard hand in hand to preserve safety, security and roof of our ocean on which we all depend. Ladies and gentlemen, the ocean, our planets largest eco-system which holds to small island developing States, as much as it is owned to the majority of world's population which we live on coastal zone. We survive on it and depend on it for our wealth, food, health, water supply, energy and air but the world knows today that the seas are under a threat. Numerous speakers have referred to it and for some of the States their existence is actually threatened and some say may be due to human action. For the first ocean previously thought of be able to withstand all forms of human pressure, pollution and abuse can collapse, irrevocable. According to the first Global interrogated marine assessment, world ocean assessment 1, our civilization is running out of time to avoid the detrimental cycle in decline in oceans health, then we have dramatic repercussion on the ability of the oceans to keep providing the support we need and we are all responsible individually and collectively, poor and rich, big or small. We all need to change our behaviour and our relationship vis-a-vis with the ocean. The good news is that the things have began to change with more global political will mobilized to bring about the global transformation and change that is required in our vision in our behaviour. Last week, I attended the fourth edition of our ocean conference co- hosted in Malta. Incidentally, a young lawyer, an environmental organizer, Afroz Shah was there to speak on the panel to speak on marine pollution. He inspired everyone with his individual action in picking up chunks of plastic garbage on the shores of Mumbai and how he started a movement which is spreading all across Mumbai to clean up the beaches. Afroz Shah believes that we should not only depend on Government, rules and institution and interventions on each and every one of us. Afroz Shah asked himself, what am I doing to change this? And then it goes out there again and again to pick up the garbage. Malta had another impact on me, a young scientist Emily Pan spoke about her experiences. TongYan where she found that this country has turned the consumerist like all the rest of us, since islanders and importing most of what it consumes have not put in place a solid waste management system to take care of all the import consumed waste. Our young scientists speaks about how fellow islanders traditionally practice of burning waste was in adaptive of burning the waste, the plastics which causes harmful smoke, this brought her to study the toxic substances found in plastic and how the plastic garbage ended up in the ocean was consumed by fish that ended up on her menu. She decided to test her blood and 34 harmful substances found in plastic to her surprise in contaminations 29 of the 34 substances were found in her blood strain. Now, for most I take it to the habit of avoiding meats because the use of genos by the producers. I would only eat meat when I am taken to place in July this year, where you are sure of the camel and goat meat that they would serve you because you will be in free range and organic. After Malta, this islander of whom I spoke to you know have decided to start avoiding fish, can you imagine the state of health of islanders, whose main source of protein come from the ocean but that might not sound too depressive. Our ocean conference in Malta, had an another seas country and had a overwhelming success and I would like to highlight for you which you can study in length on its website. 437 tangible and measurable commitments were made. 7.2 Billion Euros in financial packages, 2.5 Million Sq. Kilometers of additional marine protected areas, the 32 alone accident commitments 550 Million actions throughout the globe. Together with this individual membership and European investment banks, EU pledged more than 2.8 Billion Euros. Other countries tabled around 200 commitments while NGO's and foundations, research institutions and international organizations announced 87 commitments as a major game changer, the 2017 conference for the first time mobilized at scale the business community in the conservation of our ocean. Corporate leaders responded with one hundred commitments from plastic reduction to satellite monitoring. Seychelles core commitments as announced by the President and himself a panelist of maritime security who has to adopt a comprehensive and national maritime security strategy within broad mass. The next ocean conference will be held in Indonesia another Indian Ocean Association Member State comprising of more than 17000 islands followed by FINS partner Mr. Kansgar discussed Norway. In 2019, before returning to another Seas country allow in the year 2020. I spoke about importance of Oceans and seas and how it is the decomposition is adversely impacting on our States. To do justice to the subject, I was invited to speak on Island Governance and State and I need to further elaborate, small island development States has a agenda characterized by a combination of small size limited national resources, limited technical and human capabilities. Inhabitants vulnerability to natural disasters and small economical scales. There are management challenges and issues therefore require strong and effective environment governance. So what are the marine and environment and climate change issues since seas? For sea, the sea level rise is admirable the most certain and potentially devastating climate changing that is happening. According to the IPCC report, during the 21st century sea level will rise atleast 0.18 meters and perhaps as much as 0.59 meters and these are the scenarios, several seas are expected to loss different portions of the land due to sea level rise including Kiribati Mashall islands, Tokelau and the Maldives. Even larger seas with mushy land area will avert the sea level rise such as Fiji, Patricio and some more will have problems because most settlements and infrastructure are in coastal zone, while the inland regions would experience severe ecological changes in settling all the immigrants. Chemical changes would also reduce low lying islands inhabitability, oceanic absorption of atmospheric carbon dioxide is leading to ocean classification which is likely to warm coral reefs and detrimental effects on coral islands. Another physiological impact across all seas will be invasive alien species. Additionally significant ecological impact across all States be likely to be warm oceans, they are resulting in considerable coral depleting. These events have the capacity to eliminate more than 90% of the corals on a reef. Destroying the eco-system, leaving islands exposed to waves and storms and some other storms and eliminating menaces. Increase surface temperatures leading to more intense storms, once the storms formed as well as changing storms track could lead seas closer to equator, such as Tokelau, Aruba and others experiencing more storms because these seas have limited cycle experience. Consequent events are liable to have much greater impact, than on more experiences until a humid island can adjust. To further compound the above and at the same time the seas are faced with diminishing sea level of support from the international community as a result of their relatively high levels of theirs per GDP capita. The high GDP level capita of some seas are development partners as an indicator of their success. But in reality these indicators apart from been excused in small populations lack of progress, many areas. Last but not the least, as it has been already highlighted and discussed the areas beyond natural jurisdiction which covers most of the oceans requires a new approach. Currently the principle of common heritage of mankind as defined by under the UN clause and she was diagnosed or private entity have right to resources in ABNG and that management of this common heritage should be for the betterment of human kind present and future in practice this has lead to what it is called strategy of the commoners and whereby no one is responsible so no one cares, resulting in deterioration of ocean health in some cases. This in contrary to what intend was which was the first two corporations between nations. What can seas do if they face such challenges? What tools and solutions can seas apply in area of environmental governances? 1st let us know that now that there is now great appreciation of the importance of the establishment global development frame work that takes into account the circumstances of seas. The United Nations frame work convention of climate change recognizes a particular vulnerability of seas to the adversely effect of climate change and thus stimulates the specific needs and concerns should be given full consideration. In vision, the seas will need international support both multi-lateral and bi-lateral and development factors in vulnerability criteria should affect in their programmes which supports small states. A new legal binding instrument is currently being developed for the conservation and sustainable use of marine bi-diversity in areas beyond natural jurisdiction. This process is an opportunity is to address the limitations of sector based approaches laid the foundation for sustainable development in pace way technological advances and set out a regime for benefit sharing and ensure the protection of marine environment and facilitate corporation and coordination among various institutions where the ocean mandate and thus promoting the principle of good governance. The prep-period of two years is coming to an end and negotiations will start in 2018. So seas and their partners need to be on the watch. It is in fact insisted interest to ensure that there is a equitable international order. In a globalized world, it is an acquitable rule faced order that will ultimately govern our security by way of conclusion, I would like to mention two examples of innovation and could be considered by purely a Seychelles experience if you allow me to share. Marine special planning as a structured participatory and evidence based decision making tool and can bring success together and facilitate collaborative eco-system based decision making and the resolution of conflicts and the environment increasing the pride at national and international level. The Seychelles experience is interesting case and Seychelles is funding its marine special death for climate change and adaptations and Government permits to expand marine bio-diversity protection to 30% of its exclusive economic zone and territorial sea and an extent of 4000 square kilometers by 2020. Seychelles is also finalizing a new global financial instrument namely the blue bond which will raise funds for management of marine areas and strengthen fisheries in Seychelles including support for private investments in aqua culture. This is expected to leverage and capitalize further public private publications with a blue economy in Seychelles.

16

"Use of advance technology and Inter-state Protocol for sustainable fishery"

— *Shri Jan Fredric*

Abstract

"The Paper deals with use of advance maritime technology for fishing in Norway, for sustainable and ethical fishing practices. Author highlighted importance of cordial relations between states associated with deep sea fishing, bottom trawling.

Key-words*: use of advance technology for sustainable fishing.*

Article

I would like to state the case of Norway. My topic is on advanced technology and is it possible to do that. If you look at the Ocean Norway to the North we have the (Explains the boundaries of Ocean Norway) if we compare it to India, Norway' s Ocean is of the same size. If you look at Maldives it is not too different from India. We export about 90 percent of our fish production by sea export. The number of fishing vessels and fishermen in Norway are not that many compared to India but if you look at this particular island, we see that fisheries is very important, in this community there is nothing more than doing fishing for sustainable management. So, it is very important for the sustainable management of the fisheries and to have the Blue economy in Norway. In Norway,there is economy also in Gas, Shipping, Agriculture, Agriculture contributes about 35 percent of the GDP, about ten percent of employment and about 70 percent of export from Norway. We share about 90 percent of the fish catch and to do that we have to mainly cooperate with the neighbouring countries. We have established different mechanisms to do that, you need to have very stable and cordial relations between the States. Norway also has business potential of several fisheries sections and it is important to have international focus So, between Norway and Russia there is cooperation. The first agreement was signed in 1975, the objective of the agreement was to establish a Commission to address things under this agreement and thereafter in 1976 we had a more detailed agreement signed.

17

"Development and Integration of Maritime Assets for Global Competitiveness"

— ***Shri Krishna Kotak***

Abstract

The Paper deals with development and integration of Maritime Assets and its regional growth. Paper gives historical perspective since the time of Vasco-De-Gama to Colonial Period. Classification of Maritime Assets into Hard & Soft – and India's capacity building is explained. The Challenges being rail connectivity to handle 50 mn tonnes of cargo which calls for at least 2 train per hour. All the five soft assets are interdependent. Thus, it is pertinent to ensure meager intervention and maximum digitalization. India needs to take care of deficiency in regulatory aspects such as comprehensive policy on SAGARMALA and E-Governance goals. Also need to have positive approach to adopt best global practices. Need more emphasis on skill development and adhering to international standards in ship building, Port designs, navigation, fuel system and cargo handling system.

Key Words: *Maritime Assets, SAGARMALA, Digitalization and E-Governance, Rail connectivity, capacity building.*

Article

For the last 2000 years the Indian Ocean, the Bay of Bengal, the Arabian Sea, have been a vital meeting point for people from all over the world and therefore it is expected that the first meeting is being held in Goa. In today's time and age, people talk of business which is shipping, we talk about globalization, we talk about Port maintenance.500 years back this same very Goa was an important Port and the supply gene of the entire continent of India. It might interest you to know that the Deccan Empire which was 400, 500, 800 kms from Goa, use to receive their Arabian steels and various other types of equipments through Goa to move to Hyderabad and Pune. That was how 500 years back even then Goa was a trans-shipment hub, as the shipping people would like to call it and that was 500 years back. It is wonderful to see that Norway is a part of this gathering. Like India, Norway also has a Maritime history. It is a matter of record that at that time the ship designs that Norway, 1800 years back had, was leaders in the world and therefore for India it is wonderful to have partnership with Norway because India would look forward to sharing and growing in various fields where Norway is truly or worldly.

India in the last 70 years has grown, has gone forward, has created excellent professionals whether they be doctors, whether they be Scientists and has created Institutions which again is a matter of pride for all of us Indians and therefore I add that the voice of the leadership is very essential in showing the progress of India and in forward of the time and not in distance of the future that our leadership will also share with the world that India has also produced the best Maritime, Logistics and co- professionals. The subject which I have been tasked with to share with you dignitaries, is of the Development and the Integration of Maritime assets and its regional growth. To go little back into history, this is a map which has been there since the first century A.D. and the different three groups at that time which covered various trades of India, I come to the normal period, I talked about Goa being a trans-shipment terminal, this was the time when Suez Canal did not exist. This was the period when Columbus mistakenly discovered America while the search was for India. This is the period when Vasco da Gama landed in India and interestingly with the assistance of an Indian sea farer managed to navigate himself from the African coast to India. This is the era when the Gama Kings had already established trading routes up to Java, Sumatra and all the way to China. This was the time when Surat was also a large trading Port and the British under the peak time took the opportunity to establish a Port in Surat. Now we come to the Colonial period 18th to the 20th century. A lot of these Ports were built. Some of them were expanded, some of them shifted. Containers take tiles, spices, rice, these were the commodities which moved. Coming to the topic of today, this land seeks to share how the various Port cities of the world have developed and though this slide does not in details portrait the ports in Africa apart from developed, we all know that there is tremendous amount of development and growth which is taking place in Ports like Djibouti, Mombasa, Dar es salaam and so many others and this brings me to the aspects of Maritime assets. In India we have the television, if any one of you watch the Indian television, it is many times said that their questions are longer than their answers. So, it is on that ground to reach to this stage it has taken some time so please have some patience.

My subject is Maritime assets. We believe that there are two types of assets. No. 1 is the hard asset No. 2 is the soft asset. Within the hard assets we have direct assets such as berths, equipments, yards, various types of connectivity issues within the Port and as far as the indirect assets are concerned you have warehousing, you have road connectivity and you have rail connectivity. What we have tried to do, we have made out two charts for you which tells you where we are as far as our capability and capacity is concerned. There are two Charts. This one shows you what is the container handling capacity. As you know a large part of our day-to-day trade in the world has moved towards containers.

As I was mentioning this is the Chart which share with you the Maritime assets and we are proud to share with you that today in India we have 50 container berths, with a key length of almost 15 kms and a handling capacity of almost 25 million tons and on the bulk side cargos that are handled we have almost 140 berths with a length of 39 kms and a cargo handling capacity of almost 700 million tonnes. In the indirect assets we have adequate amount of warehousing. Our Hon. Minister has created a frame work where roads are connected to every single Port and that is in short the connectivity of Ports by roads is top class. What are the challenges that we face is the rail connectivity to our Ports. As we all know there are Port evacuations, - it is for all practical purposes the life line of a Port. We can bring in the larger ships with the maximum amount of cargo and handle it at the fastest possible speed. But if that cargo fails to get evacuated then that Port cannot handle any cargo any more. We all know that in the normal times the scale of economy is the key. To make a Port by and large you need to handle approximately 50 million tonnes of cargo that is the minimum economy. Therefore, that to be handled and evacuated in time, basically the challenge to us is going to be 40 trains per day reaching into that Port which is almost two trains per hour.

Self-assessment in rating. In India we would like to believe that our infrastructure in the Port sector is comparable probably to the best in the world. You will see a lot of our Ports which are competing with various international champions. As far as connectivity is concerned we continue to work on the rail connectivity to help us.

I come to the aspect of soft assets. There are five soft assets which all of us know. All the soft assets are closely inter-linked with each other. You cannot have ease of doing business if the regulatory frame work does not support the same. Research and development is not considered if we are weak in the human resources, technology also cannot be introduced without the regulatory frame work or without the necessary human resources. For ease of doing business what have we done in India? We have figured out that what constitutes ease of doing business is to have the least amount of documentation, meagre intervention and maximum digitalization. What needs to improve is deficiency, regulatory and interconnection such as Comprehensive policy like the Sagarmala and e-governance goals that ensure ease of doing business. The data shows that the regulatory frame work is enabling, calculative, inclusive, it is holistic and it is immediate. Global power breaking developments do take place in India. Human resources, this is one area that the Government and the Hon. Minister has emphasized a great deal towards Skill development and various Institutes are being re-energized into taking its place in the leadership role.

Research and Development - We all know that shipping, Maritime. logistics are undergoing incredible changes. Every half a decade have seen changes in port designs, ship designing, navigation, fuel systems, cargo handling system and the various practices . There are only two questions that we need to ask ourselves, Are we ready for the change and in some case can we change ourselves.

Technology - With our objective of reduction cost of digitalization of minimum human intervention and of single window cargo movement technology will be the key driver. This is a global race, every customer has a smart phone, every stakeholder has a smart phone, every banker transacts with a smart phone. The time has come that India needs its own Port Community system and India needs a Shipping Transport and Trade handling system. This is our assessment of where we are and we have tried to cross our commitments and we are confident that in the next two years you will see this meeting pointing to fulfilled actions. In conclusion, the interpretation of Maritime assets connected with connectivity is going to be the key. We know that cargo handling charges in the Ports are globally comparative and we also know that our rail transportation charges are less than the highest in the world. We also know that out of the total logistics crossed that inland transportation rate constitutes about 80 percent of our logistics cost. For the future we already know that a turnaround has started but for 2022 India should be handling 2 billion tonnes of sea borne traffic and 30 million tonnes. Our Port based infrastructure is already capable of handling this traffic. Connectivity will be the key. It is a race against time, we are becoming a highly interconnected world and the kind of participation in this hall confirms the same. Our success will depend on how quickly and effectively we can adopt and adapt these changes and especially for our neighbours and our global partners.

18

Prospects of co-operation between Coastal and Landlocked Countries

— Shri M. Ashraf Haidari

Abstract

The paper deals with the prospects for co-operation between coastal and landlocked countries. For security and growth of all in the region, such co-operation is mandated as this opens up a lot of commercial opportunities. Norway and India are the two countries.

Key-words*: Landlocked countries, SAGAR, Norway, Afganistan.*

Article

We have heard an inclusive approach which promotes corporations and partnership between coastal and landlocked countries to resolve our ocean problems should be utilized in order to address some of the key challenges that confront us into blue oceans. We strongly believe that Afghanistan as a landlocked country because our security is peace and prosperity depends very much on those of our immediate and near neighbours most of which are littoral. For most for example, maritime security on much coast as pointed out yesterday and this morning and are inter connected with and landlocked countries. Afghanistan is a prime example, over the past 40 years (not audible) on one of the most naturally endowed countries of the world and absence of peace to enable sustainable development that secures the future of our youthful population and we are one of the most youthful populations of the world and best youthful in our region. Poverty is there in our society and this provides perfect enabling environment such as maritime security challenges, terrorism, drug trafficking, arms smuggling and human trafficking among others. Over the past 60 years, Afghanistan is a victim of state sponsorship of terrorism as a proxy, of a coastal state the Taliban has killed our innocent people and by destroying the infrastructure that should help and connect Afghanistan with our resourceful regions in the North and in the South to increase trade, business and investment. This state sponsored terrorism allowed something 20 other terror networks, with global and regional reach including presence in the blue oceans to operate half of our Afghanistan at the same time it imposed insecurity enable and corrosive environment, mass drug cultivation and production in Afghanistan which is unfortunately 90% of the regional and global demand for drugs which are trafficked across the oceans in the region and beyond because of this imposed security challenges in Afghanistan and also major sources of refugees and asylums often ferried by human smugglers to Europe, Australia and elsewhere. As we see, what is imposed on, countries like Afghanistan directly affect maritime security that is why we appreciate India's constructive involvement in Afghanistan that people have seen in years to address the security challenges that are in front of Afghanistan. It would be hard to secure global peace and stability which ensures maritime security. We also appreciate the role of friendly countries as I said Norway and Afghanistan, Norway has contributed both forces and development aid towards stabilization and sustainable development of Afghanistan, as we stabilize with essence of coastal and non-coastal countries construction free strive to maintain international peace will be able to exploit our massive natural resources. Potential for revenue generation and economic growth and thus enable us to serve as round about modem initiatives including road to create and spread in prosperity across the Asia. As we look to our neighbours in the South and Central Asia, we are simultaneously strengthening the national, global and regional economic activity, President and world leaders and the recent 77th session of the United Nations General Assembly in late September. He added that Afghanistan became the maritime facility hub of the 21st Century for transport and energy, water and mining for the benefit of the entire regions economic prosperity and security. The President highlighted the Afghanistan's transmission wise the central Asia's, South Asia, power project and under construction the railway has been reached our border the g a s and pipeline under construction and the full operationalization of Chahabor Port which last year we hosted a conference investment in Afghanistan were we drew the attention of domestic and form business representatives to the following potential and best opportunities for Afghanistan and I would mention some of these to the representatives of the private sector in this gathering. 85-90% of the Afgan population lives in raw areas, they are engaged in the agriculture sector which plays the vital role in the livelihood of the 76% of the total population. More than 300 million dollars annually flows out of Afghanistan in the pursuit of medical treatment abroad and much of it here in India and at the same more than million pharmaceuticals' are imported annually to Afghanistan. Afghanistan annually produces 6 million power electricity but there is a huge potential to produce upto 23 thousand mega watts of hydro-power electricity and the past decade of Afghanistan has experienced growth in its construction industry. The construction sector has contributed 7-10% to GDP in recent years according to the US geological survey, Afghanistan perceives of minerals 1 trillion dollars whose value in our Government to 3 trillion dollars. Public procurement forms 90% of GDP, 50% of national budget, more than 90% of the considerable growth in Afghanistan are imported from regional countries and beyond, so these are some of investment opportunities that we invite those in interest and investing in the bridge of Afghanistan, so with that I conclude and look forward to any questions to asked for Afghanistan in the conference which is very much focused on maritime issues but with enormous relevance to the issues that are happening in Afghanistan.

19

"Sustainable Ocean resources strategy in Norway – a case study"

— ***Shri Ole Henaes***

Abstract

"The Paper discusses Norway's Ocean resources management strategy and 'Project Innovation – Norway'. For sustainability, post Paris Agreement, businesses including navigation, need to be part of integrated solution. An overview of energy, fishery is taken. Fish health management calls for use of advance technology especially for endangered species. Governance through organized licensing system for fish farming, cage farming in Norway is analysed."

Key-words – *Fish health sustainability, fish farming, cage farming.*

Article

In February this year our Prime Minister and our Government presented an Ocean Strategy. Our Government' s ambition is that Norway should be the number one country when it comes to Ocean Space Industries as we call them and as far as we know this is the first Ocean strategy made by any nation so we are quite proud of it. First a few words on Innovation Norway. Innovation Norway is the mission of the present Government to start ups, the business processes and business clusters. We have Offices in countries like India, we are here because we feel in win- win situations, we can create economic growth both for Norway and for India and for all the countries. We have nine Offices in seven countries; we have two Offices here in India. One is in Delhi and one is in Mumbai. Two Offices in China in Beijing and Shanghai, we have also in Singapore, Jakarta and Tokyo. In 2015 with the Paris agreement we had a turning point, we had to look into what we are doing in our Government and the way we brought sustainability. We have the navigation systematically goals, they are the foundation of the strategy of Innovation Norway and Norway working with businesses. If we have to hand over a green planet and a green planet to the kids and to the children that lit the lamp, we need to take this seriously and businesses are part of the solution. So, I am not going into details as to what India is doing, you have heard it, but the thing is history about Ocean India. So, here we are with innovation, how we are going to contribute, what work do we have to perform, and what do we have except harsh environment.

As I mentioned we are concerned with the context of sustainable development of our International Ocean industries. And we strongly believe in the research and holistic approach of the policies and the frame work. In our three Offices in Asia we have under Innovation Norway also a researcher in Cooperation where research comes in, we have one of those in India in our Delhi Office, As mentioned we were in agreement with fish workers and Norway being not the super power in the International development of Ocean policies is extremely important to us. I will now just mention a few example of what we do in Norway and how we account central elements with Blue Economy.

Offshore wind we do not have any particular incentives in Norway to develop offshore wind in the ocean waters. So our focus in offshore wind is in utilizing the offshore fleet to install operate and to do service of offshore wind mills and in this industry we look at it more at sea out of home.

Regarding fisheries, we are concerned regarding International Regulations, International Agreements and we think it is extremely important to have them in aid of fishing. There is an agreement done for legal fishing but as it is signed by quite a few nations now and agreements like that are important for the sustainable growth of the Blue Economy.

Norway is the second largest exporter of sea food in the world. The export figures last year were 11.6 million US dollars. As said by the earlier speaker most of our nation's GDP actually comes from the oceans. 70 percent. We have a very oriented export economy. 70 percent comes from the Ocean. If I may go further Fish health sustainability is crucial. This brings along with it equipments technologies, that contributes in the global aquaculture industry and also in the other species that we have in Norway. This is fish farming, this fish farming needs a licence. The licence is there with the Government, research based to make sure we have proper fishing with safety and we check the environment. It is very essential for the farmer to have this licence so that he knows he has to invest in the system like that. So he can make that investment because he knows he can do business for many years. We can meet the environmental challenges by having a system like this. So we want to bring innovation in Aquaculture more so we want to put it out in the open waters. So, we have something called the Development licences and an innovative investor can have if he or she comes up with this focus of farming. The picture to the top left here has been way to China it is not involving and to start to operate with not too long and it is interesting mix of technology from ...Industry for the Maritime Industry and the Aquaculture industry. This yellow structure has a diameter of 110 metres the height of that construction is 68 metres which basically means that in 68 metres comes a huge construction it will take one point 5 million fish and a biomass of 8.3 million kilo biomass its huge. In this Cage to produce maximum amount of fish in this Cage the investor needs 8 licenses. Of course that means this investment is 100 million US dollars.

The picture and the statement by our Prime Minister. How to develop in this direction? How strong Industrial clusters will be crucial for us to succeed, we must be able to develop technology and knowhow. We will use the Ocean space to develop not only ocean products but new industries. Second we needs to safe guard our efforts between research, development and innovations. Further we must continue to be policy followers. As a policy Norway has a strong way to manage our resources well. It takes hard work to stay in the forefront. In the future the Ocean will be a source of food, medicine and energy as we harvest and use these species and find new ways of using energy. We will introduce medicines and health products not yet seen from the resources found in the Oceans. The oceans are the key for the sustainability developments of our planets. United Nations Sustainability gives us directions on the way to sail, we need few transportations and sustainable usage of the Government and we think that Norway is in the process to continue such a course and we are here to participate and to contribute and to cooperate. Thank you very much.

20

Maritime Engagement of Landlocked Countries

— Shri. Ram Thapliya

Abstract

The paper elucidates relationship between humanity with maritime engagement. The difficulties of transport in case of landlocked countries like Nepal, essentially makes them count as a friend like India. Sea blindness could be dangerous. Having indirect access to ocean would make India – Nepal relationship strong.

Key-words: *Landlocked countries, Nepal – India relationship.*

Article

I represent a landlock country and I realize now how much it is important to give into maritime and in the Sagar Discourse. The reality is that many of the landlock countries are busy enough for the inter-land peace, integrity and friendship. I like to remember, when the Prime Minister Mr. Modi visited Nepal and he delivered his note in the Parliament. Out of many he discussed about water and human life. In Hindi, he said, Pani and Jawani, he enlightened it very nicely as landlock countries as Jawani and sea and oceans are the Pani. I just would like to talk little bit of what I learned about this conference. I was not sure what I was going to present over here. Particularly, I served number of time as a advisor the Prime Minister on many times on international relation disaster and security. I realized that rich or poor, peace or conflict, I was listening to number of presentations and our environment, what are we today? Our history and our geography and I really realized myself humanity and social science are directly related to the Sagar Discourse and I come to conclusion yes, we are. Even though many of our priorities of developing countries and landlock countries are in different sectors. Attitude yes, live in human dignity. It is a privilege to be based in this society. So Sagar, as I remember every morning, my father and mother they are praying for sun, moon and water, although we are not really not practicing that much maritime issues in the land lock developing countries because we don't see them physically. Our appreciation defiantly to what you have done today, yesterday and on the first day is a very interesting and it is our honour and privilege for us to be educated on these issues. I think injustice and fairness are the challenging issues are basically one of the key role player in the global power like India and many other countries need to focus on. The ability to influence the decision making. We are there in there corner and highest paid in the world and basically looking around and seeing and observing what is going around. Can we contribute? Yes, we can. I focused on our infrastructure development policy and realized its negative impact on Sagar Discourse on maritime and blue ocean. As a politician myself, we used to believe that tree does not vote for us but now I realised that it is our future. It is our generation's future, it is my children and my grandchildren. Sagar Mala itself is a beautiful phenomena. I like to put and propose myself here as landlock country as we are the flower of Sagar Mala, as a result landlock developing countries continue to face a lot of challenges since my colleagues mentioned before me. It is most of the time lacked behind maritime development and external trade. Distance from the coast is another challenging issue for us. India is a largest democracy in the world and we are very lucky to have a wonderful neighbour that would never feel that we don't have access to sea. Sometimes in the universal situation of the flag, the reality is different, the reality is dependent on neighbours infrastructure, cross border political relations, neighbours peace and stability. These factors combine to have different challenges and priorities and therefore maritime issue may not be priority into the national policy or maybe but that was my experience. Maritime issue are global change and sustainability issue that is why 5 years ago in the university under my leadership we started a course, a curriculum, Master and Ph.D focused on crisis management and our major specialization is global change and sustainability in environment crisis and bio-diversity issues. Temperatures are already rising and are expected to continue to rise in South Asia also. for Nepal it means that nation may see 10% GDP loss from glacier melt and climate extremes according to the Asian Development Report. I think the developing countries especially the landlocked countries are very busy for the internal issues, political stabilities, democracy and rule of the law but if you really see the capacity of us how much we are busy and engaged internal this Sagar can give you some idea ahead. I will say that issues, yesterday and today even on the opening ceremony after listening the speech given by the Hon. Ministries and also our scholars there are more issues that needs to be discussed and I believe that it is the time for landlock and developing countries like us to bring those issues back and try to understand the mainstream development activities within our own periphery. There are risks which I never realized 15 years ago all these disaster issues, the mountain glaciers issues melting and I have come to conclusion that are we effected yes, are we responsible yes. The vulnerability capacity is very different. I have realized that how prepared we are? If not now, then when? Do we have a common view, common understanding, common effect on this blue ocean. Do we really realize the importance and the existence of this oceans? I think it is very important as a landlock country that we should implement the maritime approach through across country action. We should really incorporate into our development and infrastructures and different approach and those cluster approach should heavily influence the security, benefit and respect of Sagar. I would say that yesterday I had also gone through the presentation of a person in the leading university in India and I thought myself while I was taking a note, maybe some of the issues are here very effective. Some of the issues which are here which we should focus on and respect, some of the issues which are here which we should incorporate in our law and rule. In conclusion there are key challenges for peace and stable sagar. I am hearing about nuclear weapons and I am hearing misuse of nuclear forces by democratic practice and none the less we live in mountains. We have never realized that we are not that far from the sagar and directly and indirectly we are effecting on it. So I thought persistent theory is very important for us to respect. Adaptation theory is major challenge for any of the sea country and they have their own disputes and own democratic perceptions and therefore it is very for us to think about it.What we believe to get it together and why we need to focus on terrorism theory by Sagar and through Sagar. So central structure of the phenomena based on this Sagar Discourse I come to rise myself that goals are very important and our goals should be benefited by it and helping those like us who live slightly or physically distance from Sagar. Maritime policy in prospect should be more concentrated and maritime environment and technology.

21

"Connectivity and integration of Indian Coastal Economy"

— Shri. Sanjay Parashar

Abstract

"The Paper deals with connectivity and integration of Indian Coastal Economy. Asymmetry in eastern and western coast is analyzed. Co-operation across region on for insurance and security mechanism, importance of Green Coastal Shipping and Coastal economic zones is emphasized. India also needs more E-Governance for more transparency like in Singapore. Coastal Ship Owners Development Fund can be refocused on, as this would catalyze coastal economic development. Use of Satellite system for cargo clearances is suggested. Use of social media to study behaviour of coastal community will help building community understanding and trust. An overview has been taken of industry from ship building to ship breaking and ship repairs via dry docking. Fishermen are referred to as first line of defence and intelligence and also important component of coastal economy."

Key-words: *Green Coastal Shipping, Coastal economic zones, Satellite system, use of social media, fishermen – first line of defence.*

Article

I will focus on connectivity and integration of our coastal economy. My country is blessed with fantastic coastal. If I look at the map and the East and West coast, there is a bit of asymmetry. The natural resources are higher on the East coast and the finished coast by the law of nature has taken on to the more of export or import by the West coast and this is somewhere I feel the coastal shipping steps in and being a Master Mariner for 15 years in the office with the kind of circle I have, I would say the coastal economy when I used to sail and see in other countries when I first time joined Sweden or when I went to Norway, I used to feel as a youngster or when do I see this in India and I am so lucky that in my lifetime I have had a Government and a Minister, who is known not just as Minister of Shipping but a Minister with action. So, that is how I respect you Sir and my fraternity respects you. I am glad that Norway is our Partner. I will not go to the four pillars which are been declare by the Government for Sagarmala, I will focus on the fifth one, why the fifth one? What do I do of the four? The bottle line comes how do we ship the cargo? How do we ship the people? So if we have to do this, it has to come through ships and I think that is the place where the countries who are wanting to do partnership not just for few years but strategically for many years need to actually do a proper kind of work which stay on for years. When it comes to coastal shipping insurance, where 60 billion dollars the Government is going to invest, let me tell you if the private players want to come in, it is a trillion dollar industry. Insurance of ships, the hub is Europe, I had been to Maersk, fantastic building, which we have started in India trying to nurture but it will take time. Can the European, can the people who are miles ahead of us with their experiences partner us? Green coastal shipping is the fantastic successful thing happening in Norway because the kind of plan they have rails and roads is secondary and shipping is primary. For us shipping is primary now but maritime equipment can we have this Coastal Economic Zones, which the Government has nominated on the Indian coast with so much of the skilled development. Can we have something as breeding ground for this and I personally feel, the soil which we see now is suddenly bound to change. That is how I see this import duty. The kind of accountancy which makes painful procedures for us with GST and other things coming in and we the business community settling down, I think the grading very soon as shown in the earlier slides like Kotakji's, should go very soon. E-governance, I am glad Hon. Minister himself says, well this must happen soon. Its already happening we are seeing a drastic change, 3,00,000 seafarers have already seen this change. Now, this is the time to see this change from the coastal shipping, coastal economy side. When it comes to bureaucracy and decision making we have still lots of glitches. We need to work lot on this. Private equity, well I tell you today shipping the business people like to see how much returns. Let me tell you, you can have leisure in shipping but shipping is not one generation job and it will take some time to percolate down and the day it happens I see the interest rate from 13% coming down but if there are strategic partners and emissaries have to succeed it certainly cannot be out of global competition staying at 13% we certainly need it at 4% or 5%. Research papers have remained intact, there is something new which is happening in India in last 2-3 years. I have not seen in my life so many kinds of seminars happening whether on Coastal Shipping or Blue Economy. I think this Government's push has made the citizens like us to be the soldiers of land trying to do research with our real experience and I feel this grading will also in the coming days improvise. Well, we had a fantastic thing in the 1970s, the Coastal Ship owning Development Fund I think certain years back it got shut down. I feel it is time to revisit this as it is an action plan and in India this can be a catalyst for us. The failure reports, let me tell you something new, failures are bound to happen and I am probably one of this in this field and we got nothing to hide in this. Failure reports are to be shared. So that there is no repeat and the corrective measures, the private incentives which come in by learning from other failures actually becomes are stepping stone and if I tell you one of my experiences in this particular issue of our failures, one I shared with the Hon. Minister on the Ro-Ro thing, it took him exactly five hours to change two policies of India, whether it was pertaining to the Port charges or whether it was pertaining to bringing down a regulation on the traders. So I feel if an action can be done in five hours it depends on how right and proper your feedback is. This Government listens and we have at FINS we have first hand for you and when it comes to the National Shipping Board 1959 it was from the Parliamentary Act, I think they got a good job to do and I am very pleased to see a National Shipping Board, a Board which just not formulates a policy, which goes back to the Government with a fantastic feedback so that the corrections are done at the right time. There can be nothing except dynamic changes which are required in the real time basis to happen and I would say that whatever D.G. Shipping has authorized for so many years over years on the coastal shipping probably it is time for us to really see the actionable things on that and probably implement it. I would say the Associations have to come out of that fear and comfort that it is only for live Members, well with today's technology. let me tell you with the RTI Act, let me be very clear, Industry belongs to every citizen of India, so let us not just pursue an agenda for just the Members, agenda for the members is different and proposing and agenda for the countries is different. I think it is time for the role of think tanks to be more wider than what has been there over the years. This is something which everybody knows. Even our Hon. Prime Minister says it sometimes, that we would like to see ourselves graded as one in the top 50 or probably you know one of the best in the world. The times are changing. Well, if Indian Coastal ships and foreign ships have to come in, I think the problems that we face at the Ports or with the Authorities and the transparency that has to come in, have to come in very fast. £-Clearances for the ships the way it is done in Singapore, thousands of ships come in and thousands of ships go and we have only 12-13 major Ports and if I look at the e-... that is notice of arrival I saw it 13 years back in the US, why not use that satellite system in India. I feel it is the most secured system. If US Navy can use a Maersk PC TC for 25 years to do their job why can't we have a new over box thinking with our strategic partners with the kind of assets that are required rather than harping just on the Government coming with 60 ships to deliver what the Defence needs because the needs of the defence forces have changed. But the ships what are available with Indians or Indian flags have not really reached that stage. So, we certainly need lot strategic partners and not just partners and I think the Ship Construction, Sir I am glad, in your Ministry you have cancelled contracts if the speed has not been met and I am sure the kind of pressure that is coming on to develop a Ship Making in India, will probably in few years see trying to match the best in the world because the three Ship building countries among the far East will be our challenge, not just actually making it for India and I think the Make in India we have probably lot of hope happening here. Marco & Salvage in Bangladesh is a fantastic example for us. Why not share their resources. Sunder Shree Delta we have issues happening there, if we have to do operation we need specialized ships. My perception is in coming days what you did in the European Union I think it will be replicated all over the world because if humanity has to do well it has to do well going beyond boundaries and as just now said by my colleague from Bangladesh, the trust factor is risen worldwide. Unfortunately, we got only 100 coastal ships and I think today's demand is 300 coastal ships if it is today's demand just imagine where do we go in 2025. National Shipping Board has done a little bit of research and discipline on the website only for your view on logistics and berths for shipping in due course. Well, Hon. Minister himself knows a lot if he can display it on the website saying I have got 12 thought points I have got major actions let me tell you half of the actions are done and the rest half will be seen very soon. So, if we are saying we have got a problem with these logistics there is well research done by the National Shipping Board and I would say the simplification and whatever research that has been done if FINS is asked to works with us the Shipping Board we have got enough of the troubles that are available and if the other countries want to partner it and see how in the next 10-40 years it is going to be we are absolutely for it.

What started in 1986 actually started working after April 2016 when I had launched a summit with my friend Kapil Sharma in April 2016 and I think this is the first moving infrastructure globally all over the world because when we talk we talk about one sixth population of the world. So when we say billions rest be assured it will be trillions soon. When we talk about 2025, I think the troubles what we see for shipping we see the same inland vessels the small vessels. The social media has changed, the way we look at life. I think husband and wife we talk more on Whatsapp now-a-days, so well the coastal shipping does need the local language, the local Wikipedia and I am glad, one of the persons from Pune who is probably also working with our authorities is getting out to that for the body language, a state has a Wikipedia, the language what the people understand, the fishermen understands and there probably the social media not only for coastal economics I think even the behaviour of the things which are going to come in probably if I see 2030, I would not see Whatsapp ten years back, I think it would be the biggest conduct for the marketing of the business. The Navy and the coastline is the game changer for me and in that I see the fishermen being my first line of defence. The kind of equipments they have, the kind of action and intelligence they give I think that will be one of the fantastic outcome of involving samudar putras, why we call them soldiers at sea because they are the ones who are miles and miles away and they know exactly what is happening out at sea. They know what is right and what is also not right and fishing Sir the dignitaries from overseas are trying to confess let me tell you, you guys have been the rulers with the trawlers, our 37 percent is still with the boat. Your funds are already nominated. There are Fisheries Cooperative banks, I think this is the time for you to come and see economically what is viable for you. Eleven million metric tonnes of fish production, well, we may find lot of vegetarians here let me tell you when you go to the coast, fishing is a very- very huge Industry. 40 lakhs, that is nearly 4 crore families actually are involved in this. Just imagine this particular business going three folds. So, for me the big coastal boom will be actually for the fishermen, the 40 lakh families on the coast and I tell you my coast are secured if I see this happening for coastal economy to the last man standing as fisherman. If India-Pakistan-Bangladesh has to be one, I think we have to do the maximum ship parting. What has to start has to come to an end. Six years old ship being scrapped at Palam. We do this business, let me tell you the kind of R&D equipments that were uploaded, we have done fantastic work. So, even as an Industry from Ship Building to Ship making in India has a potential and this being another billion dollar industry, being restricted not just to Gujarat now, I feel India will remain a top player, you like it if you don't like it we can think of ourselves for those purposes but Hong Kong Convention is a reality for India very soon, our 141 lakhs 50 yards are already for the Hong Kong

Convention. If I look at the domestic and international tourism I don't need to say much the rest have said so many things, we probably look at it happening in a big way. This is what I feel we need. These are the excellent points. E-governance has to go top up. (Hindi) Every youth of India is going to wait for you because we have moved only the correct way of conducting business. That's the new generation here. 30 percent of cargo movement, e-governance, the right things the strategic partners can follow but let me tell you the biggest gate way to all this is stable Asia and strategic Indian coastal economy. (Hindi) and I think I have all the confidence to say with the powers we have done the homework, India is a Maritime power.

22

Prospects and Practice in Maritime Industry – A Case Study

— *Shri. Sarosh Zaiwalla*

Abstract

The paper deals with prospects and practice of maritime law. The pre-requisites for international success being Indian-ness and silent courage in the case study discussed. The paper also takes an overview of history of Indian maritime industry. A specific mention of China in this context is also made.

Key-words: *Maritime law, maritime industry.*

Article

Conference organizers and the distinguished guests, this is the last session and I promise I am going to be to the point and as short as possible. Before I start, let me say something more about this session.

Some six weeks ago, I was in Singapore attending as a special invited guest, a session like this; a dialogue called 'Raffles' dialogue which brought together 35 high level achievers from all over the world to include the Singapore Foreign Minister and the former President of Malaysia. Attending the Singapore event I said to myself why India should not have such a dialogue. We had some very interesting discussions from different fields of life on what the world needs to do to make it a safer and a better place for our fellow human being. A couple of weeks ago, I was interviewed by BBC and I was asked what is the secret of the success of my firm in London and I said it was my Indian-ness. I refused to change my firm's name. Many other Indian lawyers who came and started in UK had anglicized their name. There was a solicitor from Calcutta who requalified in London and he started a firm called Morgan Walker and I asked him why Morgan Walker? He said it is an attractive name because there was this white complex and he therefore named his law firm putting together JP Morgan and Johnny Walker. Therefore one finds that many of the Indians who came to do work anglicized themselves. I have been accepted for two things, one is I have been what I am and not pretended to be something I am not, i.e. I have not tried to change my culture to English, although I do respect the English culture.

The second most important thing is courage, and this must be silent courage. You have to have integrity in order to take action. As a result today, in England there are 104 reported cases where my firm has been involved as an Indian origin firm in changing the English law. Today we are acting for Iran and Russia. When an Iran bank lost its challenge regarding their alleged involvement in nuclear proliferation, after they had challenged their sanctions listing through one of the big English law firm, they lost in the High Court and the Court of Appeal, they then instructed my firm for the appeal to the Supreme Court. The appeal was heard by 9 out of 12 Judges of the Supreme Court.

The Judges by the majority of 5 to 4 declared the UK government's conduct not only unlawful but irrational. As a consequence of the UK Supreme Court Judgement we are today handling for our Iranian Bank client, the largest ever claim in the English Court, which is 4 million USD of damages against the UK Government. I bring this to light because as an Indian origin English firm we have showed what we are capable of achieving if we not only do our best but do our best with integrity and courage, without fear of becoming unpopular with the establishment. This is very important because most people want to be popular. When the International Arbitration Court in The Hague award 50 billion USD against the Russian Federation some 2 years ago, in a claim brought by the Yukos shareholders, all the lawyers they consulted said to the Russian Government that they could not challenge the award. So they came to my firm and sought my assistance. Today the award has been set aside by the Dutch Court. Now that again is an Indian's achievement. What I always wanted to do is to put the Indian footprint, which is very, very essential in the field of International Law.

Now, when I came this morning, I had prepared my speech to talk about the Maritime threat. My firm was established as a Maritime law firm and I started as a Maritime lawyer for the President of India. I was very lucky because it was at a period where India was going through a food shortage caused by a major famine and President Johnson of the United States had decided to donate food grains under what was known as PL-480 scheme of the US Government. Under this scheme the US would supply free wheat to India but India had to arrange for the ships to pick the donated wheat from US ports. There were about 250-300 ships every year and every ship had an arbitration. I was appointed as the Indian High Commission lawyer by the High Commissioner Seyed Mohamed, who was himself a lawyer, a non-- practicing English barrister. He saw an Indian Parsi boy starting a law firm in England with an Indian name and he appointed me as the Indian Governments solicitor without me having any contacts in Delhi.

Now, that brings me to a second point which I think I would like to say to this audience, particularly the Indians. We need to change our culture in one respect and that is when Britain ruled India, it is a fact that there were just 4000 white civil servants including British Judges ruling 400 million Indians. Therefore, they had to have a culture and a system to keep ordinary people at a distance from the ruling class which caused the birth of the Patronage Culture in India. As a result, today in India we have a patronage culture by which those in power kept their distance from those under them. We need to change this culture. In the west things work on merits. Therefore, one finds that Indians who go abroad do very well, and we need to now accept the need to do away with the patronage culture in India and we must have a merit based culture.

I have prepared a speech but a lot of it was said in the morning so I am not going to repeat however I am going to say a few important things about the Maritime history of India. The fact is the ancient Vedic Civilization had a strong connection with the sea and the Maritime abilities. Even in the language, the Vedic Sanskrit words such as samudra, salil, sagar, and sindhu indicated the sea for Raj Rivers. This is very interesting. The word "Sinduka" also meant sailor, which became the name "Sindbad" for the sailor of the Arabian nights.

The Indian Maritime trade actually flourished many years ago along with many other trades and its advancement is hardly recognized or accounted for today. This is very unfortunate because we only have memories of what happened in the last 300 years but when I did some research, I found that way back during the Rigveda and Purana's time, there was also an advance Maritime trade, not only that but the Indian ships were respected very, very much. The fact is that India's Maritime trade actually flourished more than most people realized in the ancient days of culture.

In the ancient Indian Vedic books we find the information of complete arrangements for the boats maintained by the navy and the State 2000 years ago. Ancient Indians travelled through various parts of the world not only for the purposes of trade but also to propagate their culture. In the period 984, 1000 years after Christ, the Chowra king dispatched great naval expedition which occupied parts of Burma and Samudra by suppressing the piratical activities in Samudra borders. Now my understanding as somebody already mentioned is that this is a true story and you can get it from the British Museum from the autobiography of Vasco Da Gama. He sailed for a land which he believed was prosperous in the East and whilst he was passing Madagascar, he saw a ship which was 3 times bigger than his ship. So through an interpreter he said let me speak to the captain. The captain received him, his name was Chandan Bias and he said I want to go to this rich country, where is it? And the captain said follow me and that is how he came to India. This is an admitted fact.

Now when did the Indian Shipping & Maritime industry go down? It went down after the Moguls came and there was an invasion and were a lot of internal fights. Really it went down which, I am sorry to say, as part of the British rule. This is very, very interesting because the British found that the Indian ship buildings were much better than their own. I am going to read out minutes from the diary of the East Indian Company. The Board of Directors of East India Company wrote in their minutes that all the fear and respect that the Indian seamen had towards the European behaviour was lost when they saw our social life once they came here. When they returned to the country they will propagate bad things about us amongst the Asians and we will lose our superiority and the effect will be harmful. At this, the British parliament committee had a special act passed forbidding Indian sailors being employed by the British ships. They also prevented the building of Indian ships by making a law that Indian ships cannot bring goods to England.

But that is all now history, so we are not going to speak and be concerned about it because we now have to look towards the future. Modern Indian shipping started in 1910 with the formation of Scindia Shipping Company, many of you know Scindia shipping. This was the first Indian shipping Company. Sadly Scindia Shipping does not exist anymore. The last chairman of Scindia Shipping was Sumatiben Morarjee, a doyan of Indian shipping. Scindia went bust because it failed to modernize its business culture. Sumatiben Morarjee and the founder, Narottam Mararjee were also close to Mahatma Gandhi. I was very lucky that my firm acted for Scindia Shipping and I had an opportunity to meet Sumatiben. Then came the downfall of Scindia. It ran out of cash but the Prime Minister, Rajiv Gandhi who was the then Prime Minister of India had sent Sumatiben to me, to see if they could find finance in Europe but we could not. Now of course thankfully there are many other Indian shipping companies.

I was going to speak on the other aspects like the law and all those things but it appears everybody has spoken of it previously and the young Iranian lady is going to speak on the crew who find themselves in financial difficulty, so what I am going to do is to share my experience with you as somebody who sees India from the outside and just like President Trump's words, tell you what I think we can do together to make India great again.

I was lucky to be involved with China where I was renewed by the Indian High Commission in London as a solicitor for the Government of India for many years. For my sins, I acted for the Bofors case and when that happened VP Singh's Government came. I had a choice to make with the High Commissioner. The High Commissioner was Kuldip Nayar, he said you're a good man, decide if you want to act for the Indian High Commission or the Bachchans. But like a typical Parsi I said that there was no conflict because the Bachchans were suing a third country and so I said no, I am not going to drop Bachchans as a client of my firm. This resulted in the Indian High Commission sacking us as the Indian Government Lawyers, lock, stock and barrel. Now strangely, 2 months after that the then Chinese Ambassador in London invited me for lunch and said "why don't you help China to build up a legal system?" At that time in 1991, believe it or not China did not have a legal system. The Ambassador sponsored my trip, he arranged everything, put me in the Beijing hotel in Beijing where all state guests in those days stayed. The Beijing hotel is now becoming modern and had a red carpet and I spent a week over the Christmas holidays in China. When I came back to London, the Chinese Ambassador and I got along very well and he said why you don't start an office in Beijing. There was an English office in China already. Clifford Chance had started but they were acting for the British and the Europeans. There were only 4 law firms in China at that time and the lawyers were not loyal but were appointed as lawyers from the communist party. And that brought me very close to China. I made several trips to China and informally advised China on how China could develop an international legal system and how to work with foreign lawyers.

Fortunately for me at that time by sheer luck, I was also very close to the British Prime Minister, John Major and I had the opportunity to arrange, by coincidence, the first ever dinner in the British cabinet room for Asian businesses. I made several visits to China with the British Government

Ministers, including two with Michael Heseltine, when he was the deputy Prime Minister of Britain.

Now, I am going to tell you something about how China works and what we should do to resolve the boarder crisis but before I do that, I want to tell you again of a true incident. I was going to China with the British Rail Minister, Sir Richard Needham and suddenly the trip was cancelled because China was very upset about what the government was doing on the ongoing democratization process. So I met the Chinese Ambassador who was a friend and he said, "Look this is not right" and I said, "can I help?" he said "yes". Thereafter we had a two private second general discussions in my office, between representative of the British Prime Minister and with the representatives of the PRC Government. Within two meetings we resolved the issue. Soon after the Chinese asked me if I can help to resolve India's border issue, to which I let them know that I will try. I informed them that I, as an Indian would like to see this issue resolved. Their story was that they want just the right border of Tibet. He said the McMahon line which at present constitutes the border between China and India and is just a line drawn by the English Brigadier McMahon without any scientific study of what the border was between Tibet and India. I agreed work together with the Chinese Ambassador and send a private note to India's External Affairs Minister through Maneka Gandhi an Indian Government Minister, who was my client at that time. To our surprise, we did not get a response. I met India's External Affairs Minister Jaswant Singh later at a private event in London and when I asked him about my note he said, "My boys are not interested".

This brings me to important thing which was to understand the Chinese culture. For China 'face' is very important. The Chinese do not want to lose an argument and therefore India has to find a way to give and take and I think I have another true example. When the West wanted China not to exercise veto, the British negotiated that China will get a contract for construction of a gathering station in Kuwait in return for China not exercising veto in Security Council and that is how one deals with China on a give and take basis. Once we prepared the note, the Chinese assured me they just wanted the border to be clarified and agreed. Unfortunately, we did not get a response from India side. At that time China was very keen. We of course in India have a heated argument regarding the McMahon line, even if it was just drawn, it was drawn at a time when Tibet was an independent country. Now Tibet is now part of China and McMahon line was agreed as a border between India and Tibet when Tibet was independent

Country. So China has no right or any claim to ask for adjustment of what the border of Tibet was and that is something which we can do. It is better to resolve this dispute with China through dialog and if necessary through the law than to just keep the dispute boiling.

The other thing I will share with you is what China fears most is the west, especially United States and Briton, is going to break China. This is why they said "we are going to protect ourselves, we do not going to rule anything." I have a very vivid recollection. I used to meet the President and the Prime Minister in those days of China. When Chinese President, Zhang Shi Ping came to London, the Chinese Ambassador reminded him that I was acting for China and the President told me in clear English, "I am glad that an Asian is representing us, China". He then went onto say, "what we want is to be treated with respect not to dominate".

I think that is really China's philosophy, to protect themselves and I think all of us in the West, even possibly India, is getting hyped up that there is a military power. What they want is a trade route and I think there is a risk if we continuously say "we need to attack, we need to attack:" So what we need to do is to meet the Chinese, talk to them in a sensible manner on a give and take basis. China believes in the face that you cannot lose the face. It is okay, it is just the border and I am sure they are not interested in really fighting it out so that is one thing which we should do. I recall at one of my meetings with the Chinese Ambassador he stressed to me that there is no economical reason why Chinese Government wants to resolve the border dispute with India.

Now before I end, I am also going to share my experience of an issue of Kashmir and the issue of Pakistan and it is important to recognise that India is a secular country. I hope I will be understood when I say that today there are more Muslims in India than in Pakistan. A few years ago there was an event which Lord Hasket held in the House of Lords to discuss the Kashmir issue at which I was invited to speak. I said that Pakistan Muslims are doing a great disservice to Indian Muslims by supporting insurgency in Kashmir against India. By this they have made Muslims in India insecure. I say this is because if there is a referendum the Kashmiries in the valley might vote for Kashmir to join Pakistan but that would have serious consequences for Indian Muslim who will be made insecure and if there is a backlash against them from the majority Hindu community then even the Indian army will not be able to protect the Indian Muslims. This is because in India most villages have a small community of Muslims.

We need to educate the world about this fact. Another point which I want to make is that we should have an international television station which is non-political, something like the Japanese have, the NHK. The Chinese now have two international television channels including the CGTN, no political views but shows all about achievements. India should have similar international television channels showing the good side of India, the bad side of India, and what can be done and what cannot be done and what is being done. Also all the tourist spots in India could be highlighted along with historical difference in cultures of different Indian States. This is important for India.

I would like to share with you when Benazir Bhutto became my client. I was instructed to bring her from Dubai to London when she was convicted by the Pakistani court. I got to know the very natural soft side of her and she told me that the Kashmir insurgency is funded and she told me of how it is funded by Saudis, the Wahabis and therefore the Indian government needs to recognise this and work on getting stopping the Saudis from funding the Jehadis insurgency in Kashmir.

I would like to suggest, for those who care for India and for Asia, this is now the time that India must remove Article 370 of the Indian Constitution. I even recently wrote to the Indian High Commissioner in London with this regard to which I never received a reply. Article 370 restricts the economic development of Kashmir. If you bring prosperity to the people of Kashmir, they will come to know that what matters and what matters is the economic prosperity of the people. I used to work for a tour company when I was a student during the holidays and I know Kashmiris are gentle people by nature; they are not fanatical people and make them prosperous.

The final story I'll tell you is when Dalai Lama came to me and why he wanted a private meeting with me on his visit to Scotland. The Dalai Lama asked me if I could arrange a second channel dialog with China to enable him to return to his homeland Tibet. Dalai Lama told me that he is aware that one of the few non-Chinese person China trusts in Europe is me and he said he trusted me. I started the second channel dialog but nothing really happened thereafter. Some 5 years ago when I was invited to China to observe the new Chinese political leadership takeover I was discreetly told that China is not interested in any dialogue with Dalai Lama as China is of the view after the death of the Dalai Lama there will be no Tibet issue.

So with that, thank you very much for listening to me. I would say please continue with this dialogue and also working towards bringing in more non-Maritime and more experts from other countries to be a part of the dialogue. We need to make India great again in order to put Indian footprint in the globalisation of the world.

23

Security and Peace in Context of Maritime Governance

—*Shri. V. A. Bhat*

Abstract

Index of human development as well as index of human happiness includes security and peace. Security here means not preparedness for war but maintenance of peace. Development of small islands gives strategic depth to the nation. The economic progress requires political weight of the government in carrying out the programme further.

***Key-words**: Maritime governance, small island development.*

Article

The index of human development as well as the index of human happiness includes security and peace as an important ingredient of the assessment of human welfare. So, when we speak of security it is not preparation for war. It is a fight for maintenance of peace. It is an arrangement and pre-planning for meeting a host of requirements leading to human welfare and security. I will be mentioning few issues wherein we have the much needed attention to be given for application of science and technology which have been developed in Research Institutions as well as in the institutions of excellence in our country in the area of administration of Government Departments as well as private establishments and companies. It call for tuning of our approach and implementation style in Government Departments as well as in companies and institutions. One of the first map made of the Indian ocean of the days of Ptolemy is one of the few scientific applications of technology and science for navigation as well as other developmental purposes. So from the day of map making and its application for various purposes based on high estimation we have moved on to the era of satellite and carcosite but the need for utilizing this mapping ability for detection, for implementation of various programme and for diversified purposes is left to our imagination. In almost potential available for application of satellite data need to be made use of all around. Coming to the importance of trade routes in the Indian Ocean. We have large volume of trade taking place requiring protection from various agencies. I am grateful to the Observer Research Foundation for some of the data which have been used in these maps. In terms of component of trade, the direction of trade, the growth pattern of this trade we need policy making in the External Affairs front of the Indian Government, the involvement of island countries which are located in Indian Ocean etc. to come together to be able to use them for mutual benefit. Where do we stand in Indian Ocean in terms of the movement of cargo ships? It is next to in its intensity only to the Atlantic and generally when we say the speed, the safety and counteracting the potential for ship jacking or Naval or maritime terrorism the importance from the point of view of global prosperity is also very important. It is not merely the security of island State and India which is involved, it is global security which is involved in this. What do we need to do in this regard further is that we need to set up a multipurpose Defence establishment in great Nicobar island. Please note the strategic depth it would give over the entire Indian Ocean almost it will have the significance of Iyagogasiya in terms of maintaining the stability of political and military relationship in the oceans as well as being the guardian of peace in this area. The potential for fishing has been discussed and the potential for the development of the merchant, marine establishment can be known by looking at this graph where we see the Indonesia as well as the Singapore are having such an amount of capability in comparison with others which will be an inspiration for the others in the region. For long it have been thought that trading happen only between developed countries. As student of international economics will read theories of international trade long back. The realities were different. Today the realities are different. There is an enormous amount of trading within the developing countries. So, what we do to develop this monsoon market place. We have this concept of IORA which has come. We have now Blue Economy co-operation which has been listed out here but the important thing is to back it up with the political weight of the Government in carrying out the programme further as well as in evolving a strategy along with island countries. So the island countries are of two type those which have become independent or those which are still part of the main country with whom they were associated earlier. So in terms of the interaction with those which are part of another major country we have another dimension in terms of diplomacy and external relations. What is it that we should do further in this area is that we should not think that sea is a boundary for the country. Traditionally it has been read in our text book that we are bond by such and such boundary, we have sea here and we have kind of impression that is because of the mountain and the sea we are well protected. So the fear of the sea is something which has to be overcome. Competitions for children, event for commemorating major events by having sea swimming as a promotional federation activity etc. is something which is very important for developing that spirit of concurring the sea or adventure in the sea. Developing a multipurpose establishment at Great Nicobar gives enormous depth adding another 600 kilometers to our integrated command at Port Blair when plane get lost like that of the Malaysian Airplane. We need long endurance aircraft to be able to be operated and wonderful asset in Great Nicobar it should be developing as a Versatile Defence Establishment. We should also develop a satellite umbrella over the Indian Ocean which enables a constant monitoring of all the ship as well as all the activities in the ocean. For facilitating this we can establish another Launchpad in the southern tip of the country which gives us additional advantage of carrying additional weight. We will be able to launch a bunch of small satellites, low earth orbit satellites for that kind of monitoring. National Institute of Technology at Chennai and others knowledge institutions has enormous potential to suggest how research and development should be carried out in the area of unmanned vehicles in the sea, marine archeology, ocean energy, etc. and the last point is again in terms of leveraging our advantages of operating from Great Nicobar as well as from the southern tip of India for making Indian Ocean a zone of peace is most important thing I want to highlight and conclude because our earlier attempt to declare it as zone of peace is only a matter of word. Only when it is backed with strength of infrastructure and intervention that enable us to guarantee security for us as well as for the ocean countries.

24

Role of India in South China Sea – A Vietnam Perspective

— Shri. Vo Xuan Vinh

Abstract

The paper is about Vietnam perspective on maritime law with respect to South China Sea. The author proposes a more vital role for India in this region and envisages a stability provider's role. This is not only from security but also from trade point of view. Freedom of navigation in SCS is discussed. The paper refutes China's claim of historical right.

Key-words: *South China Sea, Vietnam – India, UNCLOS.*

Article

I could talk something on the legal background so therefore from political and international relations approach. I think that my personal view point when you have some idea because I have research at Look/Act East Policy in 10 years from now, especially on the maritime domain between India and Asia Pacific and now the Maritime security in Indo- Pacific. It inspired me a lot and I have tried to attract something about the Indian Maritime Security ambition especially in the Indo-Pacific particularly in the South China Sea.

You will now preparing for something in the future, not only present but also the future. The important thing is for the maritime security strategy to have some change in quality and that in 2007 mentioned by the freedom to be able to seek deployment of naval set in the maritime environment only. But when we come to 2015 with another Maritime Security so now you say that in order to provide freedom to be able to see in 2007 military strategy now we have a different strategy in the 21st century. And the light of necessity to ensure that you are moving something to prepare for the future and from my personal view point, it seems that India now is ready to be a global player in maritime domain that is from my mind. It also reflects a lot in Indian ambition in terms of maritime domain we too can do a change. So if we focus mainly on primary area in Indian Ocean right from 2007 you move it, expand it to many other reasons, including the South China Sea and West Pacific and in 2009, 2015, maritime strategy now I do have primary and secondary area.

The secondary areas, I think that includes a lot of areas surrounding the Indian Ocean but also is related to South and China sea and West Pacific Ocean also that also reflects very clearly the Indian Maritime ambition. And now we move to the South China Sea a very important area in the strategy and let us look at this policy. You know that trade is also important to India's economic factor. As I learn that recently trade accounts for around of 40% of India's economic growth and the economy in the Pacific contribute to more than 30% in a total trade. So it (India) is very important for India's economy. As you know that more than 90% Indian trade is sea borne trade and more than half of that it worked. So it also was not through straight America, to the South China Sea or somewhere else. So it is very important there for India and also you know that why tourism is so very important to India's economy and you have a lot of blocks.

In the South China Sea inclusive economic zones offered by Vietnam. In Vietnam inclusive economic zone and you need the security to protect in the South China Sea also and you know that gas power also counts in South East Asian countries. So you have to protect in some means with the community and the Indian community there in the Indian service. So this means that the South China Sea is very important to India but about the challenge.

And now coming to the ruling on the Philippines and China case and what it means for us for international community in general and to India in particular.

Here is about the ruling of the PCA. There are other points but here I jotted only some significant points from its meaning to freedom of navigation of the Oil and Gas exploration of some other balanced operation among India and some countries in the South China Sea.

Blue port in Asia Pacific away of freedom of navigation that is must be that is you are practicing the freedom of navigation. The second is as I mentioned before that there are a lot of channel based like terrorism, piracy that we have to protect. The Oil and Gas Exploration project is in the exclusive economic zone of Vietnam. So through. In the High sea, in international sea, in the South China Sea you can conduct that. I do know that in the framework of East Asia Summit there is a member with other country, with China, Japan, South Korea, New Zealand, Australia, US, and Russia. In that framework you also have some mechanism, some agenda like they have statement. Milan is something not related too much on military but is something that is friendship. So Milan is not in Indian Ocean and so it could move to Asia Pacific that is my last idea and everything I speak today is that with the engagement of a lot of countries into the region, Indian Ocean, Indo-Pacific, especially South China Sea is not to contain any specific country. The thing is that we have comprehensive and joined efforts to have to protect good order at sea. That is my idea. Thank you so much for your kind attention.

25

Importance of Chabahar Port for Regional co-operation

— ***Shri Arun Kumar Gupta***

Abstract

This paper discusses the importance of Chabahar port in Iran.

Indian Ocean is a very important shipping region; choke points make it extremely strategic. Development of Gwadar port in Pakistan has been mentioned. Chabahar can offers an alternative North – South Corridor route– 30% cheaper. Financing and economic feasibility of this project is also discussed in this paper.

***Key-words**: Chabahar Port, Iran.*

Article

The Indian ocean is the 3rd largest water body. It is very important for us, it is our backyard and obviously we are very concerned to what is happening in the region. Indian Ocean is very important shipping region, a lot of ships are passing through it and choke points make it very strategic. This august gathering will know about it, what is happening in the Indian Ocean region - Myanmar, Pakistan's Gwadar port, China Pakistan Economic Corridor, huge investment by China in Sri Lanka's Hambantota Port, this is all happening in our Indian Ocean Region.

The traditional sea route to Russia has been through Bab el Mandeb, Suez Canal, English Channel and up north to Baltic sea - it is very long route. In the year 2000 the concept of International North South Corridor was formulated by Russia, India and Iran. Presently 13 countries are signatory to this Agreement. Under this route ships from India would go to Bandar Abbas, thereafter through Iran, up north by road or rail. Then again we have two options; either through Caspian Sea or surface transport to reach Moscow, St. Petersburg etc. It is a short distance with corresponding time & cost savings. It is a multi-modal transport where the cargo has to be discharged and reloaded. Moscow corridor is operational but transit time has to be further reduced. Then only the logistic costs can be brought down. The advantages are distinct but we have to make it more attractive. Unified custom documents, better rail connectivity etc can perhaps help. All the member countries of the International North-South Corridor are working towards further enhancing the efficiency.

Now about Iran, it is a very beautiful and a gifted country. A lot of natural resources with a very different but interesting political setup. There are several good ports in Iran. Some ports are in the North on the Caspian sea coastline, e.g Bandar-e-Anzali, Nowshahr, Amir Abad etc. Then we have Abadan - once upon a time Abadan was like Paris of the East. Abadan and Khorramshahr are both on Arvand river, also called as Shatt al arab river that divides Iran and Iraq. When there was war between Iran and Iraq, then Imam Khomeini Port was developed which is east of Abadan. The most important port in Iran is Shahid Rajaee Port also known as Bandar Abbas. The Chabahar Port is located on the Mokran coast of Sistan Baluchistan province. We will talk in detail about Chabahar in coming slides.

India has been talking to Iran since 2003 about Chabahar but somehow we could not finalise the deal. Again in 2104, the discussion started and finally on 6th May 2015, a MoU was signed. India and Iran have close cultural relation. Once upon a time, India used to share border with Iran when Pakistan was not there. Culturally also we are very close and language is not very difficult. It is a very pleasant language. We have been very close culturally, politically and the commitment to friendship is always there. India has stood by Iran in its difficult times.

A joint venture shipping company (Irano Hind) was formed in 1975 when Prime Minister Indira Gandhi visited Iran. This company has done quite well since inception. However recently because of sanctions, the company has suffered. India has always helped Iran in the maritime sector. I remember, officials from Shipping Corporations of India were deputed to Arya National Shipping line as Technical Advisors. During the pre-revolution in Iran, the national shipping line was called Arya National shipping line. Now, it is called Islamic Republic of Iran Shipping line. Chabahar has a maritime academy faculty from India has played a vital role in its establishment. So, that is the closeness India has with Iran.

Now coming back to Chabahar. The MoU which was signed on May 2015 had broad parameters of the future Contract. However it took us one year to convert that MoU into a Contract. You might say that one year is too much but I would say that it was a real achievement. Discussing each item and each clause, several rounds of discussions sometimes in Delhi, Mumbai and Tehran. Finally on 23rd May 2016, when the Hon. Prime Minister Narendra Modi, visited to Iran, this deal was signed and concurrently another deal was signed in which President of Afghanistan was also there, i.e India, Afghanistan and Iran trilateral transit agreement. This agreement is yet to be ratified by Iran however Afghanistan and India have already done so. This Agreement is very essential for Chahabar as we expect lot of transit cargo.

I will now come to my organization – IPGL. It is Government of India entity under administrative control of Ministry of Shipping. JNPT port holds 60% equity and Kandla Port 40%.

Chahabar Port as I mentioned earlier, is in Sistan and Baluchistan Province of Iran. We have Baluchistan Province in Pakistan also where Gwadar Port is located. In Chahabar, the culture is quite different to what you find in Tehran region. Chahabar is a bay and it has got two ports - Shahid Beheshti and Shahid Kalantari. Shahid Kalantari is an old port where dhows come from neighbouring countries. There is one berth also which can accommodate container feeder vessels.

Shahid Beheshti Port at present has got one berth which can accommodate vessels up to 60,000 DWT to about 12 meters draft and small berths to accommodate dhows. Shahid Beheshti Port is being developed and there are big plans for its development. I want to again make it very clear that Chahabar is a city which has got two ports.

Our agreement has been signed between India Ports Global Limited (IPGL) and Ariya Bandar Company (ABI) and is confirmed by Port and Maritime Organization of Iran and Indian Ministry of shipping. The main contract is basically a lessee arrangement between IPGL and ABI. The contract is to equip and operate two terminals in phase 1. Under the contract India will provide a loan of USD I50 Million equivalent that will be given by Exim Bank of India from Export Development fund. It is a loan, which is returnable. There is a sovereign guarantee on it. Further Indian side will equip the port with equipments worth 85 million, 4 RMQCs, 14 RTGCs and other equipments. Iranian side is responsible for putting up the infrastructure facilities, There are slides which show that jetties are almost

75-80% complete. Operation of 2 terminals we expect to start by December 2018 or beginning 2019.

We will form a special purpose vehicle in Iran to run this port and we propose to have a private partner. India Port Global which is based in Mumbai will not directly operate the port and will be the parent company. However, we will be responsible for everything. SPV will be formed in Iran to run this Chahabar Port. All the dredging has been done, we have a draft of 14meters at the multi purpose terminal and 16 metres at the container terminal. The length of container terminal is 640 meters. The second terminal is 600 meters. This is all about the phase one which is presently being developed.

Chahabar is very close to Kandla Port - about 550 nautical miles. Kandla and Mundra very important ports on west coast of India. Another important port is JNPT, which is about 785 nautical miles away. There we have 4 container terminal almost touching 5 million use per year. JNPT is ranked among top 50 container terminals in the world. Chabahar is very close to Gwadar, the distance is 72 nautical miles.

As you see in this slide the yellow is our terminal and which is phase one. This is followed by phase 2, 3, 4 and 5. This is the break water which on the inner side has berth. Then we have a finger jetty which can accommodate dhows on either side. This slide is just a model. Here you can see bollards are already there. Fenders are being put the pavement are being done. Internal roads are under construction. The Chabahar Port is in use and there is a plan to do a formal inauguration by the Iranian side.

India is giving wheat aid to Afghanistan - I think 1,30,000 MT. The first shipment from Kandla is supposed to arrive at Chabahar by this month end. The port to be successful should have free zone. Our main objective is to serve Afghanistan which is a landlock country. For this reason Iran, India and Afghanistan trilateral transit agreement has been signed. In Afghanistan, India has already made a ring road to serve the four major cities. From Chahabar there is a road up to Zahedan. Zahedan is virtually at the border, where the three countries meet. From Zahedan through the Zabol and Zaranj, we connect to the garland road which links the Mazar-i-Sharif, Kandahar, Herat and Kabul of course.

Well there have been a lot of questions, what are America's views on Iran, yes, apprehensions are there but at least for Chahabar Port I feel, there will not be any issues. America also wants that Afghanistan should not suffer and basic objective of Chahabar Port development is to support

Afghanistan. There have been statements lately from President Trump that they support India's endeavour in Chabahar.

Road connectivity there is no issue but rail connectivity from Chahabar to Zahedan is not there. However, work is going on. There is a possibility that India would participate and IRCON may take the project.

Now beyond Chabahar let us move to Myanmar. India is developing Sittwe Port to get connectivity to its North Eastern region through Kaladan river. Inland Waterway Authority and IPGL are working very closely on this project.

In Bangladesh also we have examined Payra Port and definitely India is going to help Bangladesh for the same. Hon. Minister did mention about the inland water ways. and how we are working very closely with Bangladesh. Now cargo will go from Kolkata Haldia to Agartala.

IPGL did examine a Nacala Port in Mozambique. Not only the port has to be developed but we have to develop the railway line. Its hinterland is very rich in minerals specially coal, so we are talking to the users if they are really interested then only we will go ahead.

26

Transition of Global Power and the Rise of Indian Ocean Region

— Lt. Gen. V. M. Patil

Historical Background

1. Oceans, the largest assets on this planet, have impacted the evolution of man-kind and civilisations through the millennia. Whether the human race enjoyed peace and prosperity through cooperation and collaboration or suffered exploitation and slavery through violent conflicts and conquests depended on the powers that be from time to time.
2. During the first millennium, oceans particularly Indian ocean were highways linking civilisations through culture, commerce, trade, linguistic and religious engagements of people to people levels through cooperation, collaboration and connectivity across vast geographies.
3. Second millennium witnessed explorations in search of resources and wealth leading to conquests and exploitation through colonisation of Asia, Africa and Latin America by imperial powers. Last century of this millennium had the taste of greed for wealth resulting in two world wars ending with nuclear holocaust and cold war between capitalism and communism. It engulfed the third world with countless violent conflicts. During this period, Indian Ocean region (IOR) was influenced by the British, Pacific ocean by Americans and Atlantic ocean by Western European powers.
4. Thanks to the explosion of science and technology, globalisation of economy and connectivity resulting in the collapse of the

Soviet system and emergence of multipolar world, third millennium is faced with several mega trends as under;

- Transition of global power from political and economic balance of power is undergoing tectonic shift leading from unipolar to multipolar world.
- Decline of Atlantic basin in military and economic spheres.
- Africa and Central Asia are yet to mature into stable political economies.
- Middle East is in turmoil with unpredictable consequences unleashed by the Islamic radicalisation. No power on this planet, at this time, appears to have any clarity and strategy to effectively tackle this threat.
- Asia, polycentric, multipolar and rapidly evolving in terms of size, resources, diversity and regional influence, is destined to play a decisive role in this millennium.

5. Asia, with Pacific and Indian oceans, has two distinct spheres of influence within, each maintaining separate trading and political systems while interacting with each other. The collapse of the Trans Pacific Partnership has thrown up new challenges for Indian Ocean region (IOR). It has emerged as one of the world's busiest and most critical trade corridors, rapidly surpassing the Pacific and Atlantic Oceans. Indian Ocean with its greater economic connectivity with South East Asia and Pacific region in the East as well as Westwards with Africa and Europe is destined for greater strategic role in the maritime spheres. According to Admiral Alfred Ma-han (one of the renowned strategists of US in the 19th century), "the destiny of the world will be decided on the waters of the Indian Ocean".

India's Challenges, Opportunities and Responsibilities

6. For Indian Ocean to realise its full potential, India, which is its centre of gravity, should play "Facilitator's role". It should ensure security, stability and mutually beneficial economic growth leading to peaceful coexistence and prosperity for all its stake holders.
7. Honourable Prime Minister Narendra Modi's words, "Blue chakra of India's national flag represents the potential of blue economy" clarify India's objectives in the IOR. While focussing on political economy and tapping of blue economy leading to harmonising of

regionalism and nationalism into "Global Family" -Vasudaiva Kutumbakam promoting interdependence across the oceans.

8. In 21st century, South Asia with India as its centre of gravity is one of the fastest growing regions of the world. Consequently South Asia and ASEAN countries present an emerging opportunity bringing "benefits" similar to those experienced in the past by Atlantic and Pacific basins. These opportunities have to cope with a rising China with its global ambitions covertly projected through soft power advances such as – OBOR (one belt one road), CPEC (China Pakistan Economic Corridor) and maritime silk route. This is real challenge for next decade or two.
9. According to political economists, it is estimated that Asia will surpass North America and Europe combined in terms of global power based GDP, population, military spending and technology investment by 2030. Of the four largest economies of the world-China, US, India and Japan, three are Asian powers. Therefore greater opportunities and responsibilities for India to evolve an universally acceptable "Indian Ocean Order (IOO)"by involving all the stakeholders of the IOR.

Indian Ocean Order (IOO)

10. Eminent historian of the Oceans on this planet Richard Hall has declared that, "Now the monsoons of history are blowing afresh, as the balance of world power swings back to the East. The start of the 21st century is seen as a ushering in a new 'Age of Asia'. In which the natural unity of the Indian Ocean can once more asserts itself. "Before reviving the Indian Ocean as a geopolitical concept, it is essential to address the challenges of connectivity, economy, security, politics, culture and identity- all of which are critical to its possible resurgence. Towards this end, India should, with other stakeholders, take a lead in the evolution of "Indian Ocean Order (IOO) structured on the basis of existing international laws and then sanctified by the United Nations. IOO should be a strong, transparent and rule based architecture, which should ensure the following:-
    - Friendly cooperation among all the stakeholders,
    - Mutually beneficial to all members,
    - Adversarial competition which generates tension and differences is avoided through dialogue,

- Multilateral mechanisms to avoid and if possible prevent unnecessary conflicts,
- All nations adhere to and pursue their territorial claims in accordance with international laws,
- Structured and systemic cooperation during natural disasters and calamities,
- Maritime security cooperation against threats from non-state actors and rouge elements,
- Freedom of passage through "sea lanes" to all nations,
- Mitigating effects of climate change,
- No nation be permitted to construct/ create artificial island bases in the IOR, which can generate conflicts by disrupting naturally established EEZs as per international laws,
- All stakeholders must ensure that the IOR remains "Nuclear weapons free Zone",
- With two choke points – Straits of Hormuz in the West and Malacca in the East, no nation, non state actors and rogue elements be allowed to disrupt the sea lanes in the IOR,
- IOR member states should create transparent mechanisms to prevent and preempt maritime piracy, illegal trafficking, hijacking of ships and merchandize,
- Institutional arrangements for sharing information and intelligence on line and in time for ensuring secure, safe and smooth passage of shipping,
- Finally 100 should be able to ensure that it remains "secure and stable zone of peace" beneficial to all member states under the UN charter.

27

Sagar: Indian Stakes in Indian Ocean

— Lt Gen P.G. Kamath

There were times, when a sea was considered a barrier and countries derived naive security from oceans bodies. Indian seafarers always considered oceans as bridge between countries. In 10th to 13th century, the Cholas influence encompassed South East Asia. Sri Vijaya Empire in today's Malaysia, Singapore, Brunei and Indonesia and the Khamboj Empire of Cambodia were the result of the seafaring activities by Chola empire builders, who projected their soft power to distant lands. The influence was so widespread and benign that a road 'Jalan Raja Chulan' is named after King Rajaraja Chola in Kuala Lumpur in Malaysia to this day. The capital of Brunei is Bandar Seri Begawan is also a distorted version of Sanskrit version of 'Abode of Sri Bhagwan'. Lord Vishnu's temple at Angkor Wat in Cambodia is also an evidence for spread of Chola influence: Also, do not forget the island of Bali that virtually has preserved its 'Hindu cultural and religious heritage' standing as a last bastion of Hindu identity, when Islamisation deluged thousands of Indonesian islands and the neighbouring countries of Malaysia and Brunei. In this region of the world, the Islamization took roots peacefully without the elements of violence, which otherwise is a characteristic of such mass conversions. The Hindu empires, which held their sway for a thousand years and later the Islamisation of the region could take place due to spread of Chola and Arabic influences through the medium of sea. Hence huge water bodies of sea and oceans are bridges that bind the planet into one whole.

Though the Indians used the sea to spread its influence and carry out trade to distant lands, they did not envisage it as avenues of threat. Indian history is always replete with instances of how foreign forces invaded; such as Greeks, Huns, and Mohd Ghori, raids by Mohd Ghazni followed by the Turks, Mughals, Persians and Afghans to vindicate the requirement of secure land borders. Later the Chinese offensives both from the North and North East reinforces our thought process of land centric threats facing the country. Even now, we are concerned about the offensives from land frontiers, where we are preparing for a two and a half front war with simultaneous offensives by China and Pakistan and the externally supported insurgency and terrorism fulminating internally. The situation portrayed; no doubt needs deliberate consideration, however, the threat can be overcome and the war can be won by intelligent use of all the three services operating in conjunction with other elements of national power. It no doubt; needs strong land forces as the land can only be held and occupied by boots on the ground. No technology can hold ground, as has been proved beyond doubt in the unending US war in Afghanistan for the past 16 years with President Trump further giving an impetus to enhance ground force levels in the restive country.

In India, we rarely talk of the Portuguese, Dutch, British and French, came to our soil from seas. Interestingly, they could come only after the decline of Chola's Naval Power in the 14th century. Chatrapati Shivaji also raised a Navy in mid-17th Century, which no doubt played havoc against Portuguese and British Navies, however one has to agree that the 'Maratha Navy' was basically a 'Coastal Navy' that too; 'a dark brown water navy' with no bluish tinge in its capabilities. We finally lost our independence, when we lost our command over the seas. No other Indian Raja of the various coastal states ever had a navy worth its name except probably the Zamorin of Calicut who had a small naval fleet. This gave a field time to the European Powers to come and colonise our country. In 1741 the Dutch Marine forces sailed from Ceylon and lost decisively to Travancore State Forces of Raja Marthanda Verma in the land battle at Colachel that virtually ended the Dutch aspirations in India. Due to our lack of sea power, we could not prevent its landing but managed to win the land battle. Thereafter the British ruled the waves and established an empire, where the sun never set. It was possible for them, as they were a naval power.

Our strategy for a two and half front war needs to be drawn with ocean as prime focus. Then; what do we do for a country that has not formulated its 'National Security Strategy' in the last seven decades, since our independence? It is this strategy that empowers us to optimize all elements of National power and orchestrate to achieve our National Security Objectives. Strangling of Pakistan from the seas and cutting of energy and trade routes to China from the Indian Ocean is adequate to get a favourable victory on the land frontiers in the envisaged two and an half front war. Our ability to choke all the entry points into the Indian Ocean; the Straits of Malacca, Sunda, Lombak and Timor Sea would give us the capabilities to choke the Chinese trade. It would result in domestic glut of manufacturing goods, overfilled warehouses and large scale retrenchment of labour causing serious internal strife. China's obsession of 'Communist Party's control over the nation is enough to see its red lines much before such a situation could occur. Internal dissent is the 'Achilles Heels' of China and it is hyper-sensitive to such a situation, however remote the probability of its occurrence. The ridiculous Chinese constitution that empowers the 'Chinese Communist Party'(CPC) to own the 'People's Republic of China'(PRC) entailing the entire population to be the members of CPC is very difficult to comprehend to a civilised world but has been made into an artificial and enforced reality in China. This weakness of China has to be exploited by Indian in its two and half front war strategy.

It is not necessary to implement the strategy as we need friendly relations with all in our neighbourhood. India just need to develop capabilities to empower ourselves to execute the strategy. Such capabilities are enough to prevent a war and ensure the safety of our land and sea frontiers: Strength deters wars and weakness invites it. These capabilities take decades to build and the earlier we take a decision; the better it is for our country.

India's dependence on Indian Ocean is overwhelming. 90% of our trade by volume and 90% of our oil imports are carried on the seas. The SAGAR initiative is for security and growth for all in the region. There are 21 countries in the Indian Ocean Rim Association(IORA) and India need to knit them together so that all the countries together maintain peace and harmony in the Indian Ocean Region. India need to actively promote this association to ensure that these countries do not give their territories as foreign bases to big powers. Already US, UK, France and China have made bases in the Indian Ocean. They are security concerns to the countries of the region. Ideally the Indian Ocean Rim Countries should ensure all the countries of the world have freedom of navigation and trade in the Indian Ocean with IOR Countries being the net security provider to all the ships, which are traversing the Indian Ocean. Providing logistic support to all ships traversing the Indian Ocean and trading with them will ensure mutual prosperity of the region. India should initiate Annual Naval Exercise with all countries of the IORA to ensure inter-operability and coordination to rise to be the net security provider to all shipping traversing the Indian Ocean. All the countries of IORA have high stakes in the Indian Ocean and

India with likeminded countries like Australia, Indonesia, Iran and South Africa have to provide the lead.

Pandit Nehru had said prophetically "To be secure on land; we must be supreme at Sea". It is sad indeed that he could not implement his own wisdom on national security and neglected the Armed Forces severely, demolishing his vision of India with dreams broken and pride shattered at the time of his death. It is time we achieve the vision of SAGAR to all the countries of the region.

28

The Strategic Flipside of the Sagarmala

— Dr. Manish Srivastava

The idea of Sagarmala is to modernize and develop the Indian ports, integrate them with the industrial clusters and connect it through road, rail, inland and coastal waterways so that the ports become the drivers of India's economic growth story. India has a long coast-line, and, if the experience of the developed world - like the US, Japan and so on- is an indicator, a port-led industrialization and development has its own share in a States' economic growth. The Sagarmala project is conceived with this intention. The projects will be implemented in a phased manner over a span of 20– years period, and has essentially four key drivers: (a) optimizing multimodal transport to reduce the cost of domestic cargo, (b) minimizing the time and cost of export-import cargo logistics, (c) lowering costs for bulk industries by locating them closer to the coast, and (d) improving export competitiveness by locating discrete manufacturing clusters near ports. By virtue of its geography, India enjoys a strategic location on key internationl trade routes. The Indian coast-line is 7500 kms long and stretches across 13 Indian states. Unfortunately, New Delhi has not been able to optimize its port-capacity and the inland waterways transportation. Historically, transportation by water ways has remained underutilized despite the fact that it is significantly cheaper compared to road and railways. The Sagarmala National Perspective Plan indeed identifies specific opportunities for transportation of commodities by coastal shipping and inland waterways.

However, there is a flipside to the Sagarmala project. As such, India's maritime geographical positioning is both an advantage and a challenge. Despite a massive coastline and geographic primacy in the Indian Ocean, India has devoted little attention on the security and the strategic aspects of its vast maritime frontiers. The close proximity of international shipping lanes to India's coasts attracts other powerful countries to dominate the region and create a potential situation of conflict on issues ranging from maritime geopolitics, security, trade, and ocean –resources and right to navigation in the coming years.

As New Delhi attempts to integrate its economy with its East and South-east Asia, we now see Comprehensive Economic Partnerships with the 10 members of ASEAN, ranging from Myanmar to the Philippines, as also with Japan and South Korea. ASEAN-led forums like the East Asia Summit have led to an Indian strategic role across the Bay of Bengal, which traverses the Indian Ocean and western Pacific, crossing the disputed waters of the South China Sea. India also cannot ignore the fact that China is vigourously opposed to our participation in economic and security forums linked with ASEAN, including the ASEAN Regional Forum and the East Asia Summit.

Beijing also wants to outflank New Delhi on its western shores, through a network of roads and ports. The Chinese strategic objectives are based on developing a Silk Road that links China with Central Asia, Pakistan Occupied Kashmir, the Persian Gulf States, Russia and the Baltic States. China is simultaneously building ports across the Indian Ocean, in Asia and Africa. The Gwadar port in the Balochistan province of Pakistan is close to India's sea-lanes, linking India to the oil-rich Persian Gulf, from where we get over 70 per cent of our oil supplies.

Ideally, it would be useful if the major Asian oil importers — India, China, Japan and South Korea — cooperated on developments that threaten the security of vital sea-lanes and energy corridors. But, given existing tensions and suspicions, this may be too much to expect anytime soon.

At the same time, the Indian ocean littoral states face significant policy and governance challenges from multiple sources, including territorial disputes and rivalries among naval powers, intensifying environmental pressures on marine and coastal infrastructure and resources, piracy and trafficking on the open ocean, and weak and failing states on shore. To navigate the complicated maritime realm of the Indian Ocean, policy makers throughout the region will need to collaboratively develop strategies to address these interconnected strategic, socio-economic, commercial, and environmental trends that will continue to shape the region in the coming decades. The current strategic landscape therefore calls for a rapidly evolving security landscape characterized by both of soft and hard power, ranging from maritime partnerships and trade initiatives, to bi-lateral and multi-lateral disaster management exercises, to active efforts to demonstrate sea control and credible combat power.

Therefore, for New Delhi's the challenge would be to develop viable security architecture across and beyond its shores. As part of broader 'maritime governance', New Delhi should bolster her naval strength and expand maritime partnerships with other countries at a bilateral and multi-lateral levels. Naval modernization, expansion of civilian maritime infrastructure, development of island territories, and naval assistance to other countries should form the core of this strategy. New Delhi has already engaged friendly navies through Joint naval exercises like Malabar 2014. This needs to be further intensified, but there should also be an advance professional interaction and understanding between our sailors. A blue water navy capable of power projection is a flexible strategic tool, but it requires diplomatic investment in forward bases and friendly ports in addition to the financial and human investment.

Second, New Delhi should also augment its coastal defences. The Coast Guard suffers from capacity constraints due to inadequate procurement and infrastructure. It is incumbent upon the respective state governments to recognize the exigency of sea-borne threats and take effective steps to augment the capabilities of marine police, which is one of the first respondents during crisis.

Third, India should maintain congenial political relations with its maritime neighbours in the Indian Ocean region, and particularly, in immediate neighbourhood like Sri Lanka and Maldives. India also needs stronger partnerships with other island states, like Seychelles and Mauritius, which are being wooed by China with a renewed vigour. Recent initiatives to provide security assistance to India's maritime neighbours – such as the Seychelles, Mauritius and contributing towards multinational anti-piracy efforts in the Gulf of Aden are steps worth taking.

Fourth, India needs to deepen its military security cooperation in the Indian Ocean with USA, Australia, Japan, and Singapore. India should engage more through multi-lateral initiatives such as the Indian Ocean Rim Association and the Indian Ocean Naval Symposium to convey its maritime strategy.

Fifth, the threats to navigation and maritime freedoms, including in critical straits and exclusive economic zones can be countered through adherence to international laws by all parties as well as through monitoring, regulation and enforcement.

Sixth, rising competition for seabed minerals reveals the need for creating a regulatory regime, developing safe and effective ocean-development technologies, finding ways to share benefits of the common heritage, and ensuring environmental protection. It should be treated as a part of global commons.

India's geo-strategic significance as a stabilizing power in the Indian Ocean is now widely acknowledged. India now needs to be prepared to shoulder its responsibilities.

29

Saving the Oceans

— *Pradeep Kumar Gautam*

Introduction

The oceans provide priceless eco-system and spiritual services. They also provide many material, livelihood and esthetical services like biological resources such as fish as protein, plants, energy, material resources, recreation, tourism and so on. But all these services are under threat now. Rising population and consumerism, resource scarcities on land and sea, adverse climate change and pollution of various sorts in this era of the Anthropocene is a reality. Humans have appropriated for themselves most of the planet. Due this past action or karma, we all now have to face new risks, and challenges. At present it seems that no state-centric sovereign attitudes can even hope to resolve the problem. It is one massive tragedy of the commons. The biggest self-created economic, cultural and societal failure. This commentary will suggest some ideas as to how we can save the oceans.

Demand from the Ocean

If the entire humanity was to consume according to the standards of developed industrial economies, it is unlikely that the available resources will be sufficient to even satisfy minimal basic demands of all. The earth's shrinking biosphere which includes the oceans will not be able to satisfy the human needs. For sea food alone, 'by 2030, the oceans will need to supply 152 to 188 million metric tonnes of seafood to nourish a growing population'. Mankind's ecological footprint due to rising population and expectations may need resources of more than one earth to support itself.

In this extractive scenario, the fragile oceans assume the greatest importance. Why this is so is that unlike land, oceans are both out of sight and thus out of mind. Although a discourse and concept of blue economy and sustainable development is now in policy circles but it has missed the point from the perspective of the ocean itself. In the 2017 the National Maritime Foundation in its annual maritime power conference had the topic of Blue Economy. Although noble ideas such as sustainable development were deliberates with sincerity, the reality was that the ocean was seen more as an object than a subject.

The reason for this is not far to seek. In the present mindset, ecology is considered as a break, while economics is an accelerator. Ecology, has no political boundaries, it is long-term and 'strategic'; while economics is short sighted and is motivated by pure national cum commercial interests . Thus economics may ignore or be blind to a process of habitat destruction, overfishing and resource collapse even if adds the rhetoric of sustainable development. Ecology on the other hand, to many, appears to be abstract (vague notions of unmeasurable eco-system services) while economics as concrete (methods such as gross domestic product and commodification of nature). But one thing is certain. There seems to be a dialogue between the two and thus SAGAR Discourse 2017 is a commendable and imaginative step by India in the wake of the UN Ocean Conference which was held in June 2017.

Waste and the Ocean : A Tragedy of the Commons

Biologist Garrett Harding had conceptualised the 'tragedy of commons' to say that 'freedom in common brings ruin to all.' United Nations Environmental Programme (UNEP) of 2014 in its report had warned that 'plastic waste costs marine eco-system $ 13 billion in damages... The estimated 10-20 million tonnes of plastic waste that finds its ways into the oceans, smothers coral reefs, routinely entangles marine wildlife, and more insidiously, degrades into 'microplastics' that transfer toxins into food chain'. However, like a cyber attack, plastic waste landing at the coast and no-more pristine beaches can not be attributed to any one sovereign country alone, as waste knows no political boundaries. Both developing and developed economies are part of the problem. Surely we can not live with business as usual (BUA). In 2017, UNEP reports that 'the overall natural capital cost of plastic use in the consumer goods sector each year is $ 75 billion.' Awareness and education may be the first step in preserving the shrinking space of global commons and common heritage of mankind like the oceans.

At the domestic level, most mistakenly or mythologically believe or presume the oceans to be a large sink or a bottomless waste-basket having some magical property to devour waste. Coastal regions surely provide the best empirical indications. 80 percent of coast pollution is due to agricultural run-off from land, sewage and untreated effluents from cities and industries. The waste-stream dumped on the once pristine beaches by high tide and the garbage-waste that remains on the beach with surreal pock marks, when the tide recedes (low-tide), is a good indicator of the problem as noticed in Mumbai everyday. Further south, a visit to the coast off Daksin Kannada it is easy to spot 'sprouting' waste such as plastic piling up on the once pristine beaches. This trend is increasing exponentially, and is out of control. Such common sense observations of environmental neglect, even if anecdotal, clearly shows that we are all now part of the problem. The challenge is to be part of the solution. Five trillion bits of plastic are in the oceans with 8 million tonnes added each year. Researchers have estimated: 'By middle of the century the sea could contain more plastic than fish by weight.'

Climate Change and the Ocean

The emission of green house gases into the atmosphere is changing marine environment like ocean acidification. 'The Paris agreement is the single best hope for protecting the ocean and its resources...the limits agreed on Paris will not prevent sea levels from rising and coral from bleaching. Indeed, unless they are drastically strengthened, both problems risk getting much worse. Mankind is increasingly able to see the damage it is doing to the oceans. Whether it can stop it is another question.' Geoengineering technologies such as carbon capture and storage and solar radiation management are yet to be tested and may have very serious unintended consequences on the eco-system. While research on the technological options must be pursued what is also important is simultaneous demand side management and want limitations under the term lifestyle changes. The worrying aspect is that Indian wisdom may also be now taken for granted. It is an appropriate time now to draw upon and revisit Indian wisdom to address contemporary problems of environmental degradation.

Indian Philosophy

Recent scholarship is highlighting what probably out ancestors knew as traditional ecological knowledge:

> 'Natural ecological systems on Earth succeed - often where human do not – because they adhere to the following guidelines : They do not

> consume resources faster than they are regenerated by the environment; do not produce wastes, especially those that disrupt the environment and the climate system, faster than they are assimilated or removed by the environment; are highly diverse, making them more robust in the face of changing conditions; and power nearly everything they do with the Sun'.

Indian philosophy has the triple concept known as Trivarga - the notion of Dharma (moral ethics), Artha (material wellbeing) and Kama (desires). Today Artha, which is basically about growth and development or fulfillment of material and economic needs are met. Kama is desire and expectation of a good life. But there seems to be no end to desires. Frugality and simplicity is losing value. It is here that in the triad of Trivarga, the concept of Dharma has to be understood and invoked as a new moral ethic for creating awareness and some form of regulatory mechanisms that could balance both Kama and Artha. If we control our desires to manageable levels, the resources can support mankind in a sustainable manner. This is also understood as pragmatic want limitation.

The Rudolphs point to what Mahatma Gandhi in his book Hind Swaraj had argued:

> The main fault of modern civilisation is that it pursues world mastery rather than self-mastery. It sets no limits on desire and on growth. One hundred years after the publication of Hind Swaraj, it is becoming increasingly apparent that limiting growth has become a condition for global survival. More production of goods and services means more pollution, more global warming, more climate change and the exhaustion of resources, not least land and water.

But the question is how does the balance of Kama, Artha and Dharma play out? In modern civilisation artha and kama, according to Gandhi, assert their autonomy from dharma. Gandhi clearly urges that Dharma must reassert itself and not be overpowered by Artha and Kama. It is to the credit of Gandhi that he explained the whole issue in such simple terms using the ancient Indian vocabulary derived from the concept of Trivarga.

In a deeper framework, the time may be thus ripe is to recall the mantra of Mohandas K. Gandhi, 'For my material needs, the village is my world, for my spiritual needs, the world is my village'. With this understanding in public domain via education, leadership by action and example, and appropriate institutional mechanism, it is certain that people will get conscious of their ecological footprint, connect with eco-system such as the oceans and will also focus on zero waste and revisit the difference between need and greed. This is not idealism but a real challenge of realism.

John N. Kittinger et al, 'Committing to Socially responsible seafood', Science, Vol. 356, Issue 6341, 2 June 2017

1. https://oceanconference.un.org/programme
2. As quoted by MIU Manikarachchi, in a presentation on 'Habitat Protection and Ocean Ecology' during Annual Maritime Power Conference- 2017, 'Blue Economy : Concept, Constituents and Development', New Delhi, The National Maritime Foundation.
3. Divya Gandhi, 'Plastic waste costs $ 13 billion worth of damages a year to marine eco-systems', The Hindu, July 3, 2014.
4. Samir Nazareth, 'Plastic Realities : We need to urgently and drastically cut the use of plastics', The Hindu, July 20, 2017.
5. All the fish in the sea', The Economist, May 27th 2017, p.9.
6. 'Deep Trouble', The Economist, May 27th 2017, p.9.
7. Jonathan Foley, 'Living by the lessons of the planet', Science, Vol. 356, Issue 6335, 21 April 2017, pp. 251-252,
8. Lloyd I. Rudolph and Susanne Hoeber Rudolph, 'Gandhi and the Debate about Civilization', Economic & Political Weekly, Vol. L, No. 30, July 25, 2015, pp.78-82.
9. Anthony J. Parel (ed.), Gandhi: Hind Swaraj and Other Writings, Foundation Books, New Delhi, 1997, p. 66. See editor's note 122.

30

Evolving Geo Political and Geo Strategic Equation in Indian Ocean and Pacific Region: Impact on World Peace

— Lt. Gen. (Dr) D. B. Shekatkar (Retd.)

Since the beginning of 21st Century Asia Pacific region has emerged as a region of further economic growth, trade, commerce, new geo-political geo-strategic and geo-economic equations. From South China Sea to Mediterranean Sea almost – all nations big or small are facing some form of conflict resulting in enlarge zonal/regional rivalries and conflict. Alongside Arabian Sea, Red Sea the emergence of "Arab-Spring and the recent events added entirely new dimensions to internal and international conflicts, change of ruling regime in various nation states : totally instigated, supported sustained and even militarily intervened by outside powers who wish to change the ruling regime of any nation to suit and enlarge their so called national interests, No nation can remain untouched from the new emerging philosophy of world governance and emerging world order.

In the 21st Century due to the new philosophy and concepts of War, Interventions geographical boundaries are increasingly losing credence and relevance. Economic linkages are resulting into myriad – social, political, religious, cultural and psychological interference. The Indian Ocean Region (IOR) is now redefined as Indian Ocean – pacific Region, due to the so called Strategic and Economic interests of some nations resulting in Zone / Region of conflict. Therefore, when we now discuss and analyze evolving geo-political and geo-strategic equations which are changing the geo-economic power equation it will be prudent to include Mediterranean Sea theatre, Gulf of Suez, Persian Gulf, Gulf of Oman, Arabian Sea, Gulf of Aden to Straits of Malacca, Indonesian Water and even South China Sea as a region of Strategic interests to entire world due to global implications and economic interests. Existing vast and strategic expanse will get extended further because of Social, Cultural, ideological, economic, trade and industrial interest which collectively can be termed as geo-political and geo-strategic interest. It also must be considered that in the 21st Century due to increasing connectivity, interdependence and interoperability an extended IOR and Asia-Pacific Region is a home to approximate four billion people and accounts for 62% of GDP. By 2030, the world's leading economics are likely to be in this region and balancing pivot. The new emerging environment and realty calls for a reorientation of mindset regarding area of interest, area of dominance and area of influence, strategic dimensions combined with influence extent of sustainable and lasting outreach.

There are as many as 46 countries on the periphery of Indian Ocean – Pacific Region. Majority of them are glued to religious and ideological leanings and attach-ment. Most of the nations have yet to achieve a reasonable standard of living and sustenance, economic growth, internal peace and stability. The Oil bonanza which descended on some of the Gulf countries and North Africa region created another dimension of financial and ideological support to fundamentalism, Radicalization and terrorism. It also ignited the hunger and fueled the greed towards weapons and mechanism of mass destruction and disruption of masses, displacement of masses and refugee problem. Most of these countries have got involved are sucked into inter-state and intra-state conflicts which have adversely impacted security environment the world over. Many countries are facing land boundary and maritime disputes.

The strategic assets, economic, industrial, financial, nuclear assets of majority of nations are located along sea cost. Despite this fact and reality these is lack of understanding and unity of approach in Indian Ocean – Pacific region for collective Security. If we wish to excel as a stable, peaceful, and progressive region we must accept that "IOR at Pacific Regions" destiny will be a world's shared destiny. This will require greater regional cooperation, connectivity of minds, thoughts, actions and age old philosophy of human survival "Share and Care". In this regard "Sagar Discourse" annual dialogue being organized by Forum for Integrated National Security (FINS) is step in right – direction to engage meaningfully not only with Indian Ocean Region but also with Asia Pacific Region. Towards West India wish to engage with Oman, Yemen, Djibouti, Somalia, Kenya, Tanzania,

Mozambique, South Africa, Mal-agasy, Mauritius, Iran, Persian Gulf of Arab Region, Afghanistan and Central Asian Region.

The forces of instability and destruction are active in Asia-Pacific Region due to interest and encouragement of few major powers. India has the potential and ability to act as deference and support diplomacy and geo-politics. In the 21st Century conventional diplomacy and geo-politics is being and will continue to be supported by armed power and "military diplomacy". This has been witnessed recently in Afghanistan, Iraq, Pakistan, Tunisia, Egypt, Libya and now in Syria. India has the capacity, capability to position itself in Gulf region to ensure stability and progress of the region.

India's commanding geographical position in the IOR gives us a unique opportunity to bring to gather the forces of stability in ensuring Security of Sea lines of Communication and coastal region of other nations as well. Sea piracy in straits of Malacca to Somalia coast poses very serious threat to international trade and commerce through Sea. We need to tackle this problem through regional collaboration and achieve a good degree of success. The terrorist separatists and insurgent groups are still very active in Philippines, Indonesia, Myanmar and Bangladesh. A new theatre of conflict has emerged due to appearance of coloration of ISIS, Al-Qaida and other terrorist groups in Middle East, Europe and North Africa. This has a bearing on world peace, economy, and trade. The very existence and Security of some nations is under threat. Therefore new geo-political equation will have to be considered and evaded to ensure Sea, maritime of costal security. A study of world map shows that there are four communication bottlenecks that are of vital important from the point of view of geo-strategic and geo-economic implications to all nations in IOR and Pacific region. The Cape of Good Hope, The Strait of Hormuz, Bab al mandab and strait of Malacca. With emerging ambitions of a lone power in Asia-Pacific region, geo-strategic, geo-economic interests, India has no other option but to play a lead role and pay special attention to the possible zone of conflict and to the island Group which provides the land base, staging points and jump off areas for operations. This was evident during invasion of Afghanistan in 2001 and Iraq in 2003, assault on Libya, Yemen and new operations against ISIS in Syria and Iraq; the concept of enforcement of "No Fly Zone", imposition of economic sanctions and trade barrios.

Diego Garcia and Maldives will remain of special significance in the IOR. Japan, Tai-wan, South Korea, Vietnam, Thailand, Philippines, and Indonesia will play a significant role in South Chinas Sea and Pacific region. Both USA and China are enamored by Pakistan due to strategic location.

Geographic "Location" of any nation is every-thing when it comes to security and strategic considerations. Pakistan's location and connectivity is linked to US strategic interest in Afghanistan, Central Asia, Iran, China and India. Same holds good for China too. China is keen to use Pakistan as captive and exclusive transit Territory to Iran, Middle East, Arabian Sea, and shortest route to East Africa and North Africa coast. China – Pakistan Economic corridor can always be used as Military Corridor by China. India with its strong maritime and air capability has been attempting to play useful role in establishing peace and stability in the IOR. However, due to mutual distrust between the RIM countries they have prevented the creation of an overall security umbrella or architecture in the region despite inter-dependence and common security interests. India therefore has to play a key role to develop binding relations with IOR countries as well as Pacific region countries. US leadership wants a stranger presence in the region to counter greater threats to peace and stability. US new diplomatic and military strategy is explicitly geared towards tracking and countering threats from terrorists and terrorism. Unlike others the USA does not have any territorial ambitions and aggressive uncontrollable greed. The emerging trends and likely threats have encouraged USA to reorient and refocus the military resources from Atlantic to Pacific and Indian Ocean. India is a major trustworthy nation in the region with geo-strategic advantage and that adds to responsibility of India to play a lead role to ensure regional and maritime security. To marginalize and neutralize Pakistan's geo strategic importance, it will be in USA's long term geo-economic and geo-strategic interest to improve good relationship with Iran and make a constructive and powerful presence in Afghanistan and Central Asia. The US will have to manage and balance the relations and dependence on Saudi Arabia. It will be in the long term interests of Saudi Arabia and entire Middle East to end hostile attitude and hostilities towards Iran to protect the interests of coming generations in the entire Middle East. India can and must be invited to play a major useful and lead up role in establishing new friends and purposeful relationship between USA – Iran and Saudi Arabia. At present there is no other country which can match India's Soft Power; Hand Power, Strategic Proximity and Smart Power to build a new stable, peaceful Middle Eastern Region. Improved and friendly relations between USA and Iran will change geo-political and geo-strategic power equation in Middle East; Central Asia, North Africa and South Asia. This will be good for entire Middle East and world. It may sound impractical and unachievable at the moment, but the understanding and united action by USA NATO and Russia against ISIS is an example of Common interests. Few years back before emergence of

ISIS as a major Challenge it was unthinkable that both USA and Russia will face a common threat to ensure stability, peace and security there is a need to ensure power balance. Historically in International Relations a Power Imbalance has always led instability and eventually to War or Conflict. The events since 2001 across the world suggest that in 21st Century power imbalance will not only encourage interstate War/Conflict, but also more importantly unconventional War, low intensity conflicts, regime change internal conflicts supported from outside. A stronger and combative power will always ley to achieve total dominance and influence. While India has never been nor in future would wish to dominate any one, but at the same time India must ensure that no one else is in a position to dictate terms to us or to our neighboring countries.

Finally it is recommended that a cooperative and convergent approach to integrated and comprehensive security of IOR and Pacific region will be potential source of regional peace, stability and prosperity. There will be a shift from confrontation to cooperation, from destruction to reconstruction, disengagement to reengagement which will lead us and our coming generations towards a bright, positive, meaningful and prosperous future for Indian Ocean- Pacific region. Sagar Mala conclave, dialogue a step in this direction.

31

India and Maritime Security Issues in the Indian Ocean Region

— Dr. Shrikant Paranjpe

Indian Ocean, that at one time had been described as a 'British Lake' became a thorough fare for maritime trade that crossed through the Suez Canal and the Malacca Straits connecting the growing economies of the East and the West by carrying raw materials, oil and finished goods. It had seen a great power rivalry between the United States and the Soviet Union during the cold war years and now has become a major global focal point of a conflict over resources, trade and environmental issues.

India

India had been a consistent critique of the 'power vacuum' theory that had been propounded by the United States to justify its presence in this region after the British 'withdrawal from East of Suez' policy. The argument that the littoral states did not have the naval capabilities to replace the British and maintain order in the Indian Ocean Region (IOR) was contested by India. Indian call for a Zone of Peace in the Indian Ocean was an attempt to establish an order in this region with the participation of the littoral states. However, these efforts had limited success due to the intra-regional conflicts that persisted in the region amongst the relatively relevant regional powers like Iran, Pakistan, India, Malaysia and Indonesia. The then South African apartheid regime was not included in the efforts of cooperation and Australia was looked at suspiciously as it had ties with the United States. The post-cold war era has seen the emergence of regional aspirations of littoral states for a greater say in the issues of stability and order in the IOR. Today the littoral players have started to emerge as relatively significant ac-tors willing to have a dialogue both, amongst themselves and with the extra regional powers. The Indian Ocean Naval Symposium (IONS), a concept promoted by India, is one such initiative.

One can identify two levels of security challenges that are experienced in the IOR: One is the spill over of issues in the domestic conflicts within the littoral states and the adjoining waters of the IOR and two, are the concerns that are faced in the IOR directly. The former would include such concerns as the conflict in the Middle East including the Gulf region, Afghanistan, South Asia and the South China Sea. The latter includes piracy; illicit trafficking of narcotics, small arms and humans; environmental degradation; maritime boundary disputes; disruption of maritime trade; and linkages with terrorism.

In sharp contrast to the importance that the Indian army has been given in the plan-ning for defence, Indian maritime forces have been given a raw deal throughout. A strong plea for an active maritime policy, as articulated by K.M. Pannikar, and Swatantryaveer Savarkar remained a lone crusade in a land-bound defence perspective. Understanding of India's security policy has for long been dominated by considerations of defence of land frontiers. This is partly a product of the long history of aggression or migration from land routes either from the North West or from the North and North Eastern regions of India. Partly, it is a product of the equally long history of a 'secure' Indian Ocean due to the British presence and the relatively small and coastal naval presence of Indian rulers. Consequently, much of the work on Indian security policy has focused on the land forces as against the sea power and its utility.

At a popular level, the history of Vasco da Gama landing at Calicut in 1498, conflict with the Zamorin of Calicut; the Dutch entry in 1641; and the subsequent British and French arrival are points of academic curiosity in the history of India. They do not cause the same stirrings as those caused by the various onslaughts of the Afghans, Turks, Mughals through the North West frontiers. This is despite the fact that, per-haps, it was the sea routes that in the long run became the instruments of eventual growth of colonialism in Asia.

Maritime Security

There are certain defining features of the maritime environment that India needs to exploit. Ocean, unlike the land is not politically controlled. It presents a free access to any land mass. Maritime forces therefore, are the only instruments of power that can be deployed almost anywhere in the world without any accusation of intervention. The importance of navy rests on its ability to influence the events on land through its control over sea. For India, this would imply its ability to ensure safety of trade ves-sels, the guarding of the Exclusive Economic Zone (EEZ), defence against 'State' and 'Non-State' incursions on Indian Territory in terms of its immediate national security concerns. At the regional level, it involves the ability to retain a sphere of influence and establish stability and order in the littoral states of the region on the premise that instability in those areas constitutes a direct threat to Indian national interest. At the global level it presents an opportunity to demand space in the decision making circles of the world.

The unique geo-political position of India in terms of its peninsular presence in the Indian Ocean and its growing military capability presents an opportunity for India to emerge as a key player that would maintain order in the Indian Ocean region. In geo-strategic terms we can identify some important choke points that would be of interest to India. In the west are the Strait of Hormuz, Suez Canal and the Red Sea, Strait of Bab-el-Mandeb and the Horn of Africa; in the East are Malacca Strait, Lombok Strait, Sunda Strait,; and along the Indian coastline are the Six Degree Channel and the Nine Degree Channel. These choke points represent the tac-tical level area that India can 'look after' in order to maintain order in the region.

Various initiatives that seek to create a cooperative perspective about the Indian Ocean Littoral Community and the possible role that India can take in the region also tends to be defined within the space of these choke points.

Indian Navy's first Maritime Vision was expressed in the Naval Plans Paper of 1948. Indian Navy was to consist of cruisers and destroyers, structured around small aircraft carriers with the objective of protecting India's sea lanes of communication. The rationale at that time was that of 'territorial defence' – a view that continued to dominate India strategic perspectives for over two decades. It was only in the 1971 Indo-Pakistan conflict that the Navy played a significant role. The primary tactical success in 1971 came from the use of missile attacks in the Arabian Sea. The Navy entered the war with five Alize aircraft that were the main source of domain awareness. The limited domain awareness facility was some-what a handicap during the war, a matter that came to be corrected over the years. Amphibious operations, which can enhance options and opportunities, were not used during the war. Even the knowledge of submarines had been largely undeveloped.

Indian Navy's Maritime Strategy today speaks of the need to project power as a means of supporting foreign policy objectives. The areas of primary interest that have been identified by the Indian Navy as areas that need attention include: (a) The Arabian Sea and the Bay of Bengal, which largely encompass India's Exclusive Economic Zone, Island Territories and their littoral reaches; (b) The choke points leading to and from the Indian Ocean, they being the Strait of Malacca, Strait of Hormuz, strait of Bab-el-Mandeb and the Cape of Good Hope; (c) the island countries; (d) the Persian Gulf as a source of oil supply and (e) principal international sea lanes that cross the Indian Ocean Region. The secondary areas of interest include: (a) The Southern Indian Ocean Region, (b) The Red Sea, (c) The South China Sea and (e) The East Pacific Region.

Over the past years one can cite some examples of Indian Navy's actions in terms of its strategic mission. India acted in Maldives to restore the democratically elected government in 1998; activities in the context of Sri Lanka both, as rescue missions and tackling threats from across the border; rescue mission to evacuate Indian, Sri Lankan and Nepali citizens from Lebanon in 2006; and the anti-piracy mission taken up since 2008 off the Gulf of Aden.

The Indian Navy envisages four types of roles for itself: Military, Diplomatic, Constabulatory and Benign. The military role is the key role that any Navy is expected to play, it may involve deterrence, active engagement, securing territorial integrity, safeguarding sea lanes, etc. The diplomatic role entails use of naval power in support of foreign policy. While the constabulatory tasks are secondary, the increasing incidence of maritime crime has brought this dimension to the fore-front. The objectives here are coastal defence including the defence of EEZ. Anti-piracy is one of the key tasks in this context. The benign role is essentially humanitarian in nature, providing rescue and relief operations.

The Vasco da Gama landing had opened up India to the Western world. It was the beginning of a new era in the sense that the earlier sea route trade contacts of the Middle East had only a very limited impact. Unfortunately, the enormity of the entry of a Western Power in this manner did not strike any resonance in the Indian mind. A nation that at one time had seen a glorious maritime history under the Cholas and the Pandyas lost out on its maritime perspective. It is that mind-set that needs to be rekindled, and an awareness of the maritime domain to be created.

32

India's Security and the Indian Ocean

— Cmde. R A Maslekar (Retd.)

Landing of terrorists on Mumbai coast in November 2008 and subsequent mayhem caused in the city by killing of scores of residents jolted the country's security experts and political masters from their somnolent attitude towards securing the vast coastline. The historical mindset that threat to India's security would emanate only from the northern land borders had led to neglect of coastal defence infrastructure and myopic security appreciation. India has over 7500 kms of coastline giving it a large economic exclusive zone. Additionally the Lakhadweep and Minicoy islands on the west and Andaman and Nicobar islands in the east of the mainland further add to the EEZ. The country is able to generate considerable offshore economic activity in terms of marine products and contribute indigenously to its quest for energy security. India has also been allotted a large area in central Indian Ocean to explore sea-bed for rare minerals. Large number of minor and major ports, while not yet adequately modernised to handle greater volumes of trade, have been instrumental in the country's economic progress based on exports and imports of goods. It is also because of the Indian Ocean that the country gets the south west monsoon current bearing life sustaining rainfall. It would thus be pertinent to state that the Indian Ocean and its constituent Seas and Bays have a direct connect with India's march towards being a developed country in the near future. Any disruption in this connect will have disas-trous ramifications to India. India's national security will be under threat if any of the components of its comprehensive national power gets denuded or degraded through adversarial action. It will be manifested as disruption in energy as well as goods trade through piracy deliberately sponsored or aided by those inimical to India. Although the world had witnessed high levels of piracy along the coast of Horn of Africa and in South China Sea, the reach of this scourge was seen close to Indian shores when one Pirate mother ship was sunk by Indian navy close to Minicoy Island in the year 2011. Illegal deep sea trawling for marine products in the Indian EEZ adversely affects its export potential and is a direct threat to wellbeing of millions of its citizens whose livelihood is dependent on the ocean. The possibility of Illegal migrants occupying un-inhabited island territories is quite high due to deficiencies in round the clock surveillance and monitoring capabilities. Instances of some of smaller islands of Andaman and Nicobar being occupied for some duration for fishing activities have been detected in the past. These illegal migrants colluding with terrorists cannot be ruled out. Increasing marine pollution because of oil spills and other effluents due to ever rising shipping traffic along the sea lanes of communication passing through Indian EEZ is yet another threat which the country is unable to obviate. Offshore oil drilling rigs and processing platforms could be targeted to cause serious disruptions to India's indigenous energy production. Indian strategic thought has to delve deeply on importance of Indian Ocean to India as its life line as well as a threat. Writing in the 1940s, K M Pannikar, a noted historian had argued that "while to other countries the Indian Ocean is only one of the important oceanic areas, to India it is a vital sea. Her lifelines are concentrated in that area, her freedom is dependent on the freedom of that water surface". One of the great freedom fighters, Vinayak Damodar Sawarkar, stepping on the shores of Andamans while being interned at the Cellular jail in 1911, had envisioned these islands as sentinels of mainland security. He had written in his autobiography "My Transportation for Life" about the need to develop Andamans as India's forward naval base in order to dominate the maritime area around and guard any naval incursion on the mainland from the East. The late prime minister Jawaharlal Nehru summed up India's concerns regarding threats from the maritime front when he stated that "History has shown that whatever power controls the Indian Ocean has, in the first instance, India's sea borne trade at her mercy and, in the second, India's very independence itself." To summarise, India's key security considerations include:-

- The accessibility of the Indian Ocean to the naval fleets of the world's most powerful states. Steady rise in Chinese naval footprint in the Indian Ocean Region.
- The proliferation of conventional military power and nuclear weapons among the region's states

- The large Islamic populations on the shores of the ocean and in its hinterland which have come under influence of the radical and extremist leadership.
- Illegal immigrants and human trafficking.
- India being made a conduit for illegal trade in arms and narcotics.
- The oil wealth of the Persian Gulf. Critical dependency for energy security by many developed and developing countries.
- The importance of key straits such as Hormuz and Malacca for world trade and their possible effect as choke points.

Supplementing its diplomatic and political initiatives, India is shaping its growing military capability for envisaged threats emanating from and in the IOR. These forces should be able, should the need arise, to prevent militaries especially the air forces and navies of hostile nations to have freedom of operation in the Indian Ocean. They should be able operate in distant waters with impunity to safeguard Indian maritime and economic in-terests and if need be project power over mainland of hostile nations. Most critical capability is to have all round surveillance, interception and interdiction capability over key choke points, on vital islands, around the littoral, and along key sea routes

India seems to be playing a catch up game in terms of its capacity building to counter likely threats to its interests in IOR. It has to be very clearly understood by the policy makers that the strategic scenario may not unfold as envisaged and hence the nation needs to be prepared for the unexpected. The interests of outside powers in the IOR may grow to such a level as to be in direct confrontation with those of India. It would then depend upon the wisdom and all the diplomatic acumen of the national leadership whether India stands firm or acquiesces to the adversary. Hence, if India sees IOR as primary area to pursue its national interests it is quite apparent that there is no escape from building adequate deterrence, and a credible and effective military response.

33

Control and Cooperation Strategic Narratives and Maritime Stability

— *Prof Dennis Rumley*

I. Introduction: Great Power Control and Cooperation

This paper has two principal aims:

To describe and evaluate a number of Great Power strategic narratives on maritime control and conflict, primarily in the Indian Ocean and South China Sea To initiate a dialogue on a new narrative of cooperative maritime security

II. Great Power Maritime Strategic Narratives

What are Strategic Narratives?

A strategic narrative has been defined as "a means for political actors to construct a shared meaning of the past, present and future of international politics to shape the behaviour of domestic and international actors". Among other things, Great Powers use strategic narratives to project their interests and to create identity groups and enable the establishment of normative orientations.

Strategic narratives can meet a number of functions in attempting to control the way in which space is perceived and managed and how states might/should behave [TABLE 1].

1. Ability to shape behaviour
2. Manage public view of state action
3. Ensure a leadership role among allies
4. Perpetuate interpretations of the world

5. Claim control over extra-state maritime space
6. Limit frameworks of critical analysis
7. Design an illusion of external threat
8. Facilitate a cooperative relationship

TABLE 1: Functions of Maritime Strategic Narratives

Examples of Great Power Maritime Strategic Narratives

I will briefly discuss ten examples of strategic narratives for the United States, India and China [TABLE 2].

1. US Monroe Doctrine (control)
2. One Ocean (control)
3. Asian Monroe Doctrine (control)
4. Panikkar's 'steel ring' (control)
5. China's sphere of influence (control)
6. US 'pivot' to Asia (control and cooperation)
7. Indo-Pacific (control and cooperation)
8. India's 'Look East'/'Act East' (cooperation)
9. String of Pearls (cooperation and control)
10. OBOR (cooperation and control)

TABLE 2 Great Power Strategic Narratives

The two most obvious commonalities among these examples is that:

1. They are all underpinned by or imply expansionist motives. While such expansion might lead to greater inter-state cooperation, invariably it will create negative perceptions that will result in Great Power reaction and even conflict. They all claim control over/precedence in extra-state maritime space. While international maritime law gives some guidance in this area, there exist considerable challenges to global oceans governance especially in terms of fisheries, species conservation, deep-sea mining and ocean environmental protection. The end result is that, in spite of considerable effort to the contrary, the Ocean Commons remain insecure in the broadest sense of that term.

1. US Monroe Doctrine

There is a view among some analysts that the Monroe Doctrine should be restricted to the United States. Others have argued, however, that the

Monroe Doctrine is essentially an Anglo-Saxon concept, available only to Britain and her former (white) colonies – Australia, pre-1994 (or pre-1961?) South Africa and the USA – the gateways to all of the world's oceans.

The US Monroe Doctrine - the declaration of the "sacred text of 1823" as one scholar has called it – laid the basis for American expansionism in the Western hemisphere. It has been regarded as "an assertion of legitimate regional hegemony", and that "the United States managed to climb to world supremacy in the face of British imperialism by carving out its own sphere of influence under the Monroe Doctrine". In effect, the US Monroe Doctrine states that the Western Hemisphere is the sphere of influence of the United States and that it will not tolerate any new colonies within it.

However, in 1994, a Yale Professor, Gaddis Smith, argued that with the end of the Cold War the Monroe Doctrine should be torn up.

2. One Ocean

There are large spaces on the earth outside of the jurisdiction of any sovereign state – most of the world's oceans, the atmosphere, outer space and the Antarctica – that lack strong global institutions to govern them and thus rest on "fragile foundations".

In 1903, Ellen Semple's geo-political analysis for the Indo-Pacific was built around two central propositions. First, that the United States can obtain pre-eminence in the region by a process of dominating the Atlantic and the Pacific. It is important to note that Semple was much ahead of her times in anticipating a 'future history' where the United States, ably assisted by technological advances and innovation, would be working out its geostrategy in terms of 'oneness of the world ocean'. Indeed, Lewis, among others, has reminded us of the "constructedness of oceanic categories" and that there are no 'real' divisions "across the undivided Ocean Sea".

US World Ocean dominance is therefore a central goal for the United States. None-theless, the UNCLOS agreement is potentially of paramount importance in attempting to manage the control of Ocean space and in terms of maximising Ocean stability and security. As at 23 May 2017, 168 states had ratified UNCLOS. The United States is the only Great Power yet to ratify UNCLOS. This reinforces the One Ocean point made above. It also calls into question the legitimacy of the US critique of Chinese behaviour in the South China Sea in terms of UNCLOS.

3. Asian Monroe Doctrine

A renewal of interest in the concept of an Asian Monroe Doctrine arises in part as a responseto at least four global geo-political/geo-economic shifts:

(i) A shift to a post-Cold War world – ideology no longer bifurcates global space; although during the CW period the so-called "Brezhnev Doctrine" formalised the Soviet sphere of influence in Eastern Europe.

(ii) a shift to a post-colonial world – the emergence of post-colonial nationalism

(iii) a shift in the global distribution of economic power – a shift in global economic power away from Europe and the United States to Asia

(iv) a shift to a post-unipolar world – the relative decline of the United States

As Mearsheimer and others might argue, it is unsurprising that, given these shifts, that Asian Great Powers would wish to possess their own Monroe Doctrine. However, the geo-political configuration of Asian Great Power Monroe Doctrines was principally an outcome of historically perceived extra-state maritime control 'set' in the colonial or even the pre-colonial era. This is the case with both India and China.

As David Brewster (2014) and others have pointed out, a key figure in the creation of the original Asian Monroe Doctrine narrative was Chester Bowles, a former US Ambassador to India in the 1950s and 1960s. Apparently, on a number of occasions, Bowles tried to persuade Nehru that, with the informal backing of the United States, India should institute an Asian Monroe Doctrine that would encompass the whole of Southern Asia and the Indian Ocean, partly as a hedge against China. However, Bowles' concept for India had already been pre-empted by the thinking of Indian geo-political doyen, K. M. Panikkar.

4. Panikkar's "steel ring"

K. M. Panikkar, who according to Raja Mohan, is still "an inspiration for Indian naval thinking", argued in his classical essay India and the Indian Ocean (1945) that, since India was "dependent" on the Indian Ocean and since "whoever controls the Indian Ocean has India at its mercy", then it follows that "The Indian Ocean must therefore remain truly Indian". He also argued that:

> As a matter of course that only on the basis of a regional organisation of which India will be the secure and firm foundation can the safety of the Indian Ocean be assured.

He suggested that such an Indian Ocean regional organisation offers the prospect of regional security and the creation of peace, freedom from colonialism, food security, economic development and public health could be primary goals.

At least two important issues arise out of this. First, in the 21st century it seems that India is unwilling to act unilaterally in taking on a regional security burden. A regional solution appears to be preferred. Second, given Panikkar's insights and their continued relevance:

> If for China the Indian Ocean is not an Indian lake, New Delhi's imperative is to contest impressions in Beijing that the waters east of Malacca automatically fall under the latter's sphere of influence (Pant and Joshi 2015).

Panikkar saw that the primary responsibility of the Indian Navy was to guard the "steel ring" created by Singapore, Ceylon, Mauritius and Socotra. This was India's sphere of influence or indeed Monroe Doctrine. In short, Panikkar argued for the creation of a circle of "Indian nuggets" long before an American strategic consultant conceived of a Chinese "string of pearls".

5. China's Sphere of Influence

The Geographer, Norton Ginsburg, in 1968 published an interesting piece on the Chinese perception of a world order. This traditional view was unsurprisingly Sinocentric but was unique in the sense that it held this view long before the modern European state had come into existence – that is, it was held long before it was assumed that state power extended to delimited and demarcated political boundaries. While in the Western model, all areas of the state were of equal value, in the Chinese case, some regions were regarded as being important than others (Figure).

The centre of the system (zone 1) was 'China Proper' (the 18 Provinces or hub of the Sinocentric universe) and the 'periphery' to this centre comprised subordinate areas or "client states" in a zonal arrangement with zone IV being 'The Outer World'. The "traditional frontiers" ran through the Sea of Japan, encompassed the South China Sea and included most of Southeast Asia.

Robert Kaplan has argued that China is in the process of applying a "Monroe Doctrine-style sovereignty" notion in constructing a Greater China, the heart of which is the South China Sea. Kaplan's view is affirmed by another US commentator, John Mearsheimer, who has suggested a clear linkage between China's behaviour in the South China Sea and the 19th US Monroe Doctrine.

6. US 'pivot' to Asia

In late 2011, President Obama announced that "the center of gravity for US foreign policy, national security, and economic interests is shifting towards Asia", that there would be a US "pivot" to the Asia-Pacific, a "rebalancing", and as Hilary Clinton declared, this was a part of "America's Pacific Century" (yet another narrative). The pivot was clearly a response to the rise of China, for the US to become involved in the South China Sea dispute, and an attempt to reassure as well as coopt regional allies. From a maritime perspective, the US navy would move from a 50/50 split between the Pacific and the Atlantic to a 60/40 split. Some critics of the policy were in disbelief that the US had actually left the Pacific and needed to come back and that the 'pivot' appeared to be a return to outmoded Cold War thinking.

7. Indo-Pacific

The Indo-Pacific regional strategic narrative is intimately linked to the US 'pivot'; it is a contested geopolitical concept and like all regional concepts, it is a construct designed for particular purposes.

Among other things, the Indo-Pacific is a US regional construct - originally developed by German geo-politicians - is designed to fulfill at least 6 essential functions:

1. Provide regional focus and purpose for US security policy
2. Re-use and re-imagine an old geopolitical concept – i.e. 'pivot'
3. Incorporate India into its 'contain China' strategy
4. To leverage the co-option of other regional states – e.g. Australia
5. Act as a framework of leadership for regional state defence strategies
6. Create a regional control mechanism as part of a 'New Cold War'

8. India's 'Look East'/ 'Act East'

While the Indo-Pacific strategic narrative implies control and conflict, India's 'Look East'/ 'Act East' narrative implies the expansion of cooperation especially in terms of reinvigorating historical ties with Southeast Asia.

Narasimha Rao's 1991 "Look East" narrative, which has been reinforced by Narendra Modi's "Act East" strategy, has been referred to as "rebalancing Indian style" and is especially aimed at:

1. Developing a range of linkages, especially with Australia, Japan, Vietnam and ASEAN, for enhancing economic ties
2. Ensuring energy security
3. Acting as a balance against China in the India Ocean
4. Carving out a more prominent global role
5. Potentially for acting as a regional stabilising force

9. String of Pearls

The "string of pearls" strategic narrative was devised in 2005 by an American security analyst to perpetuate the view of a Chinese threat to states in the Indian Ocean and especially to India. It is said to involve a three-prong strategy:

1. Develop diplomatic relations with IO littorals
2. Build IO bases
3. Secure IO SLOCS

The "string of pearls" can be described as a "flawed narrative" for several reasons:

1. Chinese strategic imperatives are in the East and South China Seas
2. The IO is thus of secondary importance
3. China is not an IO littoral and thus it does not figure in its territorial integrity
4. Chinese IO interests are essentially economic – natural resources and energy
5. The so-called 'bases' are 'ports' and do not lend themselves to military usage
6. The IO is too large and too expensive for one state to control
7. In short, the 'string of pearls' is out of touch with Chinese priorities

10. OBOR

OBOR - first announced by Chinese President Xi Jinping in September 2013 - is portrayed by some analysts as a direct response to the US 'pivot' – China's 'look west' narrative. It has also been described as a geo-political and geo-economic strategy for China to gain global prominence in third world economic development, particularly in developing economic partnerships and in the development and building of communications infrastructure.

The OBOR narrative comprises a maritime silk road and a silk road economic belt plus 6 'economic corridors':

1. China Pakistan-Economic Corridor (CPEC)
2. China- Mongolia-Russia Economic Corridor (CMREC)
3. New Eurasian Land Bridge (NELB)
4. China- Central and West Asia Economic Corridor (CCWAEC)
5. China- Indochina Peninsula Economic Corridor (CICPEC)
6. Bangladesh- China-India-Myanmar Economic Corridor (BCIMEC)

It has been argued by some American commentators that the One Belt One Road strategic narrative (comprising the land and sea based silk roads) is a cooperative rebadging of the control/conflict implications of the 'string of pearls' strategy. On the other hand, however, it has been emphasized that Chinese investment will stimulate much needed development and make significant inputs into national economic plans, thus contributing to greater global and regional stability.

III. Conclusion: towards an Asian cooperative Great Power security narrative

1. Concept of 'Great Power strategic space'
2. Perception of external intrusion
3. No one owns the SCS or the IO
4. Mutual recognition needed to minimise conflict
5. Thus, India pre-eminent in IO & China pre-eminent in the SCS
6. Initiate a dialogue on a cooperative narrative
7. Towards an India-China Maritime Accord (ICMA)?

34

Trade & Flag: "Sagar" and Pax Indica in the Hind Mahasagar

— Rear Admiral Sudarshan Shrikhande

In 1885, just over two decades after the Meiji Restoration, the Imperial Japanese Navy coined a term, Kaikoku Nippon which meant Maritime Japan. It was a movement to create catalysts for all round maritime progress for a fundamentally maritime nation. While the Japanese Navy germinated the intellectual seeds, it was the Japanese government that watered and nurtured the "whole of nation" momentum that made it a nation that arrived on the world scene. Kaikoku Nippon was a slogan that harnessed ambition and purpose for gains in several areas. It resulted in Japan building more ships, some naval but mostly merchant vessels. It modernized cargo handling and ship- turn around in existing ports and created many new ones. It created the foundations of skill development, technical and engineering education, that impacted upon and synergized railways, shipbuilding, steel, and machine tools as well as machinery. It created the internal growth of railways and later, of roads as motor transport appeared on the world scene in the early 19th century.

In comparison, as a nation, even if in 1947, we did "awake to life and freedom", we took far longer to begin the voyage of achieving India's maritime destiny. In a sense, the decision to do so, as a whole of government approach came to fruition with the first "Maritime India" Summit at Mumbai in April last year. The impetus to Sagarma-la Project, along with the very idea of "SAGAR" (Security and Growth for All in the Region) can now begin creating a truly beneficial Indian Ocean regional environment. The two key words, "Security and Growth" are profoundly inter-linked, mutually dependent, and mutually reinforcing.

The linkage between Security and Growth brings into the discussion Navies and Coast guards and equivalent maritime security agencies of nations in the Indian Ocean Region (IOR). As can be appreciated, trade routes on the sea generally enjoy freedom of navigation. Yet, the passage itself is subject to many threats and risks. Some risks and threats arise from the vagaries of nature itself; storms, cyclones, earthquakes and sometimes even devastating tsunamis. Who can forget the Dec 2004 upheaval caused by a cruel earthquake off Indonesia, on the Eastern extremity of the Indian Ocean, that carried in its powerful upwelling, a wave that caused destruction thousands of miles away on the coast of Somalia at the Western extremity of the same ocean. As nature and geographers conspired to define the spread of the Indian Ocean, the destruction along India's coasts and in the Andaman Islands as well as in many areas of Sri Lanka, united us all in a shared tragedy and in shared resources for helping each other gat back to life and work. At the centre of the mammoth relief and rescue effort, was the Indian Navy (IN), with the Indian Army and Air Force and the Coast Guard standing shoulder to shoulder. Some day, HADR may have to directly deal with consequences of climate change.

Natural disasters and the humanitarian relief that follows (HADR, in military parlance) require national capacities and capabilities that are then cooperatively put into action along with the affected nation's/ region's instruments in a cooperative effort. This is something that Indian Armed Forces are demonstrably capable of. With the medium of the Indian Ocean Naval Symposium (IONS) there are regular exercises and workshops where these mechanisms are tuned. This is one way, albeit a very important one, in which human security is ensured through relief; affected ports are opened; people are helped to re-establish their livelihoods.

Security and Growth are also linked in the other threats to freedom of commerce flows upon the seas. This threat is of piracy. Just like terrorism, piracy often has the backing of some states, of interest groups, of financiers. It is a direct threat and risk to international trade. In the past decade-plus the scourge of piracy has reduced in a maritime region around the Horn of Africa (HOA). In achieving this, there were and are multiple international, and other cooperative efforts through various mechanisms. The Indian Navy has played a most central role in rolling back piracy. In several incidents in the HOA, IN ships specially deployed, or others who were in the area, have thwarted quite a few incidents. Some resulted in neutralisation of pirates. Even more so, it was in the waters West of the Lakshadweep islands that the IN and the ICG acted robustly in multiple operations leading to the capture of more than a hundred pirates. In the aftermath of the heinous, Pakistan- supported terror attacks on Mumbai, the growth engine of India, the IN and ICG have been at the forefront of ensuring coastal security. As a silent maritime services, the IN and ICG inarguably ensured both Security and Growth even before the SAGAR acronym was created. Navies have traditionally done this for centuries in the symbiotic relationship between Flag and Trade, Trade and Flag.

However, there is a larger risk to growth and security that requires navies such as ours to be equipped, trained and deployed not only in the defence of India's interests, but also those of our friends in the region. A navy is primarily raised for conflict and war. At the same time, its most important role is as a guarantor of peace, an assurer of freedom of the seas, a provider of security to friends in time of war or under other dangerous situations. An instrument created for war works through dissuasion and deterrence. Should dissuasion not work, or deterrence collapse, then the Indian Navy will step actively into its role given that India itself is a net security provider in the IOR.

On the contrary, if we cast our eyes on what is happening in the South and East China Seas, a different picture emerges. An economically powerful China is expanding its influence with a new, oriental "trident" of economic muscle, rising military-maritime power and geo-political leverage. It is altering the maritime geography of the region through claims of which some are unsustainable, and others questionable at best. Almost all littoral nations, with relatively lesser power and leverages, are very concerned about the very uneasy environment. Much of what China is engaged in, de facto, is perceived as a risk to freedom of the seas not only by those smaller nations abutting these seas, but also countries which are geographically at a distance, but still intimate users of those seas. India is one of them, and several have been the occasions when our senior most political leaders have expressed concerns about such risks.

We will always do well to remember that 30 percent of India's trade flows through the South China Seas. As Programme SAGAR, (in terms of domestic manufacturing, better roads, efficient ports, hopefully a resurgent Indian merchant fleet built in India and flying the Indian flag), acquires traction, certainly the quantum of trade passing through the SCS, and perhaps even the proportion could increase. In turn. Meanwhile, many SE and East Asian nations are concerned about risks to their Security and to their Growth. Chinese actions, their posturing, their aggressiveness in the SCS seem to be the very antithesis of what SAGAR is about in the IOR.

A looming concern is the beginnings of Chinese maritime initiatives in the IOR which, while perhaps superficially attractive, could be double-edged swords for some of the littoral nations. Clearly, these steps are a concern for India. These are concerns that could grow even more serious in years to come.

Thus, the future both beckons us who live in the many nations that fringe the Indian Ocean for shared prosperity and Growth as well as cautions us towards adopting more pragmatic approaches to regional, cooperative Security mechanisms.

The future could provide a framework in which a Pax Indica named more after the eponymous large ocean whose waves touch so many shores rather than just the country that bears the name. In its noble endeavour to address Security and Growth, SAGAR within the Hind Mahasagar, an effective, strong and friendly Indian Navy, along with sister services shall always remain ready.

35

India-japan Ties: An Evolving Partnership in Troubled Waters

— *Chaitanya Mallapur and*
Uttara Sahasrabuddhe

Since the 1990's, India's strategic outlook has steadily evolved from being a land power to becoming a maritime power. The change was prompted by its growing trade and the need for security of its trade and energy routes. Consequently, the sphere of interest for India also expanded from South Asia to the Indian Ocean Region. "Look East" Policy redesignated as "Act East" Policy by the Modi Government – is an important pillar of India's evolving maritime outlook. New Delhi's maritime concerns include ensuring peaceful atmosphere in the Indian Ocean Region.

India's strategic location in the region has bestowed it with significant advantages. Especially when the world focus in the 21st century has shifted to the Indo-Pacific region from the Atlantic. The region has come to prominence for its geo-political and strategic significance as well as maritime trade passing through the sea lanes.

It is an energy rich region with abundance of mineral wealth and marine bio-diversity. More than half of the world's container ships, cargo and oil tankers pass through the maritime trade routes in this region. These sea lanes function as veins and arteries of global economies facilitating maritime trade.

India is seen as an emerging power in the region and the only competitor to China in the long run. The 'rise' of China's economic and political might and its assertiveness over territorial boundaries in East and South China Sea have raised concerns among littoral states in the region. The 21st Century Maritime Silk Road under One Belt One Road initiative by China is seen as its expansion in the region through infrastructure and portled development.

These initiatives indicate China's growing influence with shifting the power dynamics in Beijing's favour. The 'Free and Open Indo-Pacific Strategy' by Japan supported by India through its Act East Policy aims to counter changing dynamics in the regional politics. The strategy aims to connect the two continents—Asia with Africa—and the two oceans—Indian and Pacific.

Japan has been a major partner in India's rise. At the early stage of India's liberalization process, it offered to invest in India. The partnership has strengthened since Modi and Abe have taken over as Prime Ministers of India and Japan respectively. Japan has offered to invest in major infrastructure projects in India. These include Mumbai Metro III (through JAICA), Mumbai-Ahmedabad Bullet Train project, Delhi-Mumbai and Chennai-Bengaluru Industrial Corridors. Its Overseas Development Assistance has grown many folds in the past few years. Japan is the largest bilateral donor for India, extending loans and grants since 1958.

India must grab this opportunity to attract Japanese investments for portled development under the Sagarmala initiative. About 95% of India's merchandise trade in volume passes through sea-ports, hence, ports function as economic drivers in country's growth and development. India's turnaround time at major ports was approximately 4 days in 2014-15, as against the global average benchmark of 1-2 days. Thus, India must improve the efficiency of its ports with modern capabilities to boost its economic activity.

Japan is India's third largest source of foreign direct investment with $26 billion in-flows over the last 17 years. Similarly, it is India's 11th largest trading partner with bilateral trade worth over $14 billion in 2015-16.

The partnership has gone well beyond investment and trade. Sea borne threats in the form of piracy and maritime terrorism have made maritime security of utmost importance. Japan has now become a permanent partner in the Malabar naval exercise. Tokyo has made a nuclear deal with New Delhi – the first ever by it with any country that is not a signatory to the NPT. Together, the two countries have proposed to promote the Asia-Africa Growth Corridor (AAGC).

Rise of China has proved to be a major concern for both India and Japan. Both perceive it will jeopardize the peace of the Indo-Pacific region.

Both are not happy with the Chinese position in the South China Sea. The Joint Communique/Statement after the recent visit by the Japanese Prime Minister Shinzo Abe to India clearly points to the role of China in supporting countries like Pakistan and North Korea. The use of the word alliance in the Communique overcomes the old Indian taboo.

The stronger cooperation between the two countries is a clear message to China, at a time when the role of US in Asia is at best uncertain. The two Asian democracies are signaling that they are prepared to play a positive role in the Indo-Pacific region together. The growing friendship between the two countries has a significant geo-political context that seems to drive their geo-economics further.

India, Japan and the US have further planned to enhance cooperation in maritime security, connectivity and proliferation issues. This comes in the wake of turbulent situation in the region with increasing Chinese dominance in the South China Sea and North Korea's firing of ballistic missiles over Japan and its sixth nuclear test, conducted recently.

These uncertain and unforeseeable events in the world politics demand for resurgence in maritime diplomacy with changing times. Maritime diplomacy is now not only restricted to politics, trade and security but has widened its gambit towards climate change and sustainable environment. Both, India and Japan are committed in freedom of navigation in the Indo-Pacific region respecting sovereignty, international law, practicing free and fair trade and promoting dialogue. These evolving India-Japan ties with increased cooperation, signify concentrated efforts towards re-balancing regional order.

1. http://www.mea.gov.in/bilateral-documents.htm?dtl/28946/IndiaJapan+Joint+State-ment+during+visit+of+Prime+Minister+of+Japan+to+India+September+14+2017
2. http://mea.gov.in/Portal/ForeignRelation/Japan_Relations_13_12_2016.pdf
3. http://sagarmala.gov.in/about-sagarmala/background
4. http://dipp.nic.in/sites/default/files/FDI_FactSheet_June 2017_2_0.pdf
5. http://commerce.gov.in/EIDB.aspx
6. http://mea.gov.in/press-releases.htm?dtl/28957/India_Japan_US_Trilateral_Foreign_ Ministerial_Meeting

36

Challenges and Opportunities for Ocean Resource Management

—Admiral Dr. Jayanath Colombage

Ocean; The future of human kind

The world oceans play an important role in the sustenance of the planet earth and human kind. Humans have been using the oceans for various purposes; as a source of food, to travel and explore and to trade and acquire wealth. The oceans balance the eco-system on land to a greater extent. Over the years people have come to understand the potential and dynamic behaviour of the oceans and also the need to maintain the balance of the oceans. In the 21st century, we experience extreme drought and devastating hurricanes and floods, like in the case of category five Hurricane 'Irma', which devastated the southern part of the United States in September 2017. The ocean is vast and well over 70% of planet earth is covered with oceans containing 97% of earth's water (UN SDG 14,2016). The ocean is the largest absorber of Carbon dioxide. The ocean winds regulate and cool the climate. The ocean currents regulate the marine eco-system and nutrients that promotes the growth of ocean vegetation, planktons and the fish species, and millions of other life forms beneath the surface, beyond the vision of the humankind.

Ocean Resources and Opportunities

As per Dr Terney, 95% of the underwater world remains unexploited (Terney, 2017). This is a clear indication of the hidden, unknown potential of the ocean. The ocean is the major mode of transportation for 90% of goods. International maritime trade is the lifeline of the world; for goods or energy. As per the UN SDG 14, oceans serve as the largest source of protein, with more than 3 billion people are depending on the oceans as their primary source of protein and over 3 billion people depend on marine and coastal bio-diversity for their livelihoods (UN SDG 14,2016). More than half of the world population live within 100 kilometers off the coast. Marine ecosystems are among the largest of earth's aquatic systems. They include oceans, salt marsh, inter-tidal ecology, estuaries and lagoons, mangroves and coral reefs. Coastal habitats alone account for approximately one third of all marine biological productivity. Physical factors that determine the distribution of marine eco-systems are salinity, geology, temperature, tides, light availability and geography. Deep sea eco-systems are largely undiscovered and covers nearly 62% the globe (Terney, 2017). This area may contain more than 10 million unknown species. The ocean is also a medium for leisure; whether it is coastal tourism, fishing, diving or cruise industry. They thrive mainly on the beauty of the ocean, Beaches and coral reefs. The Indian Ocean Region (IOR) is rich in marine resources. Many rivers and tributaries have deposited large quantities of sediments and nourished the sea bed for thousands of years. Possibility exist for discovery of hydrocarbons, and natural gas and sea-bed minerals. Dharmarathna has indicated that sea-bed heavy minerals such as gem minerals, Ilmenite, Rutile, Zircon, Monazite, Manganese nodules, Phosphates nodules and crude oil and gas should be available in commercially viable exploitation quantities in the IOR (Dharmarathna, 2017). These marine resources are critically important to the sustenance and economic progress of the IOR.

Management of the Oceans

The ocean is considered as highly dynamic in time and space. The oceans have changed and are continuing to change, mainly due to climate change and human-made pollution. Presence of multitude of actors such as state players, law enforcement agencies, researchers, exploiters, smugglers of humans, narcotics and guns, IUU fishers and tourists complicate ocean management. However, the oceans need to be managed. There is a need to look beyond state jurisdictions of territorial and Exclusive Economic Zones (EEZ) and to treat oceans as a maritime common. Since the oceans are dynamic, management of it also should be dynamic. Static management practices can only be implemented in fixed locations such as oil rigs, coral reefs etc. It is necessary to study and research about critical marine habitats and threatened species. This region's regulatory framework should be catering to dynamic ocean management by using technology as a tool. Stake holder's collaboration and cooperation is a key component in dynamic ocean management. Coastal and Marine issues are politically and technically complex as there will be many interests and perceptions. Hence, human-marine management will need to combine a sound knowledge in natural and social sciences. Moreover, there will be a requirement to enhance capabilities of governmental agen-cies which are required to maintain a rule based maritime order and other institutions dealing with the ocean research.

The worlds Ocean are under threat: Challenges to Oceans Global Warming and Climate Change

There is no doubt that the world oceans are under an unprecedented level of pressure from human activities and commercial exploitation. Human commercial activities would include fisheries, shipping, marine culture, and extraction of minerals, natural gas and oil. The impact from these activities is compounded by climate change, pollution and invasive species (Halpern, 2008). The Guardian international edition of 24th August 2017 reported that a Russian tanker has travelled through the northern sea route in record speed and without an icebreaker escort for the first time, highlighting how climate change is opening up the high Arctic (The Guardian, 2017). The same article reported that the extent of the arctic ice fell to a new winter time low in March this year after freakishly high temperatures in the polar regions, and hit its second lowest summer extent last September. This may be good news for maritime trade as less fuel will be consumed by the shipping. But it is a clear indicator that climate change and global warming is real and it is now physically visible and even if we stop producing greenhouse gasses it is unlikely that the process will be reversed. The possible impacts of these could be sea level rising, changes in hydrodynamics, changes in ocean temperatures and salinity, water quality deterioration and ocean weather anomalies (Terney, 2017).

Human-made Pollution

Earlier, it was assumed that the ocean is vast and deep and can absorb any amount of garbage dumped into it. Humankind has been polluting the oceans for centuries and now it has accelerated, mainly due to industrialization and lack of understanding and disrespect for ocean health by governments and people. Oil spills, dumping of toxic wastes, and plastics have contributed immensely to deteriorating health of oceans. Polluting oceans basically begin on land. As per a report produced by the National oceanic and atmospheric administrative service of United States Department of Commerce, 80% of pollution to marine environment comes from the land (2017).

Land based pollutants can come from agriculture (fertilizer and pesticide), Urbanization (Disposal sewage and solid waste) Industries (Effluents and solid waste discharge) dirt, aquaculture projects, oil from motor vehicles etc. Thousands of tonnes plastic is dumped into the ocean on a daily basis. Plastic is one of the most dangerous pollut-ants found in the ocean. It is harmful for the environment as it does not break down easily and often it is considered as food by marine animals. Trash and waste dumped into the ocean can be washed up hundreds of miles away. Dumping of toxic waste, chemical waste and radioactive waste are also heavy contributors to ocean pollution. Chemicals can enter the ocean through various industries, as well as accidents. All these pollutants can kill large numbers of sea creatures and birds and impact the entire marine eco system. It can impact the reproduction cycle of the marine animals and behavioural changes, finally causing death. This has led to a gradual loss in marine life and an increase in the number of endangered species. Littering causes pollution in the ocean, which also causes a substantial loss of life beneath the seas. Disposal of untreated or under-treated sewage is a major polluting factor of the ocean. Sewage leads to the decomposition of organic matter that in turn leads to a change in bio-diversity. This can lead to changes to the marine ecosystem in a harmful manner. Land based agriculture is another contributor to ocean pollution as chemicals and fertilizer wash off to the ocean and could help rapid increase of algae, which deplete the oxygen content of the water and impact marine life and its survival. Marine animals, specially the smaller ones, can absorb these chemicals as part of their food and then enter the larger marine animals through the food chain. When people eat fish, the chemicals enter them and could lead to terminal diseases such as cancer. Garbage such as plastic and aluminum dumped into the sea can end up in a coastal area and would negatively impact the coastal communities and their livelihood and also coastal tourism. Even air pollution can impact the oceans. Dirt and other particles from air pollution can settle on the ocean surface and add to pollution. We cannot assume that the garbage and other forms of pollutants humankind dump into this vast, deep ocean would dilute and disappear. On the contrary, these pollutants come back to the humans through the food chain, which is sometimes even life threatening (Conserve Energy Future, 2017). Correcting harmful effects of human made pollution of the oceans will be costly. The UN SDG 14 indicates that as much as 40% of world oceans are heavily affected by human activities, including pollution, depleted fisheries, and loss of coastal habitats

(UN SDG14, 2016). There can be ocean based pollution too. These includes ships accidents (oil and hazardous matter), Explorations (Oil and Suspended matter) and Dumping (Oil and Garbage) (Terney, 2017).

Noise Pollution

Marine life is always disturbed and threatened by a combination of industrial noise, mainly from shipping, seismic exploration and use of air gun and naval sonar. Marine scientist and bioacoustics expert Clark term this phenomenon as "acoustical bleaching" of the oceans, a human-made cacophony that can tear apart the social networks of whales, adversely affecting survival and reproductive success (Schiffman, 2016). Whale feeding grounds and migratory routes are then disturbed and they lose breed-ing opportunity and choices. Further these loud noises can impact the communication ability of marine mammals which are capable of echolocation. The sound from seismic air gun explosions, which are mainly used in oil and gas explorations travels through the ocean and it changes from a big bang into a big fuzzy ball of reverberating noise. These bubbles produce a pressure that expand and contract, generating an immense amount of acoustic energy. The energy from all these explosions fills the ocean with noise (Schiffman, 2016). The exact impact of this noise pollution is not fully known and only came to attention in the recent decades. But the good news, says Clark, is that technologies are being developed to drastically reduce the noise from ships and geological surveying. The technological advances may produce quieter ships which is a main attributor to noise pollution. There should be controls of the locations, duration and for number of seismic air guns used in explorations.

New Industries and Polluting the Ocean

The population of the world in general is growing. However, the land area available for humans is rapidly decreasing due to various reasons. Further the economic conditions of the masses are also improving. This situation will require the world to extract more resources from the ocean, produce more and trade more. Therefore, industrial activities in the ocean will increase with new industries such as renewable energy, sea bed mining, blue bio-technology, blue technology and remediation and restoration of the ocean. All these activities will add more pollutants to the oceans, unless strict regulatory measures are not implemented.

Maritime Security Implications

With the increase demand for trade and exploitation of resources from the ocean, there will be many stakeholders in this domain. There will be a large number of stake holders, both from the governmental as well as non-governmental side. This additional activity in the ocean will contribute to maritime security issues as well. There is a need to understand the need for new economic activity in the ocean and the resulting security implications. Whilst the harnessing ocean resources will capture prospects and promises, security will be required to understand the risks and vulnerabilities and counter-action to mitigate or deter these threats. There will be traditional security threats emanating from state vs state rivalry and non-traditional threats coming from transnational maritime crime and other nefarious activities committed mainly by non-state actors. Hence the ocean governance and maintaining rule based maritime order is essential. Economic growth, ocean health and sustainability need to be balanced with maritime security implications. Activities in the oceans cannot be sustained unless there is security. Security will be paramount for ensuring that stakeholders abide by various regimes and protocols concerning ocean health. A single naval power would not suffice to maintain rule of law in the ocean space. Collaborative and combined efforts of bilateral, multi-lateral, regional and international mechanisms will be needed to achieve the desired end state.

SAGAR and Way Ahead for Sustainable Ocean Exploitation

The Ocean is the future of the Indian Ocean Region(IOR). Ocean divides us but also act as a connector. Countries with more effective technical and financial capacity will be able to harvest ocean resources better and make economic progress. However, whether this will take place in a sustainable manner is the question. Marine resources are not only found in territorial waters of states but in the areas beyond national jurisdiction too. This is a global common and need to be protected. It is true that United Nations Law of the Sea (UNCLOS) provide the basic framework for ocean governance and resource exploitation. But the need is to go further. The United Nations Sustainable Development Goal 14; 'Life below water' can be a useful vehicle to carry forward the agenda in the IOR. But it may not be sufficient to address today's dynamic situations in the oceans. Organizations such as Indian Ocean Rim Association (IORA), Indian Ocean naval Symposium (IONS) and Galle Dialogue should focus more on understanding the potential of marine resource utilization and opportunities and challenges and especially dangers of unsustainable exploitation and manmade pollution, which are detrimental to the ocean life. The IORA's 'Jakarta Accord' of May 2017, specially focuses on sustainable exploitation of ocean resources as a driver of inclusive and sustainable economic growth and development for the IOR and underscores the importance of regional synergies and cooperation to promote peace, stability and prosperity (Jakarta Accord, 2017).

SAGAR, which means Security And Growth for All in the Region, could be considered as a suitable platform to create a healthy discussion and come up with a plan of action to sustainably exploit the ocean resources in the IOR, in support of 'Jakarta Concord'. The IOR is in need of a network of political and economic maritime partnership to strengthen regional framework to be an effective platform. It is strongly recommended to establish an expert committee under SAGAR, representing various stake holders to study and discuss the issue of ocean resources and sustainable exploitation, and to come up with a legally binding multi-lateral framework. This is the need of the hour and the people of the IOR do not have the luxury of waiting and taking no action on this critical issue.

References

1. Conserve Energy Future (2017) What is Ocean Pollution? Available at: http://www. conserve-energy-future.com/various-ocean-pollution-facts.php
2. [Accessed: 12th Sep 2017]
3. Darmarathna, T. (2017). Potential Challenges and Opportunities of Marine Bio-diversity and Eco-systems in Sri Lanka, Lecture for Blue Economy: Prospects and Challenges for Sri Lanka, Bandaranaiyake Center for International Studies, 31 Aug 2017.
4. Halpern, B.S. (2008). A global map of human Impact on marine eco-systems, Science, 2008, vol. 319(pg. 948-952)
5. Jakarta Accord of IORA (2017) Promoting Regional Cooperation for a Peaceful Stable and Prosperous Indian Ocean. Available at: http://www.dirco.gov.za/docs/ 2017/ iora0309a.pdf [Accessed:15th Sep 2017]
6. Millennium Ecosystem Assessment. (2005), Ecosystems and human well-being: Synthesis, Island Press, Molteni
7. National oceanic and atmospheric administrative service of US Department of Commerce (2017). Available at: https://oceanservice.noaa.gov/facts/ pollution.html [Accessed: 12th Sep 2017]
8. Schiffman, R (2016). How Ocean Noise Pollution Wreaks Havoc on Marine Life. Yaleenvi-ronment360, Available at: http://e360.yale.edu/features/how_ ocean_noise_pollution_ wreaks_havoc_on_marine_life [Accessed: 14th Sep 2017]
9. Terney, P.K. (2017) Potential Challenges and Opportunities of Marine Bio-diversity and Eco-systems in Sri Lanka, Lecture for Blue Economy: Prospects and Challenges for Sri Lanka, Bandaranaiyake Center for International Studies, 31 Aug 2017.

10. The Guardian (2017) Russian tanker sails through Arctic without icebreaker for first time. The Guardian, 24th September 2017, Available at: https://www.theguardian.com/ environment/2017/aug/24/russian-tanker-sails-arctic-without-icebreaker-first-time [Accessed: 12th Sep 2017]
11. What is Ocean Pollution (2017) Conserve Energy Future, Available at: http://www.conserve-energy-future.com/causes-and-effects-of-ocean-pollution.php
12. [Accessed: 12th Sep 2017]
13. United Nations Sustainable Development Goals (2016). Goal 14: Conserve and Sustainable use the Oceans, Seas, and Marine Resources, Available at: http://www.un-org/sustainabledevelopment/oceans/# [Accessed: 14th Sep 2017]

37

Fisheries Research in Indian Ocean Region – Defining India's Role

— Dr. B. B. Nayak

Indian Ocean region is a complex region in terms of resources, trade, politics, and human races. Indian Ocean, as a common resource, has supported trade within the region and along with it, the exchange of cultures, traditions and food habits. With 40% of the global trade passing through Indian Ocean, the region is strategically very important. India being centrally located in the region has both unique advantage to be a development hub and has a daunting task of tackling a variety of security threats. In order to achieve the strategic goal, the country has to increase its presence in the region, not alone to guard the area but also to harness the resources for the wellbeing of its people. Fisheries resource is one of the most important resources that stands apart from others because it is linked to livelihood of a significant proportion of coastal population as well as to the food and nutritional security. It is therefore important to understand the fisheries potential offered by the seas surrounding India. Further, enhancing the capability to tap the resources can help keeping India's leadership role in the region.

Marine Fisheries Resources of India and its management

The fishery resources in the region have supported the livelihood of millions of coastal population. The fisheries sector contributes to economic growth in the region engaging millions of people in activities like fish culturing, harvesting, processing and trading. Fisheries resource component of IOR under India's control is significant. The marine resources of the country comprise of an Exclusive Economic Zone (EEZ) of 2.02 million sq. km, a continental shelf area of 0.53 million sq. km, a contiguous zone of 24 nautical miles and a coastline of 8,118 km. The marine fishery potential in the Indian waters have been estimated at 4.41 MMT constituting more than 47% demersal, 48% pelagic and 5% oceanic groups. The total fish production during 2015-16 (provisional) is estimated as 10.79 million metric tonne (MMT) with a contribution of 7.21 MMT from inland sector and 3.58 MMT from marine sector (DADF, Annual Report 2016-17). Mariculture has taken a new dimension in the last decade with the thrust on development of technologies pertaining to sea cage farming. Open sea farming of fin fish and shell fish species such as Cobia, Pompano, Sea Bass, Groupers, Snappers and Lobsters in cages in different locations offer promising prospects of sea farming. In India, there are 757 cages installed for open sea cage farming which has a production of 2271 metric tonnes (DADF, Annual Report 2016-17). Fisheries resources is rich and diverse in Indian coast with 735 marine species landed in 2015, belonging to 327 genus, 154 family, 41 order, 9 class and 4 phyla (CMFRI Annual report 2015-16). While the near shore fisheries resources can be exploited on a sustainable manner, there is a need felt for up-gradation of technology to harness the untapped deep sea and oceanic fishery resources. The conversion and up-gradation of existing fishing vessels promoted by Marine products export development authority (MPEDA) can contribute to the reduction of fishing pressure on the coastal waters and simultaneously help in harvesting of the under-tapped and resources like tunas, bill fishes, pelagic sharks and oceanic squids etc. Estimated that harvestable tuna resource alone could be up to Rs.3000crores

Central Marine Fisheries Research Institute (CMFRI) has focused on fisheries resource management which include GIS based resource mapping, satellite imagery based prediction of fishing ground, stock assessment of commercially important species, fish distribution response to Oceanographic forcing and culture of marine plant and animals in the sea. CIFNET meets the demand for qualified and certified personal for manning the fishing vessels. The Fishery Survey of India (FSI) is the nodal agency for carrying out the survey, assessment and monitoring of marine fishery resources of the Indian Exclusive Economic Zone (EEZ). FSI in collaboration with Indian national centre for ocean information service (INCOIS) is also working on satellite telemetry studies of tuna. The oceanic tuna migrates from Srilankan coast till the gulf of Oman and is an untapped resource and it's harvest is now promoted by MPEDA.

Changing requirements in fish trade

Management of fisheries calls for stakeholder participation to implement regulations based on scientifically validated guidelines. The preservation of marine protected areas and reserves, and implementation of fishing ban, need support from stakeholders. Sustainability of food source is also an important concern among the elite food consumers. Thus, the traceability and ecolabels have become part of food trade where consumer can identify the products which are green, safe, and environmentally sustainable. The international standards on traceability and ecolabelling necessitate declaration from the seller that the stock of the traded fish has been harvested without affecting the sustainability. Further, to facilitate traceability, it is necessary to record the area in the sea from where the fish is caught to where it was preprocessed or processed to locations through which it was passed till it reaches the consumer. The seafood traceability along the whole chain of custody from vessel to final consumer is considered to be an overarching market-based approach to combat illegal, unreported and unregulated (IUU) fishing. Estimates of the total value of illegal and unreported fishing losses worldwide are between 10 billion$ and 23.5 billion$ annually, representing between 11 and 26 MMT in volume. There is no credible estimate of the volume of losses due to IUU fishing in IOR. Illegal fishing by domestic mechanized trawlers in the inshore artisanal zone has been reported in all coastal states of mainland India. Illegal fish catches are very high in island territories, with most violators being foreign trawlers targeting sea cucumbers, shark fins and reef fish in the Andaman Islands, while shark fins are the usual target of poachers in Lakshadweep area. India has taken initiatives at multiple fronts to reduce the greenhouse gasses (GHGs). Efforts to improve the energy efficiency of about 1.5 lakhs of mechanized and motorized can add to this initiative. Design of boats, size and design of fishing gear and requirements of engine power for a particular type of fishing have to be assessed and remedial measures should be taken to improve fuel efficiency. The GHGs, most significantly carbon dioxide can lead to ocean acidification. Acidification has led to bleaching and loss of coral reefs which serve as great habitats for fishes and other organisms

The challenges

Tapping the fisheries resources in a manner that is both ecologically and economically sustainable is a difficult task. It involves credible fishery resource mapping, establishing their maximum sustainable and economic yields, developing means to harvest them, and to provide infrastructural support. Though Fisheries survey of India has been doing the fishery resource mapping very meticulously, it has very little backing from research on capture methodology and fishery oceanography. Fisheries oceanographic studies help us understand the distribution, abundance, migrations, and recruitment of fish as a response to variations in abiotic and biotic environment. Fishery oceanography, unlike other components of biological oceanography, needs different sets of research infrastructures usually unavailable with most institutions. Barring the vessels of FSI and Central Institute of Fisheries Education (CIFE), most of the vessels capable of fishing research and survey are below 20m length(LOA) restricting the endurance and space for oceanographic equipment. Exotic and invasive species, mostly introduced through shipping activities have been identified as a major threat to marine ecosystems and are to be monitored. Indian Ocean has always been vulnerable to criminals and anti-national activities. The sea route has also been used for transport of contrabands.

The frequent straying of fishermen into neighbouring country waters has jeopardised the safety of the fishermen and has also raised national security concerns. This has happened at maritime borders of Bangladesh, Pakistan and Srilanka. The coast guard performs a variety of duties ranging from patrolling the territorial and contiguous waters; enforcing criminal laws in these waters; ensuring compliance of laws relating to shipping, fishing and pollution. The said tasks are enormous given the area under its supervision.

The Road ahead

In the back drop of the above challenges, it is imperative to take key measures for greater appreciation of the Indian Ocean resources and for their sustainable and equitable exploitation. The present government has taken strong measures to have friendly and close political relationship with all neighbouring countries. This should be furthered through research and educational collaborations. India receives a handful of scholars from the sub-regions of IOR, to pursue higher education in fisheries. Enhancing capability to host more students from the region would help having goodwill emissaries, who in the long run can be engaged in joint research programmes. Better understanding of each other's concerns on a common knowledge platform would aid long term strategic partnership and sustainable and mutually benefitting use of the common fisheries resources.

Fishermen are exposed to various natural calamities and have the most challenging working conditions including the uncertainty of livelihood. Country need to invest on research on catch prediction and capture technology to better the income of this group. While poverty and poor education can make this vulnerable population be manipulated against the nation, if empowered, they can form an information network and a strong first line defence against any security threat through the sea route.

38

Climate Change and its Impact on Security of India and Indian Ocean

— Prof. Narottam Gaan

Climate change with its devastating consequences in terms of global warming, sea level rise, spread of diseases, storms and cyclones, air pollution, change in precipitation pattern and loss of habitats has turned to be the greatest threat to human kind of all other traditional threats posed by nuclear weapons. The traditional conceptualization of security in military terms controlled by states has not been able to provide security to human beings against the non traditional climate change threats. How can a missile plug the ozone hole or a nuclear weapon stop the frequency of cyclones and storms? The very inadequacy of traditional security analysis to meet the challenges of security threats emanating from climate change has led to rethinking security. In view of climate change that is taking place so swiftly the states are concerned with revisiting their strategic security analysis.

India is a vast country with a billion-plus population and it has a variety of climates and topographical features. It depends on the monsoons for meeting all its water needs, with its major rivers either originating from the Himalayas or fed by the mon-soon rains. Indian agriculture is critically linked to weather and climate. India has faced severe droughts, widespread floods and devastating tropical cyclones. The threat of climate change induced by global warming therefore looms large over India in a real sense. Although this problem has global dimensions, there are certain challenges to which India is more vulnerable and are specific to India. It would also like to ensure that the mitigation actions do not themselves become a stumbling block in the path of sustainable development.

India has reason to be concerned about the likely impacts of climate change on at least six major fronts:

- Change in the amount and distribution pattern of monsoon rainfall, which is India's only source of water
- Effect of temperature rise and change in the rainfall pattern on agricultural production and its impact on food security
- Possible increase in the frequency and intensity of tropical cyclones over the Bay of Bengal and Arabian Sea, which cause heavy losses of life and property in the coastal regions
- Threat of sea level rise to India's 7,500 km long coastline including the Andaman, Nicobar and Lakshadweep islands
- Retreat of Himalayan glaciers and its effect on the Indian rivers which originate in the Himalayas
- The possible effect on the health of the population arising from the growth of vector-borne diseases due to rising temperatures

Therefore, climate change is a pressing concern which requires urgent action. The nature of the problem is unique, the impact is all encompassing, and the risks to both infrastructure and human life are high. Recognising the immediate threat which impacts the entire world, all countries unanimously agreed on a legally binding global climate deal in the 21st session of the Conference of the Parties (COP 21) to the 1992 United Nations Framework Convention on Climate Change (UNFCCC). While a common framework may have been evolved for a legally binding agreement, actions for mitigation and adapta-tion have to be undertaken at the national level. There is a talk that the leaders of the world intend to arrive at a consensus to limit global warming below 2 degree centigrade. While India has called to base the deal on the principle of "climate justice," it has declared an ambitious Intended Nationally Determined Contributions (INDCs) which it hopes will contribute to a fair and an equitable climate deal. Notwithstanding the above, India needs to integrate climate change in its national security strategy.

Climate Change and National Security

The path-breaking 2007 report, 'National Security and the Threat of Climate Change', penned by the Military Advisory Board (MAB) of the Center for Naval Analysis (CNA) based in Washington D.C. concluded that "climate change acts as a threat multiplier for instability in some of the most volatile regions of the world" and "projected climate change will add to tensions even in stable regions of the world." As this would affect the US national security, the report recommended that "the consequences of climate change should be fully integrated into national security and national defence strategies."

This conclusion proved to be correct and over the years it has been observed that recurring flooding, drought, temperature extremes, frequent and/or more severe ex-treme weather events, sea level rise and temperature changes, exuberates the threats to food, water and energy security which impact the society at micro and macro levels. These societal impacts interact to affect national security and it is therefore essential that these impacts are quantified for national security planning. Apart from the impact on society, an increase in the frequency and intensity of extreme weather events directly impacts military assets and undermines military readiness. These findings were reaffirmed by the MAB in its May 2014 report, 'National Security and the Accelerating Risks of Climate Change', which also concluded that climate change affects the internal and external stability of a country and impinges on national security.

The US has been at the forefront of integrating climate change concerns in its national security and military strategy. In the July 2015 report, 'National Security Implications of Climate-Related Risks and a Changing Climate', the Pentagon said climate change is an "urgent and growing threat to our national security." The report reinforced that global climate change would have wide-ranging implications for US national security interests over the foreseeable future as it would aggravate existing problems such as poverty, social tensions, environmental degradation, ineffectual leadership, and weak political institutions that threaten domestic stability in a number of countries. This is viewed as a security risk as it impacts human security as well as affects the ability of governments to meet the basic needs of their citizens.

Climate Change and Ocean Management

The direst long-term threats to the collective interests of regional countries and peoples are non-traditional security risks. The combined impacts of climate change, environmental degradation, and ocean resource exploitation will profoundly affect the lives of millions in a region where many states have little capability to manage or respond to them (Gautam, 2009).

The Impact of Climate Change

The Geneva-based Intergovernmental Panel on Climate Change has concluded that the evidence of warming of the global climate system is unequivocal (Singh, 2015). Sea temperatures of the equatorial areas of the Indian Ocean are rising more quickly than elsewhere, and the likelihood of significant variances in the monsoon season has increased, which could create drought conditions for much of South Asia. There are increasing incidences of very intense storms, with higher peak wind speeds and heavier precipitation than has been typical, which could result in major coastal damage and massive flooding (2045, 2014). The changing frequency and intensity of extreme weather events,together with sea-level rise,are expected to have significant adverse effects. The scale of the potential climate change impact in the IOR is so immense as to be difficult to comprehend. The region is likely to be faced with a series of major weather-related events that, overtime, will impose human suffering and environmental damage that will cumulatively overwhelm and drain response resources and undermine resilience. The impact will be deeply felt in Asia; more than a billion people will have been adversely affected by the 2050s. The number of people annually subject to flooding in coastal populations is projected to increase from thirteen million to ninety-four million, primarily in South Asia and South-east Asia (Bureau Report, 2014). Millions of people in low-lying areas of Bangladesh, Pakistan, Sri Lanka, India, Vietnam, Burma (Myanmar), and Indonesia will be affected. The incidence of increasingly intense tropical cyclones, combined with growing coastal populations, will result in massive loss of life, damage to property, and large-scale transmigration, resulting in very frequent requirements for humanitarian assistance and disaster relief.

Marine Resources

Global warming will also have far-reaching implications for marine ecosystems (Chauhan, 2009). The effects of climate change will be compounded by increased competition for and environmental degradation and overutilization of the ocean's resources. Illegal, unreported, and unregulated fishing is predicted to increase in the Indian Ocean as stocks in traditional fishing areas are exhausted and fishermen are forced to move to deeper and more distant waters. There is already significant evidence of the wider implications of the illegal plundering of stocks by distant-water fishing fleets off Somalia. Local fisheries are being progressively dispossessed by external enterprises catching marketable fish, like tuna, to meet international demand (Ronamai, 2013). These circumstances exacerbate already tenuous food-security concerns in the IOR.

Maritime and Marine Challenges: Managing the Risks

Many IOR states have little or no capacity to fulfill their responsibilities for managing marine zones effectively. Exploitation, pollution, and water-security infringements will proceed unchecked in many parts of the Indian Ocean, both under national jurisdiction and in the high seas. Very few regional countries have the individual capacity to deal with human tragedies and environmental damage to coastal areas on a massive scale resulting from repeated natural disasters. The overall regional capacity to mitigate the risks from climate change is grossly inadequate. The widespread coastal devastation and loss of life caused by the 2004 Asian tsunami and the 2007 and 2009 Bangladesh cyclones point to the collective human security challenges that lie in the future. In those instances, many regional countries rallied in mutual support; significant response and recovery assistance was also provided by extra regional nations and organizations (Majumdar, October 13, 2014). The combined effects of climate change and marine environmental degradation pose profound threats over the medium and long terms to many IOR littoral states. Natural-disaster response and humanitarian aid will demand the application of resources and the coordination of collective efforts on scales and at frequencies far beyond anything so far experienced. Related human, food, and environmental security concerns will be greatly magnified. Vast cooperative responses will be required that will involve regional and extra regional maritime security forces.

A Direct Threat to Military Preparedness

Apart from the impact on society, an increase in the frequency and intensity of extreme weather events directly impacts military assets and undermines military readiness. Coupled with other possible impacts such as large-scale migration across borders, as seen recently in Europe, it has the potential to exacerbate conflicts around the world and is a threat to national security and stability. In the Indian context, Pai has analysed the impact of climate change on regional security and its implications for India's national security in Climate Change and National Security: Preparing India for New Conflict Scenarios and concluded that "India needs to develop military capabil-ities to address a range of new strategic scenarios"(Pai, 2008). In 2009, the Institute for Defence Studies and Analyses (IDSA) Working Group on Security Implications of Climate Change for India identified India's key vulnerabilities and highlighted the pos-sible adverse impact on the strategy and tactics of the Indian armed forces(Analyses,

2009). The Centre for Air Power Studies (CAPS), organised an event in September 2009 under the project Climate Change and the Military: Copenhagen and Beyond (Chauhan, 2009), which, was an initiative by a consortium of independent think-tanks, and the report titled, "Climate Change and the Military: The State of the Debate" that outlined the threats to the armed forces. PK Gautam has identified the impact of climate change on military operations and identified adaptation of the operational and tactical strategies and logistic plans of the military as one of the possible impacts (Gautam, Climate Change and the Military, 2009). The author opines that for the Indian Navy, Sea Level Rise (SLR) would affect naval operations at all levels of warfare – strategic, operational and tactical. Port operations, protection of coastal installations and changes in manning of ships have also been envisaged. Climate change as a threat to naval operations and infrastructure and its impact on maritime security in the Indian Ocean Region (IOR) have also been highlighted by A Singh(Singh, Climate Change and Maritime Security in the Indian Ocean Region, 2015). The threat from climate change is also acknowledged in the report on Global Strategic Trends – Out to 2045, released by the Ministry of Defence, UK, in 2014 (Ministry of Defence, 2014). It notes that by 2045, climate change is likely to have more noticeable effects such as the risks of flooding of coastal cities from the rising sea level as well as from the frequent and destructive weather events. The report titled Climate Change and US National Security by the Atlantic Council's Brent Scowcroft Centre, on international security, released in March 2016, also discusses the past, present and future of climate change and concludes that climate change is an environmental stressor and "ought to be seen as a threat to core US national security interests, both at home and abroad(Chiu, 2016)." In the recently concluded Shangri-La Dialogue in June 2016, Ashton Carter, Secretary of Defence of the United States, emphasised on the growing strategic impact of climate change. While addressing Asia's complex security challenges, he suggested that the region's myriad security challenges including "the growing strategic impact of climate change need to be addressed collectively." This placed climate change within the broader context of a range of pressing security threats facing the region(Femia, 2016). The Union of Concerned Scientists, in its report released in July 2016, titled The US Military on the Front Lines of Rising Seas, highlighted the direct impact of climate change on the military which included the risk of "losing land where vital infrastructure, training and testing grounds, and housing for thousands of its personnel currently exist". Out of the 18 militarily installations which were analysed, it was found that many of them, including the Portsmouth Naval Shipyard,

US Naval Academy at Maryland, Washington Navy Yard, Naval Air Station Key West, Naval Station Mayport, and Eglin Air Force Base at Florida are likely to experience extensive tidal flooding and extensive storm surges during hurricanes. The report also highlighted the gap between the military's current preparedness for sea level rise and the impending threats due to climate change (Erika Spanger-Siegfried, 2016). One of the main threats to naval establishments comes from the rising sea levels. The Intergovernmental Panel on Climate Change (IPCC) in its Assessment Report 5 predicts an increase in the sea level by 0.26-0.55 metres (m) by 2100 under a low emissions scenario, and by 0.52-0.98 m under a high emissions scenario. This would pose a significant threat to naval establishments located in Mumbai, Vishakhapatnam and Kolkata. Military infrastructure in these bases could be inundated, leading to a decrease in the efficiency of conducting Search and Rescue (SAR) andundertaking Humanitarian Assistance and Disaster Relief (HADR) missions. Naval bases, which are scattered across the country's coastline, are also at increased risk from the higher frequency and increasing intensity of typhoons, hurricanes and cyclones. Military stations in high altitudes, on the other hand, are at a higher risk from flash floods due to the melting ice. Droughts or excessive rainfall and extreme temperatures could threaten many training activities, and the environment for military operations may be constrained or altered in the long run. Natural disasters in India have led to devastation of infrastructure in military bases. This was most evident in the case of the Indian Navy when one of its premium naval bases at Vishakhapatnam was in the eye of the storm 'Hud-Hud' in October 2014. It was estimated that the loss to the national exchequer due to damage to the infrastructure in the Eastern Naval Command was around Rs 2,000 Crores (Report, 2014). While there was no damage to the ships and submarines, the cyclone uprooted trees and caused extensive damage to the infrastructure, including communication and power lines, disrupting the availability of essential commodities like water, petrol and electricity. While the impacts of higher temperatures, increased precipitation, changes in the salinity of water and other physical changes may affect the operational performance of the war-fighting machinery, communication equipment, sensors and other hardware, these changes would be gradual and can be offset by tuning the equipment. However, it is the uncertainty of climate change and the suddenness of the impact, which is hard to anticipate and prepare for. This requires flexibility, adaptability and incorporation of multi-functionality in the role and capability of the armed forces.

Conclusion

While India has a well defined and independent National Action Plan on Climate Change (NAPCC), it lacks in analysing the impact of climate change on national security. There is also no thought on integrating the responses to increased threats due to climate change in the existing military strategy. The US provides a good example of how military planning and operations can be viewed through the climate lens to enhance national security. It can be argued that the US operates in various parts of the world and provides security hegemony universally and is therefore impacted by the security implications of climate change across the globe. However, such an argument is equally valid for India at least in the regional context.

Integrating climate change in India's national security strategy should therefore be a priority, considering that the risks from the impact of climate change are increasing both in terms of the probability of occurrence of extreme climate events and in terms of the quantum of loss of human, natural and economic capital from climate related disasters. Early action on the assessment of risk and vulnerability, building capacity and capability to enhance resilience and adaptation will lead to lowering the impact of climate change. It can therefore be concluded that fine-tuning the national security strategy to analyse, assess, and prepare for the uncertainties of climate change are likely to reap rich dividends for India and steps must be taken to act in this direction.

References

- 2045, G. S.-O. (2014). Strategic Trends Programme Development, Concepts and Doctrine Centre, Ministry of Defence, UK.
- Analyses, I. f. (2009). Security Implications of Climate Change for India.
- Bureau Report. (2014). "Hud-hud Impact: Navy's ENC Suffers 2,000 Cr Loss. The Hindu Business Line.
- Chauhan, S. (2009). Climate Change, Disasters and Security: Issues, Concerns and Implications for India. Centre for International Policy Exchanges, University of Maryland.
- Chiu, P. E. (2016). "Climate Change and US National Security: Past, Present, Future," . Washington DC,: Atlantic Council.
- Erika Spanger-Siegfried, K. D. (2016). The US Military on the Front Lines of Rising Seas.
- Femia, C. W. (2016). Secretary of Defense Carter: The 'Growing Strategic Impact of Climate Change' Climate and Security.
- Gautam, P. (2009). Climate Change and the Military. Journal of Defence Studies, 3.

- Gautam, P. (2009). Climate Change and the Military. Journal of Defence Studies, 3(4).
- Majumdar, B. (October 13, 2014). Cyclone Hud-hud: Visakhapatnam's Naval Base Takes a Battering. The Times of India.
- Ministry of Defence, U. (2014). Global Strategic Trends - Out to 2045, Strategic Trends Programme Development, Concepts and Doctrine Centre.
- Pai, N. (2008). Climate Change and National Security: Preparing India for New Conflict Scenarios. The Indian National Interest Policy Brief.
- Report, B. (2014). Hud-hud Impact: Navy's ENC Suffers 2,000 Cr Loss. The Hindu Business Line.
- Ronamai, R. (2013). Uttarakhand Floods: Indian Army - The Unsung Heroes. International Business Times.
- Security, I. f. (2009). Climate Change and the Military.
- Singh, A. (2015). Climate Change and Maritime Security in the Indian Ocean Region. Journal of Defence Studies, 9(1).
- Singh, A. (2015). Climate Change and Maritime Security in the Indian Ocean Region. Journal of Defence Studies, 9(1).

39

Corporate Ocean Responsibility: Should it Become A Norm?

— Kritika Jain and Dr. Anupam Jha

Abstract

In this paper, authors try to explain the concept of Corporate Ocean Responsibility while highlighting provisions under the UN Convention on the Law of the Sea jurisprudence. This paper explores various dimensions of corporate social responsibility and highlights that corporate ocean responsibility is an extension of corporate social responsibility. This paradigm shift towards corporate ocean responsibility can be one of the ways by which India can attain Sustainable Development Goals (SDG), 2030 [especially goal no. 6 and 14]. At the end, the paper concludes that there is a need to come up with separate legislation in order to ensure the health of marine eco-system along with allocating liabilities on the big business houses causing damage to the marine environment.

Introduction

The credit for popularizing the approach of corporate ocean responsibility can be given to World Ocean Council (WOC). It brings together diverse ocean business community to tackle shared and cross sectoral issues.[1] This body holds every marine industrialist accountable for their corporate responsibility towards saving the environment. It makes rules and regulations for a corporation who tries to venture in the marine eco-system as no single company, much less one sector can solve those problems because they are so interconnected.[2]

The main objective of this approach is to maintain sustainable ocean resources so that it can be used for centuries without hindering the overall scientific development related to marine environment. So, this acts as a forum where they can participate and show their global commitment towards ocean sustainability.[3]

Issues involved and the Need to Create a Norm

The United Nations Convention on the Law of the Sea, 1982 establishes the legal framework within which all activities in the oceans and seas must be carried out. National and regional governments as well as global inter-governmental organizations have their parts to play in regulating those activities. The Part XI of the Convention provides for the principle of "Common Heritage of Mankind", which has become basis for many treaties, legislation and has revolutionized not only the law of the sea but the international relations also. This concept actually assumed prominence after the speech of Arvid Pardo, the Maltese ambassador to the United Nations, delivered at the United Nations General Assembly in November 1967, calling for the deep seabed beyond national jurisdiction and the resources contained therein to be declared the common heritage of mankind.[4] This principle was later embodied in Article 1 of United Nations General Assembly Resolution 2749, titled 'Declaration of Principles Governing the Seabed and Subsoil'.[5] This concept originated with reference to marine environment and later on was extended to other spheres of environment. Accordingly, one of the core components of this principle "common heritage of the mankind" provides that the representatives from all nations must manage resources contained in such a territorial or conceptual area on behalf of all human being since this common area belonged to everyone. This practically places liability on everyone who is involved in the area and especially deriving benefit from it to take extra care and thus this necessitates the need for a coordinated and shared marine world management which can be provided by corporate ocean responsibility. Thus, it can be said that corporate ocean legislation finds it roots in International law.

Corporate social responsibility contains a great proliferation of theories, approaches and terminologies. The norm of corporate social responsibility is already widely acceptable where corporations have a social as well as environmental responsibility towards environment as they operate in social setup.[6] This approach is based on the quid pro quo policy. One of the fundamental norms of corporate social responsibility points out that the concern for profits does not exclude taking into account the interests of all who have a stake in the firm. It has been argued that in certain conditions the satisfaction of these interests can contribute to maximizing the shareholder's value.[6] This same argument can be extended to corporate ocean responsibility.

The corporate ocean responsibility is based on the same ethos as corporate social responsibility. The difference is only that in corporate ocean responsibility, the responsibility that we are talking about is in the context of the ocean especially of those corporations who are dealing or doing business in that zone, in marine ecosystem, basically where they are interacting with the ocean and the species living there.

The age of free market and no responsibility have become obsolete. In this age of corporate constitutionalism where businesses are considered social institution, the corporations must use their power responsibly. Similarly, another theory which puts liability on the business houses especially working in marine vegetation is of corporate citizenship. India became the first country to bring legislation on corporate social responsibility and placed the corporations under the duty to fulfill their obligation as a social institution operating in the social environment. In the same way, there is a need to bring a legislation which will cater to the need of marine environment and make these corporations dealing with marine environment liable for their negligent or irresponsible acts.

The concept of corporate ocean responsibility is also compatible with the 17 sustainable development goals. In particular, the 6th goal which talks about "clean water and sanitation" and the 14th goal which talks about "life below water".[7] This focus on marine life preservation is rather recent as we didn't see any reference in the Millennium Development Goals and was only included in the post 2015 sustainable development agenda. Oceans provide livelihoods, subsistence and benefits from fisheries, tourism and other sectors. The Summary of the First Global Integrated Marine Assessment, or World Ocean Assessment,[8] found that the sustainable use of the oceans cannot be achieved unless the management of all sectors of human activities affecting the oceans is coherent. Managing the human uses of the oceans and seas has to be divided among many players. In the course of their activities, individuals and commercial enterprises that use the ocean on a constant basis take decisions that affect the human impacts on the ocean. They also help regulate the global eco-system by absorbing heat and carbon dioxide (CO_2) from the atmosphere. However, oceans and coastal areas are extremely vulnerable to environmental degradation, overfishing, climate change and pollution. Thus, the need to attain goal 14 has made it imperative to conserve and sustainably use the oceans, seas and marine resources for sustainable development and to create a new norm regarding the same.

One of the critical needs to assess progress in implementing national actions to achieve the SDG 14 is to collect data and information related to agreed targets and indicators. Given the diversity of targets and suggestive indicators, it can be safely assumed that there will be a need for significant amount of data and information that need to be collected and analyzed.[9] Corporate ocean responsibility can play an essential role in this data collection, information and research.

The advantage as well as challenge for a country like India in dealing with sustainable development is the need for outreach at various levels and using diverse set of approaches. While a national normative framework on SDGs is needed to channel investments, finances, expertise and outreach, it will be very important to design differential approaches to deliver the actions for impactful results. The role of people-centric approaches to sustainable development action can only be strengthened using multiple interventions at multiple levels.

Conclusion

Corporate ocean responsibility is essential not just in terms of saving the environment but also for consistent and continuous economic development as we have already seen so many examples where several marine sites have been reduced to nothing but mere hollow shadows of their glorious past. Corporate ocean responsibility becomes more imperative in the Indian context because India is surrounded by ocean from three sides and being one of the fastest growing economy in the world and one of the most developed and stable state in the south-east Asia. It is the responsibility of the Indian state to work on the creation of a new norm on corporate ocean responsibility. The maritime security should not be just limited to defending its coasts but also by adopting an approach through which liability of the corporations working in interaction with the marine life should be ensured. As we have already seen an oil spill can single handedly destroy an entire regional eco-system.[10] For instance, the recent oil spills of Sunder ban, Chennai.

As we are well aware that marine areas and resources are subject to complex combinations of state, open access and common property regimes, private property regimes and have relatively poorly defined rights of access and use. Historically, India's focus on oceans and marine resources management has been forward looking. With close to 129 institutions in the country working on marine and ocean related issues, largely supported by four ministries of Government of India, the challenge is the lack of coordination and cooperation among many of these institutions and programmes. In an unpublished study by the National Bio-diversity Authority (NBA) in 2012 it was estimated that the amount of money spent, annually, in support of biodiversity conservation actions in India is to the tune of Rs. 11,000-15,000 crores – both as direct and indirect support. However, the impact of this investment is hardly felt since the investments are dissipated, unavailable in timely manner for prioritized action. Thus, placing the responsibilities on the private players by creating norms will help in making the whole process more transparent and efficient to some extent.

The need for having a corporate integrity and lack of structure of private ownership has been reiterated at many fora. As India became the first country to incorporate corporate social responsibility in its legislation, it should not hesitate in bringing a legislation outlining the framework upon which corporate ocean responsibility can be implemented effectively. Similarly, in order to achieve inclusive results in sustainable development, it is important to forge long term partnerships with private sector and civil society groups in India. Specific and predictable guidelines should be made available just as has been done under the newly enacted Corporate Social Responsibility (CSR) law to ensure part of the proceeds from the revenue collections should be earmarked for an specially created trust fund aimed to support SDG implementation at local levels. The need for a separate legislation to specifically manage ocean environment is the need of the hour and thus a separate law is needed to provide for the guidelines and rules to place some of the responsibilities on the corporate houses.

References

1. Paul Houltus, Corporate Ocean Responsibility, Global Island News (September 16, 2015).
2. David Ritter, Oil and Water: Corporate Ocean Responsibility, Global Policy (June 17, 2010)
3. Greg Trauthwein, Corporate Ocean Responsibility, Marine Links (June 26, 2015).
4. Oxford Bibliographies: Available athttp://www.oxfordbibliographies.com/view/document/ obo-9780199796953/obo-9780199796953-0109.xml
5. Rudolph Preston Arnold, the Common Heritage of Mankind as a Legal Concept, The International LawyerVol. 9, No. 1 (January 1975), pp. 153-158.
6. Elisabet Garriga and Domnenec Mele, "Corporate Social Responsibility Theories: Mapping the Territory", Journal of Business Ethics, 2004.
7. United States Sustainable Development Goals 2030, Goal 14-Conserve and Sustainably Use the Oceans, Seas and Marine Resources for Sustainable Development.
8. Balakrishna Pasupati, "Maine Resources and Challenges to Sustainability", India and the sustainable development goals: the way forward, Research and Information System for Developing Countries.

9. India and sustainable development goals: the way forward, United Nations, Research and information System for Developing Countries.
10. Marine Insight, Corporate Ocean Responsibility and Its Importance to Marine Industry (June 21, 2016).

40

Role of India in "Asean Plus Six" in Reducing Trade Imbalance

— *Prof. Anant G. Amdekar*

Role of India in "ASEAN plus Six" in reducing trade imbalance in Indo- Pacific Region, leading to prosperity & growth through co-operation – a tool for Conflict Resolution

ASEAN has been establishing itself as a platform for Asian integrations and co-operations, working with other Asian nations to promote unity, prosperity, development and sustainability of the region, as well as working on solutions to resolve disputes and problems in the region. While mainly focusing on the Asia-Pacific nations, ASEAN also established communications with other parts of the world, to better promote world peace and stability. The organisation has a global reputation of promoting good-will and diplomacy among nations, shutting out any biased opinion or decision, and carrying the principle of non-interference.

Role of ASEAN –

1. ASEAN territorial waters cover an area about three times larger than its land counterpart. – So maintaining peace & efficient use of Sea-lines of communications is imperative.
2. Member countries have a combined population of approximately 625 million people, 8.8% of the world's population. – Hence huge market for other players – Countries need to use it to its advantage.
3. Formation of ASEAN plus Three (China, Japan & South Korea) in 1997 – To counterbalance the growing influence of the United States in Asia-Pacific Economic Cooperation (APEC)

4. ASEAN Free Trade Area (AFTA) - It is an agreement by member nations concerning local manufacturing in ASEAN countries – If fostered by respective countries then will lead less import dependence and will help in reducing trade imbalance.
5. Common Effective Preferential Tariff (CEPT) - This scheme was adopted as a schedule for phasing out tariffs with the goal to increase the "region's competitive advantage as a production base geared for the world market – again a measure to reduce import dependence of its member nations.

The above mentioned highlights narrating role of ASEAN is aptly mooted by President of Indonesia Susilo Bambang Yudhoyono in the conference held on 15th December, 2008 - "This is a momentous development when ASE-AN is consolidating, integrating, and transforming itself into a community. It is achieved while ASEAN seeks a more vigourous role in Asian and global affairs at a time when the international system is experiencing a seismic shift". Referring to climate change and economic upheaval, he concluded: "South-east Asia is no longer the bitterly divided, war-torn region it was in the 1960s and 1970s". (Quote – Unquote)

However, resurgent economic growth of China and India in last 2 decades has laid to expansion of territorial boundaries' for trade and commerce and its evident presence in Indo-Pacific region. Economic growth invariable leads to positive built up of reserves on Current as well as Capital Account. Such Capital base makes these countries to look outwards for investment opportunities.

However, these investments come with its perils – e.g. increased interference of such investing nations in the policy making of neighbouring states. Continuing interference leads to political ambitions leading to empirical behaviour at any cost – be it use of military aggression.

Growing trade and commerce activity thereby involving high economic stakes make such countries under the pretext of safety and security; deploy military power on the Sea routes –

Balancing the imbalance in Trade

ASEAN plus six (Australia, China, India, Japan, New Zealand, and South Korea).The trade bloc was formed to promote facilitates economic, political, military, educational and cultural integration amongst its members. The bloc and its partners have gained global prominence due to setup of offshore manufacturing facilities and thereby having an impetus to the intra-trade and inter-trade carried out by the bloc through maritime routes in the Indian Ocean.

Table 1: Trade of ASEAN countries

(In $ Billion)

Reporter	Partner	2014		2015		2016	
		Export	Import	Export	Import	Export	Import
ASEAN	Intra-ASEAN	330.209	277.904	287.279	239.394	276.219	239.794
ASEAN	Extra-ASEAN	963.778	963.317	884.627	861.735	874.260	846.070
ASEAN	World	1293.988	1241.221	1171.906	1101.128	1150.479	1085.865
ASEAN	European Union [EU]	132.507	115.673	127.387	100.456	130.415	103.146
ASEAN	India [IN]	43.694	24.299	40.553	19.498	37.634	20.815
ASEAN	United states [US]	121.213	90.295	125.443	83.560	131.071	80.730

Source: ASEANStats https://data.aseanstats.org/trade.php.

The Indian Ocean has some the busiest maritime routes viz. The South China Sea, Suez Canal, Babel-Mandeb, Strait of Hormuz, Strait of Malacca, etc. encompassing key choke points for energy trade and merchandise goods. These maritime route since long have been plagued with natural calamities, transnational maritime disputes and piracy. The incidence of piracy is the highest in the Indian Ocean.

Table 2: Statistics on Piracy acts in 2015

Maritime Route	Armed Robbery & Piracy Incidents
Straits of Malacca and Singapore	134
South China Sea	81
Western Indian Ocean	38
West Africa	35
South America and the Caribbean	5
North Atlantic and Pacific Ocean	4
Yellow Sea	4
Mediterranean Sea	2
Somalia-based pirates (Arabian Sea)	15

Source: Review of Maritime Transport 2016- Acts of piracy and armed robbery against ships reported to IMO in 2015; http://unctad.org/en/PublicationsLibrary/ rmt2016_en.pdf

In the wake of these developments, few more Doklam like incidences in APEC region are certainly on cards. Such scenario calls for more restraint and prudent behaviour on the part of big brothers in the region like China

& India. **The Author is of the opinion that "It requires paradigm shift in the mindsets of economically dominant nations that of – 'Instead of growth at any cost, mutual gain by improving inter-dependency be it economic, cultural, sports etc. with peace, confidence, unity & security as corner stones of growth in Indo-Pacific Region'."**

Another challange for ASEAN in this direction is - The recent ruling by the Permanent Court of Arbitration in favour of the Philippines, which found that China had no basis for its expansive claims to territorial waters in the South China Sea. The ruling has resulted in a further escalation of tensions between China and other claimant states, several of which are members of ASEAN. The ruling may prove to be a critical juncture for the region. - Milner & Schafer (2016). The ruling importantly demonstrates the strategic challenges for ASEAN, which has failed to reach a consensus on the South China Sea ruling despite several rounds of talks (Rapp-Hopper & Krejsa, 2016).

Further area of concern is, ASEAN currently trades more with other countries (80%) than among its member countries (20%). Therefore, ASEAN economies are more concerned about currency stability against major international currencies, like the US dollar. To counter such exigency, ASEAN members considered Asian Currency Unit (ACU) on the similar lines of monetary union of EU. **The Author is of the opinion that since on macroeconomic conditions, ASEAN member countries have different levels of economic development, capacity, and priorities that translate into different levels of interest and readiness, such major step requires caution, as Monetary Union is the ultimate stage in integration of markets. Experiences and difficulties faced by EU cannot be overlooked. In this regard, more matured approach and experience of India weathering South Asian currency Crisis and 2008 US Sub-prime crisis will be of great help to ASEAN member countries.**

In this context, "The ASEAN Way" Philosophy assumes greater importance. Logan Masilamani and Jimmy Peterson – Professors at Simon Fraser University has aptly summarised it as –"A working process or style that is informal and personal. Policy-makers constantly utilize compromise, consensus, and consultation in the informal decision-making process... it above all prioritizes a consensus-based, non-conflictual way of addressing problems. Quiet diplomacy allows ASEAN leaders to communicate without bringing the discussions into the public view. Members avoid embarrassment that may lead to further conflict."

Bill Hayton – Author of "South China Sea: the struggle for power in Asia" - published by Yale University Press – expressed that "ASEAN's 'natural' role is to be that of a security, community uniting all Southeast Asian countries as a bloc against rising great power rivalries".

It has been said that the merits of the "ASEAN Way" might "be usefully applied to global conflict management". Though it has its own limitations like Myanmar, Cambodia, and Laos emphasise non-interference while older member countries focus on co-operation and co-ordination. These differences hinder efforts to find common solutions to particular issues, but also make it difficult to determine when collective action is appropriate in a given situation. **The Author is of the opinion that India can use its growing economic dominance in bringing these players on a table and work out mutually acceptable solution based on Consensus and co-operation**. ASEAN plus Six is definitely a step in this direction.

Contribution of India to ASEAN members

Over the years there have been several sub-regional initiatives linking up India and the ASEAN viz. ASEAN–India Free Trade Area (AIFTA), South Asia Sub-regional Economic Cooperation (SASEC), Bay of Bengal Initiative for Multi Sectoral Technical and Economic Cooperation (BIMSTEC) and the Bangladesh-China-India-Myanmar corridor (BCIM) and the Regional Comprehensive Economic Partnership (RCEP).

India has been also keen in improving connectivity by sea for ASEAN countries, the recent Kaladan Multi-modal Transit Transport project with Mayanmar, Mekong-India Economic Corridor and the setting up of ASEAN Connectivity Coordinating Committee (ACCC) for Maritime Connectivity between India, Myanmar, Thailand, Cambodia and Vietnam which is aimed at creating soft infrastructure in order to permit seamless movement of goods and passenger traffic along the ASEAN-India connectivity corridors.

India demonstrates itself as a contributor to the Indo-Pacific balance through joint military exercises, patrolling, port calls, anti-piracy missions and humanitarian missions. It remains to be seen if such measures will be perceived as credible enough by the ASEAN countries owing to their territorial conflicts with China in the South China Sea. As illustrated in the recent Delhi Dialogue with the ASEAN members, wherein the ASEAN members are keen having Indian presence in the South China Sea and undertake a leadership role in order to maintain stability in the region.

Although India has increased proximity with the ASEAN countries, India have been emphasising the ties with its geographical neighbours viz. Bhutan, Nepal and Sri Lanka. With countries like Bhutan and Nepal being landlocked have been dependent on India for its maritime trade, they are by large in consensus with the Indian foreign policy. Sri Lanka on the other hand is also an emerging trade hub owing to its natural advantage in the Indian Ocean and is largely dependent for establishing itself as prime trade node in the region. India has also positioned itself for the neighbouring countries as an anchor to socio-economic development as well.

By the exception of Pakistan, it has been seeking Chinese aid. The China Pakistan Economic Corridor (CPEC) is an attempt made by both the Indian neighbours to gain strong foothold in the Indian sub-continent. While Pakistan is in consensus with China's foreign policy, China has adopted multi-lateral diplomacy by increasing trade with India as well in the past couple of years.

In the light of the above discussions, the Author is the opinion that "Owing to the shared interest in the Indian Ocean for growth and development, it has become highly important for the ASEAN and its partners to consider a broader perspective of "Indo-Pacific region". This perspective, currently in its nascent stage can be said to rest on three pillars of culture, commerce and connectivity between the countries. However the transnational issues amongst the countries are one of the key components withholding the development of this perspective. With China and India finding themselves emerging as important players in the global balance of power it is prudent for them to establish a foothold over the Indian Ocean in order to gain prominence in the Indo-Pacific region.

41

Reducing Trade Imbalances - To Boost India's Growth

— Dr Sudhakar Kasture

Trade imbalance is a serious concern for any developing country. If imports are more than exports, it not only puts pressure on exchange rate but also impacts the employment in the country. The situation has become much more serious due to globalization & explosion of technology / communication techniques in the last 20 years. A simple example of this is increase in import of mobile handsets and similar devices. The value for import of mobile handsets and similar devices (HS code 8517) has touched US $ 16.16 Billion in the year 2016-17.

The world itself is in imbalance when it comes to economic development & trade activities. China was nowhere on world scene prior to 1980 & today it occupies number one position in exports. The top 3 countries of the world (China, USA & Germany) account for more than 25% of world trade in goods.

Is this situation alarming for a country like India, which hopes to become a "very important" country if not super power? Considering the annual growth & our population we are likely to attract attention of all major countries as they see it as an opportunity to expand their trade. Imports therefore will not require any promotion but if import increases & export doesn't, it will create serious problem for us.

How do we analyze the situation, then?

Let's have some actual details. Our exports & imports for financial year 2016-17 are US $ 276.28 billion & US $ 384.32 billion respectively. The world statistics from WTO shows that, 30 countries (including India) account for approximately 82% of world's imports & exports. It is therefore essential to analyze the trade balance with remaining 29 countries. This is shown in the following table:-

Trade Balance 2016-17

Sl. No.	Name of the Country	USD Million India's Export	USD Million India's Import	USD Million Trade Balance
1.	China	10,196.69	61,286.24	-51,089.55
2.	USA	42,331.32	22,343.53	19,987.79
3.	Germany	7,213.14	11,583.64	-4,370.50
4.	Japan	3,855.59	9,756.21	-5,900.62
5.	Netherlands	5,084.92	1,895.71	3,189.21
6.	Hong Kong,China	14,157.57	8,205.14	5,952.43
7.	France	4,925.46	5,707.78	-782.32
8.	Republic of Korea	4,243.56	12,592.55	-8,348.99
9.	Italy	4,947.77	3,896.67	1,051.10
10.	UK	8,560.66	3,664.96	4,895.70
11.	Belgium	5,668.68	6,624.63	-955.95
12.	Canada	2,009.18	4,131.52	-2,122.34
13.	Mexico	3,473.77	2,944.48	529.29
14.	Singapore	9,568.95	7,086.45	2,482.50
15.	Switzerland	980.19	17,248.68	-16,268.49
16.	Spain	3,439.03	1,968.77	1,470.26
17.	Russia	1,932.04	5,552.30	-3,620.26
18.	Chinese Taipei	2,188.67	3,142.89	-954.22
19.	UAE	31,305.80	21,498.20	9,807.60
20.	Thailand	3,174.49	5,415.40	-2,240.91
21.	Poland	1,204.24	690.98	513.26
22.	Australia	2,966.51	11,154.48	-8,187.97
23.	Malaysia	5,234.17	8,934.93	-3,700.76
24.	Brazil	2,408.30	4,114.69	-1,706.39
25.	Viet Nam	6,815.43	3,320.56	3,494.87
26.	Saudi Arabia	5,134.63	19,945.17	-14,810.54
27.	Czech Republic	534.32	539.25	-4.93
28.	Austria	385.07	908.34	-523.27
29.	Indonesia	3,501.46	13,437.43	-9,935.97
	Total	**197,441.61**	**279,591.58**	**-82,149.97**

It is interesting to see that, we have huge trade deficit with some countries like China, Switzerland, UAE, Saudi Arabia, Indonesia etc. These 29 countries cumulatively account for 76% of our total deficit. Certain percentage of deficit is attributed to our requirement of petroleum products & our obsession for Gold & Silver. Other than these two, we import lot of machineries (mechanical as well as electrical) from China. Given this situation, the real question is how do we reduce this trade deficit?

There are few concerns:-

1. **Integration into global value chains:-** In today's globalized world goods are not manufactured in a single country. Naturally, the manufacturing process gets divided between countries & everyone wants to source the goods from those countries which are most competitive. This in turn requires adaptation of technology & process expertise. This does not necessarily mean expertise in manufacturing alone. It also includes expertise in services as well. Most of the consumer products today require 'design' as pre manufacturing service and 'branding / distributing' as post manufacturing service. The competitiveness of a country is therefore seen as a combination of manufacturing processes & services. India has a great chance as we have large SME sector. However, this is not really reflected in our trade efforts. There are many reasons for this like lack of awareness, technology gaps, skill development, transaction costs etc. etc. Unless these issues are sorted out, our SME strength would remain unrepresented in the larger context. It is also important to note that, this is the sector which provides employment on large scale.
2. **Impact of technology:-** The developed world is talking of Fourth Industrial Revolution, internet of things & use of artificial intelligence in the area of manufacturing. Robotics & big data analysis are another two factors, which add to the complexity & cost of all businesses. It's ironical that, we provide solutions to rest of the world except to our own systems. It's very common to hear that, our servers do not work & international trade transactions get hampered because of system failure. This is not happening once in a while but happening almost regularly.

   We need to understand that, international trade is an area where buyers do not wait indefinitely for any one. If we cannot deliver, the buyer has many options, hence if we need to increase exports we need to make sure that our systems should work 24*7*365.
3. **Trade Facilitation Agreement (TFA) & transaction cost:-** TFA is an important mile stone for the WTO. This agreement has come into effect on 22nd February, 2017 & aims to reduce transaction costs & red tape worldwide. This also aims at bringing impartiality, transparency & discipline related to charging of fees. When implemented fully it is expected that, it will add to $ 1 trillion worth of business world-wide on an annual basis. We therefore

need to make sure that, our exporters become aware of the provisions of TFA.

4. **Free Trade Agreements (FTA):-** FTAs are being entered left, right & center by and between countries. This has resulted in bilateral trade or trade within geographical blocks on preferential terms. As a country we have also started negotiating with many important economies of the world. FTAs offer concessions in custom duties & therefore are important tools to increase our exports. Unfortunately, we are more defensive in our approach. We need to become aggressive & present our interests supported by proper statistical data in order to have better market access. We are a large market ourselves & hence, we are definitely in a better position to ask for duty concessions to get legitimate market access for manufactured goods. Again, awareness about FTAs continues to be a big concern.
5. **Our Focus:-** We need to be export oriented. It should be our national interest & priority. While we need ease of doing business & competitiveness, we also need facilitating attitude, particularly at the hands of Government's field formations. Exporters need to be respected. (Our Hindi films show them as villains)

At the end, we must realize that, today's world is economic in nature. Trade is an important aspect of global economy. If we wish to achieve our legitimate position in the world, it cannot be achieved merely by talking about past glories. We need to showcase that, we are relevant & good trade partners. A surplus trade balance would definitely be a symbol of our economic strength.

Let's achieve this by putting our whole hearted efforts, collectively.

42

India and China Bilateral Trade Relations

— Dr. Neelam Mathur

China and India, the two largest developing countries in the world, share a number of interests especially in the field of domestic development, and economic reform. They are experiencing a period of rapid economic growth. However, both the states are also struggling to define their role in the world given their new profound influence on the global economy. Both promote the notion of a multipolar world in which they may serve as bigger players alongside the United States.

China's strategic interests in India follows from its desire to maintain a peaceful international environment create friendly relations with all the states and especially with neighbours, prevent any attempt towards the formation of anti-China blocs and finally develop new markets, investment opportunities and resources to stimulate its economic growth. It also wants to resolve its domestic problems in a coherent manner.

To achieve all these objectives, it is necessary for China to have friendly relations with India, despite the inherited bilateral issues. On the other hand, India's own focus on the internal development encourages it to cultivate positive relations with China. However, the attitude within India towards forging cordial relations with China remains mixed to some extent due to the historical legacy of China-India relations.

While the left parties such as the Communist party of India (Marxist) has always sought the friendly relations with China, but the right wing parties and some people within the security establishment view China as a major security threat.[1] From this perspective, it would be pertinent here to state these areas in which both the sides compete with each other and which is a major source of distrust, suspicion and misunderstanding between them.

Bilateral Issues between China and India

There are factors within and outside between China and India which still impacts their relations, for instance, border and Tibet issues are more prominent and recently, the water issue has also surfaced in the bilateral relations between China and India. These bilateral issues will not only effect on their present relations but have a negative impact on their future relations as well; it will also affect the process of their rise and the peace and stability in and outside the region.

Border issue

The main problem between the two countries is the Border question, which is a historical one. The Border issue is rooted in the disputed status of the McMahon Line, which defines the border between India and Tibet. India recognizes this agreement as the basis for its territorial claim while China objected the validity of McMahon Line which was drawn in 1914 Simla convention because China believes that it was not a party to Simla Convention so it is not bound to accept the boundary demarcated by Simla convention.[2] India claims 43,180 squares Kilometers of Jammu and Kashmir occupied by China including 5180 square kilometers cede to China by Pakistan under a 1963 China-Pakistan boundary Agreement. On the other hand China claims 90,000 square kilometers of territory held by India in Arunachal Pradesh.[3] There has not been a remarkable progress in re-solving the border dispute between the two sides due to the importance of Aksai Chin to China because it is the main link between Tibet and Xinjiang province of China and Arunachal Pradesh to India is crucial to stability in India's north-eastern insurgent affected areas.

After the 1962 war, relationship between China and India remained hostile for several decades. India's grant of statehood to Arunachal Pradesh in the late eighties (February 1987) which China claims as a part of South Tibet caused the hostility on the bilateral relations to such an extent that another border war seemed about to happen.[4]

In the same way, as China seeks return of Arunachal Pradesh on religious grounds, India demands the return of the sacred Mount Kailash Manasrovar in Tibet, since it is a sacred place associated with the Hindu religion.[5] However, ease on border and overall border relations began to improve following the border agreements in 1993 and 1996 between the two states. Since then, both sides have agreed to keep working on the border issue and resolved that any disagreement on border issue should not be allowed to affect the overall bilateral relations. The two sides have also pursued Confidence Building Measures (CBMs) along the border which includes mutual troop cut, regular meetings of local military commanders and other confidence measures. Further, an additional step was taken for the resolution of border disputes in 2003 when both the sides appointed Special Representatives to address the border issue.[6] Since, then the Special Representatives have held number of talks to resolve the border issue, but so far no breakthrough has been achieved. Here the main reason has been that the unsettled border provides China the strategic leverage to keep India uncertain about its intentions and nervous about its capabilities and ensuring India's good behaviour on issue of vital concern to China.

Further, an unsettled boundary also suits the contemporary Chinese interests, for China's claims in the western sector are complicated by the India-Pakistan dispute over Kashmir, and China wants to engage India under strategic pressure on two fronts that is from China and Pakistan.[7] Moreover, it should also be taken into consideration here that although India has recognized. Tibet as a part of China, at the popular level, there remains significant sympathy for the Tibetan cause within India. Due to the security threats and national interests, neither side is willing to give away their claims or compromise over the disputed territory. However, it may be once again reiterated here that from the India's point of view, "Tibet is not a critical issue in China-India relations because Indian government is neither abettor nor instigator of political cause of the Tibetans".[8]

For India, resolving the border issue ranks higher than status of Tibet. That is why during the Prime Minister Shri Atal Bihari Vajpayee's visit to China in 2003, India formally recognized . Tibet as an integral part of China. However in recent years China shown more aggressive policy towards border issue with India. In May 2007, the Chinese government denied a visa to an Indian official to visit China on the grounds that he was from Arunachal Pradesh which considers its own territory. In addition, there have been continued media reports of the People's Liberation Army's (PLA's) encroachments across the Line of Actual Control (LAC). This recent increasing aggressive policy over the disputed borders has led to a rapid melt down in Sino-India border talks and a 'mini-cold war' on the border issue was prominently visible. Again in March, 2009 China attempted to block a $ 2.9 billion loan to India from the Asian Development Bank (ADB) on the grounds that it was destined for development of Arunachal Pradesh.[9]

Thus, border issue between China and India is one of the delicate issues and needs immediate resolution so that some long lasting peace can be brought in this part of the world.

Water issues between China and India

In all the times, water was regarded as a precious commodity and is essential for human existence. That is why, its possession bestows power. The preciousness and possession in geopolitical mechanics makes water a strategic commodity and its role as a strategic asset or vulnerability cannot be over-estimated. Thus, seen in this context, water can become a source of both contention and co-operation in the context of contemporary world.

In case of China and India, water issues are becoming major area of concern between two states. In fact, many strategic thinkers are arguing that disputes relating to water will be major source of conflict between the two countries in the future. China's plan of constructing big dams and diverting the water of rivers to its own advantage has discontented in India. As there are four rivers that flow from China to India, the two countries must have a better understanding relating to water sharing and other attending benefits out of these rivers. However, China's strategic advantage over these rivers makes it possible for her to counter-balance India on many other issues. A deep analysis of the water issues between the two countries is quiet relevant her.

China trade relations are the most important part of bilateral relations between India and China. From a temporary decline in the the influx of Chinese imports in the Indian markets, the scenario seems to have changed - India is enjoying a positive balance of trade with China. The India China trade relations are regulated by the India China JBC, which ensures a free exchange of products and services between the two nations.

According to the Ministry of Commerce of China (MoCC, 2011), trade in services, which grew at a modest rate earlier, has registered a high growth in the recent years.4 Foreign direct investment added up to $378 billion cumulatively with about $108 billion in 2008. Rising current account surpluses combined with strong capital flows brought the net international reserves to about $1.55 trillion in 2007, surpassing those of Japan in the present decade. However, external sector performance was adversely affected during the period of recession.

Conclusion

It can be concluded that India's long standing border dispute with China particularly China's claims on Arunachal Pradesh through which the river Brahmaputra flows, comes in the way of meaningful cooperation on the water issues. Here it can be said that border issue and water issues between both the two states is closely interlinked with each other. In future, China is likely to use water as a tool to pressurize India and to exact concessions on boundary question. Thus, water will be the prime issue, apart from the border issues, that will determine the future relations between the two largest states of the world India and China. Besides, there life sustaining rivers coming from Tibet region of China into India will be the major stimulant of cooperating or conflict between the two.

43

Good Order and Governance at Sea in a Maritime Theory Model

— Cmde (Dr) Odakkal Johnson

Abstract

This short paper examines few issues in a crisp manner to outline an outlook that is titled as "Maritime Theory of International Relations." It begins with salient of the scope and security of the medium and then examines classic peace operations through later part of the twentieth century. Any recent review of maritime security needs to factor international actions against piracy in the period 2008 – 14. The last case study would be the prolonged journey of conflict and collaboration in the South China Sea. Such a spread would provide a possible model of maritime approach to good order and peace in a governance perspective. This is a brief summary of a larger study as a thesis in maritime governance.

Governing A Global Common

The Ocean dimension faces key challenges bringing political, military, economic and obviously academic attention. With rise of navies in the emerging multi-polar world this era has seen greater naval deployments at a range and scale larger than ever before. The maritime dimension renders the establishment of good order quite different and somewhat complex. Boundary issue and consequently territoriality is quite rigid and politically inviolate over land and air space of a nation. However, at sea, a ship of a particular nationality can traverse through even the territorial waters of another nation, under the "right to freedom of navigation." This certainly complicates both conduct and governance of maritime operations.

The Maritime Medium is Unique

Hugo Grotius (1583-1645) in his classical presentations on Mare

Liberum (1609) and De Jure Belli ac Pacis, (On the Law of War and Peace) (1625) had a central assumption of solidarity of states with respect to enforcement of international law. The neo-Grotian movement in the 20th century considered use of force as feasible in the cause of international solidarity. Thus the competing ideologies of controlled governance of the sea stands in contrast with freedom of the sea.

Shared global heritage jostles for attention with national power in the emerging world order. The maritime environment offers power to any nation state to ensure free and full use of the seas, for trade, transportation and to meet its resource needs. Yet, the ocean is anarchical and the principle of 'Mare Librum' provides a liberal, coordinated spectrum. The sea is a resource, as well as a means of transportation, information and of dominion. Increased economic activity threatens regional eco-systems and potential of an oil disaster exists in any sea area. Therefore future maritime conflicts will have a global spread.

In the words of Ken Booth, navies function as an instrument of state policy. While naval project power and show presence, they are also tools in catalysing partnerships and in building trust and creation of interoperability. A pursuit of peace and stability at sea is a significant driver for maritime cooperation flowing from a shared global as well as a regional partnership initiative.

Peace Operations at Sea

Naval Forces have contributed towards peace operations by maintaining shipping corridors, keeping supply chain open by sea, undertaking non-combatant evacuation from strife torn regions and maintaining good order at sea. The consent of the parties to dispute resolution is not necessarily required, although there will be a defined mandate to use force. The Indian stand on peace operations was that successful UN peacekeeping operations require clear and unambiguous support and mandate of the UN Security Council.

The first UN Naval Peacekeeping Operation was to render assistance to a mediation process. The blue UN ensign flew from US warships in support of Count Folke Bernadotte's mission to Palestine in 1948. The UNTEA Ops in New Guinea (1962-63) and the ONUCA Naval operations (1990) in the Gulf of Fonseca both involved mechanism for organisation and deployment of naval platforms. In a neo-realist approach there would have to be an agreement with willing cooperation of all entities. Even in a neo-liberal approach the methodology would be evolve a Code of Conduct.

The deployment of military assets in a 'what is available' working arrangement, comes out as a functional mechanism. The UNIFIL Maritime Task Force (2006 onwards) has been the embodiment of both mandate at the apex level and functional mechanisms at the operational level that has enabled effective assistance to the Lebanese Navy in securing the country's 200 kilometres of coastline.

Micheal Pugh (1994) had earlier itself enunciated that it has sometimes been practical and convenient to delegate naval peace operations to a single state. While well-evolved functional mechanisms provide a means to overcome inter-operability issue, the logic of a focussed and specific mission undertaken by integral unit is far more effective.

Response to Piracy off Somalia

The profile of piracy in Gulf of Aden and West Indian Ocean in the period 2008 – 09 indicated that incidents by Somali Pirates grew from 111 in 2008 to 217 (with 867 hostages) in 2009. The percentage of successful hijacking compared to attempted incidents however reduced due to increased Multilateral Maritime Military action and heightened awareness and precautions. There was a decisive mandate through UN Security Council resolutions passed in 2008 and later. They reflect the international political mandate for mitigating the growing crisis. The UN Security Council Resolution 1816, gave foreign warships the right to enter Somali waters for the purposes of repressing acts of piracy and armed robbery at sea, using all necessary means as permitted under International Maritime Law on the High Seas.

There were a number of regional and extra-regional players (stake holders) with a direct interest in good order off the Somalian Coast. In January 2012 Japan, China and India implemented a mechanism of Escort Convoy Coordination with one state taking the role as lead navy in a particular sector. These efforts were also a result of the trilateral dialogue during the meeting of the Shared Awareness and Deconfliction [SHADE] initiative that sought to address the topics of Asian security developments and non-traditional security issues. SHADE was a mechanism under a concise cooperative mandate made individual missions against acts of piracy at highly effective and enhanced the cooperation at an international political level.

South China Sea Arena

South China Sea is a major flashpoint in East Asia for the potential conflict of national interests and threat to peace and security. The Paracels and the Spratlys, are two archipelagoes consisting of hundreds of tiny islands, reefs, and sandbanks. The islands are desirable not for their land, which totals about five square miles, but for their proximity to some of the world's busiest shipping lanes, access to fishing resources, and the oil and gas believed to lie beneath. From 1974 to 2012 there have been 25 reported incidents of clashes in the South China Sea because of territorial disputes. While the disputes have remained largely stable and not emerged as a runaway flashpoint, the region continues to draw attention of the international community as well as academics. There is also a clear desire both indigenous as well from extra-regional powers to see peace and good order in South China Sea.

The biggest initiative for peace emanated from ASEAN and its engagement with China. Since 1994, ASEAN and China have been looking for a lasting solution to the maritime territorial disputes in the South China Sea. ASEAN and China have managed to craft a Declaration of Conduct of parties in the South China Sea or the DOC which is a non-binding declaration that was signed on November 4, 2002 in Phnom Penh by the 10 members of ASEAN and China. Indo-Pacific states have continued to evolve a mandate using multilateral frameworks such as the ASEAN Regional Forum, The East Asia Summit, ASEAN Defence Ministers Meeting (ADMM) plus, etc. On a naval-operational level, states have been cooperating through multilateral frameworks such as the Western Pacific Naval Symposium (WPNS) and Indian Ocean Naval Symposium (IONS), both of which have made a significant contribution to regional stability.

A significant initiative for peace, came from the President of Taiwan, MaYing-Jeou (2015). This calls for maritime cooperation and shared codes of conduct in order to enhance peace and prosperity. China's State Councilor Yang Jiechi (2015) has stated that China and ASEAN nations would carry out cooperation in the areas of marine economy, maritime connectivity, marine science research and environmental protection, safety and security, and people to people exchanges on the sea.

Creation of new dialogue mechanisms may also be worth consideration. A South China Sea Coast Guard Forum, modeled after the North Pacific Coast Guard Forum, which cooperates on a multitude of maritime security and legal issues, could enhance cooperation through information sharing and knowledge of best practices. The creation of a South China Sea information sharing center would also provide a platform to improve awareness and communication between relevant parties.

Sekiguchi (2013) stated that the Indo-Pacific region is known for its ethnic, cultural and ideological diversity. Diversity is an opportunity to develop new ideas of multilateral collaboration. Whereas the scenario in the South China is still evolving, there is a loud voice and a decisive mandate for peace and good order in these waters.

The model of approach

Drawing upon the best of the Neo realism (or institutional) and Neo liberalism theories, the maritime dimension presents a model of **"Mandate – Mechanism - Mission"** approach.

The first and apex consideration is a **Decisive Mandate**. A small group of key stakeholders evolve the mandate for adressing issues of concern. The second component is the working out Functional Mechanisms for progressing the overarching mandate. This would involve many more agencies and sub-components beyond the original stakeholders that drew up the mandate. This is a larger operational level process. The third and final part is to executing Specific Missions. This necessitates well defined command and control and tactical integrity. At the same time the boundary lines would have been already defined in the prescribed mechanisms and amidst the cover of the larger mandate.

This paper gives the basic findings of a comprehensive study which outlines of the identified Mandate – Mechanism – Mission as a model of effectiveness definitely in the maritime dimension. This has the scope of better relationships and forging workable partnerships for effective security and freedom of the ocean space in the emerging international environment.

44

Towards Co-operation in Indo Pacific Region - An Evalutionery Perspective

— ***Prof. Rajiv Gupte***

Abstract

Inter-state disputes come and go. Any nation's relationship with other nation is born; wax and wane, sometimes die or gets modified. In that sense it evolves- presumably in the way that can be analyzed systematically, Evolutionary paradigm is a relatively newer paradigm as compared to Realism, Liberalism, Marxism or constructivism and their variation. Theory developed here seeks to lay foundation for resolving inter-state conflicts and contributes to the bridging of the environment – agent gap with co-evolutionary perspective. While conflict resolution does not necessarily mean co – operation, the latter is almost impossible without the former at all levels. This is a descriptive and not prescriptive paper.

Strategic rivalries involve the identification of competitors as usually menacing because they invoke some potential for military threat that is not associated with other competitors (Thompson, 1998). The potency of such rivalries can be reduced by changes in strategy (Modelski, 1996). US – Japan, Sino – US, US – Vietnam, Sino – Russia have been such case studies. Strategies evolve as a consequence of selection processes operating in a context characterized by variety. Effective strategies may not necessarily be the best or progressive; but they need to affect co-evolution. The leaders or decision maker is the focal point here. The leader must choose change in strategies in some sense. That is, there must be some linkage between individuals and strategic choices (Ader and Young). Armstrong emphasizes on environmental determination, which may also modify strategic calculus. Lebow (1995) hypothesis that, conciliatory accommodation is likely when leaders

1. One committed to internal reforms that require improved relation with adversary

2. Recognize that confrontation has been counterproductive in past
3. Expect adversaries to respond positively to conciliation approach.

They have been also mentions of "mutual fear of third party" and "economic incentives."

Expectation Theory (Thompson, 2001) assumes that:

- Actors seldom functions as unitory decision makers and various domestic groups also matter.
- Actors are not hyper rational. They operate with imperfect information
- Actors distinguish other actors with competitor and non-competitors categories
- Past memory matter
- Expectation, strategies and behaviour have inertia
- Incentives in form of stocks can overcome inertia
- Shocks must be interpreted

Thus, Expectation Theory suggest that,

Deescalation = shocks + Expectancy Revision

+ Consolidated policy entrepreneurship

+Reciprocity + Re enforcement.

Also, third party pressure can contribute but, it is neither necessary nor sufficient This is especially appropriate in case of dyadic transactions. Here, shocks or innovations can change the population of strategies and they are introduced as random mutations. Variation creates opportunity for evolution in the population of strategies. With same substitution and corresponding reinforcement, conflictual dyads may "choose". The newly co – operative strategies, thus causing evolution.

Here the author proposes Rugged landscape. NK theory for conflict resolution. Fisher's fundamental theory explains the role that variation plays in adaptation

(i) There is no cardinal – this emphases that here is a lot of variation among species, (here, strategies)

(ii) Rugged landscape

Adaption is one of the basic phenomena of biology (Williams 1966); it is the process whereby an organism becomes better suited to its habitat (Dobzhansky 1968). This fundamental process is present in all living organizations, and as such, we expect to observe it in any organization that can be considered as a living one, with companies being an ideal candidate. In this paper, we have examined the evolutionary process of nations in an effort to be better suited to their operating environments. We used Wright's work (1931, 19332) to efficiently define the operating environment within which the nations move and try to adapt to: a fitness landscape consists of a multi-dimensional space in which each attribute (gene) of an organism is represented by one dimension of the space and the final position in the space indicates the fitness level of the organization (Levinthal, 1997). The fitness is defined as the overall expected performance of a nation that follows a specific strategic form.

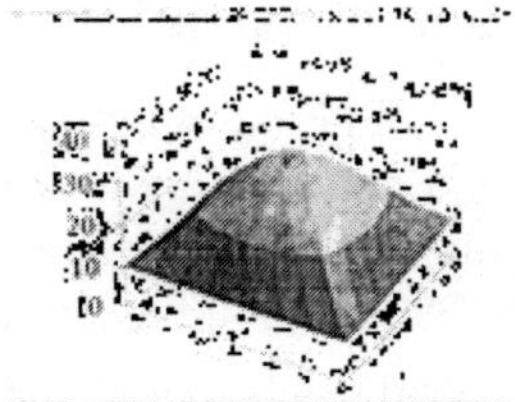

Fitness Landscape for K=0

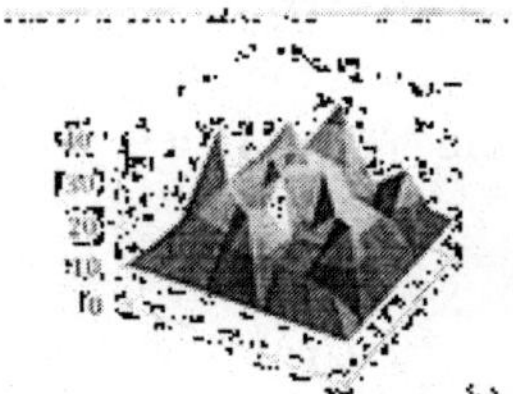

Fitness Landscape for K>0

Here, N one the binary attribute of strategies and K are the peaks of the landscape

(iii) Replicator dynamics Agents would copy those strategies which are 'fit'.

Discussion

- Interdependency spawned by action of multiple players has made landscape rugged.
- When the choices of numerous independent players interact, they have a great difficulty finding an optimal solution.
- Dynamics of co-evolution makes dancing landscape. Hence no single attractor.
- But seek local optima.
- Mutually interacting entities self-organize.
- To get to the highest point on a given fitness landscape they must consider interactions that will cause landscape to shift and change the menu of option.
- Adoptive processes is pulled towards local optima.
- When multiple agents engage in parallel processing and perform their particular optimization at the same time, they fundamentally change behaviours of whole system.

- More rugged a landscape (blocks views) more limited the support of mutual information's about the strategies of other players & the more confined given players be to the local optima.
- In stable landscape, Six Sigma is a better option, but is dancing landscape, variation leads to fitness.

Interpretation

With entrepreneurial leadership, it is appropriate to affect variation and not getting stuck to local optima. Regional co – operator & dyadic relationships at economic, strategic, cultural levels will lead to co – evolution and change the external environment. This, confirmed with Expectancy Theory will lead to further improved relations and co – operation in Indo – Pacific region.

It is therefore essential to develop many dyadic relations and manage cluster coefficient as per the requirement to modify the rugged landscape.

References

1. Thompson, William, "Evolutionary interpretation of World politics", 2001.
2. Modelski. George, "Globalisation as evolutionary process', 2008.
3. Kauffman, Stuart, "The Origins of order", 1993.
4. Gavrilets, Sergey, "Fitness landscape and the origin of species", 2004.
5. Root, Hilton," Dynamics among Nations", 2013.

45

Characterization & Corrosion Studies of Nano Structured Slip Coated Al Fibers for Passive Radar Countermeasure

— ***Dr. Sunil D. Kahar***

Abstract

Chaff is metal foils or glass fiber with a metal content which is cut into various lengths with varying frequency responses. From Second World War different types of chaff material were put into use like Aluminum foil, Silver-coated nylon monofilament, Aluminized glass. Internationally at present Aluminum coated glass fibers are widely used as chaff materials to reflect electromagnetic waves in armed forces as a countermeasure or decoy against hostile attack due to low density and high electrical conductivity. In present work, attempt were made to developed nano-structured Aluminum fiber by wet etching process using NaOH solution which was subsequently treated with organic media at different dipping time to developed coating. The corrosion behaviour of this coating was studied by potentiodynamic testing according to ASTM G 5 standard in 3.5 % NaCl solution. The film was characterized by AC Impedance spectroscopy while morphological & micro structural changes were observed with help of SEM. Studies shows that the coating developed on Al fiber using new organic media has got better corrosion resistance, good compactness and uniformity with compared to imported fiber.

Keywords: *Chaff, Nano structured fibre, wet etching, slip coating, potentiodynamic study, AC impedance spectroscopy*

1. Introduction

Chaff is metal foils or glass fibre with a metal content which is cut into various lengths with varying frequency responses. It is used to reflect electromagnetic energy and act as passive radar countermeasure.

Chaff material is used to confuse and distract weapon system which is operated by radar. From Second World War onwards Chaff material deployment is one of most cost effective against radar related threats. For example in event of rocket attack vessels or aircraft may use chaff in decoy systems for defence by projecting the chaff away from vessel or aircraft and causing the chaff to disperse to form chaff cloud, Which result in creating false target away from original target and in turn diverting rocket from original path.[1] The idea of using chaff developed independently in the United

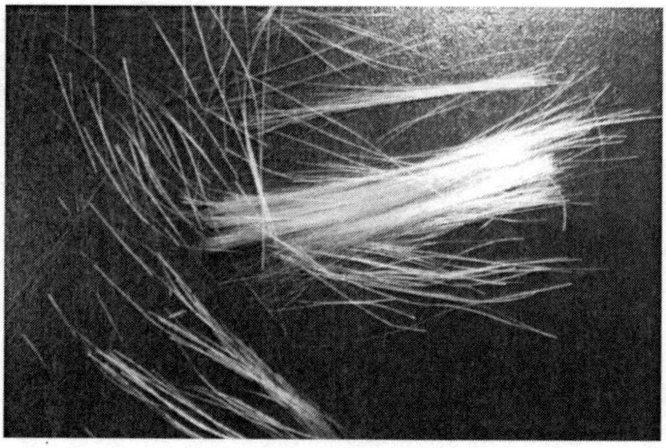

Fig.1: Aluminized Chaff.

Kingdom, Germany and the United States. In 1937, British researcher Gerald Touch, while working with Robert Watson-Watt on radar, suggested that lengths of wire suspended from balloons or parachutes might overwhelm a radar system with false echoes and R. V. Jones had suggested that pieces of metal foil falling through the air might do the same. In early 1942, a Telecommunications Research Establishment (TRE) researcher named Joan Curran investigated the idea and came up with a scheme for dumping packets of aluminum strips from aircraft to generate a cloud of false echoes. An early idea was to use sheets the size of a notebook page; these would be printed so they would also serve as propaganda leaflets. It was found the most effective version used strips of black paper backed with aluminum foil, exactly 27 cm × 2 cm (10.63 in × 0.79 in) and packed into bundles each weighing 1 pound (0.45 kg). The head of the TRE, A. P. Rowe, code-named the device "Window". In Germany, similar research had led to the development of Düppel. The German code name came from the estate where the first German tests with chaff took place, circa 1942.Once the British had passed the idea to the US via the Tizard Mission, Fred Whipple developed a system (according to Harvard Gazette Archives) for dispensing strips for the USAAF, but it is not known if this was ever used.[2] The more recent types include Aluminum-coated glass filaments, developed by Bjorksten Research Laboratories in the USA, and silver coated nylon monofilament developed by Chemring. These three types constitute the majority of chaff material being manufactured today.[3]

1.1 International Status of Chaff material

There are different kinds of chaff material that are put into use since Second World War. This includes Silver-coated nylon monofilament, Aluminum foil, Aluminized glass, Zinc-coated glass filaments and copper-coated polyester filament. Each and every material has its own limitation; Silver coated nylon monofilament can't be produced below 90 μm and same time it is very costly that is why it is not currently used. Aluminum foil chaff has very good flight motion but has low packing density i.e. less number of foils can be packed in given space which makes it ineffective against high frequency radars. Zinc-coated glass filaments and Copper-coated polyester filament offers no significant performance advantages over other chaff types as both material have high density when compared to Aluminum, Zinc is about 3.4 times resistive then Copper and is therefore near the lower limit for consideration as an efficient scattering material. Zinc has low melting point which may be a disadvantage in some dispensing situations, and it has no particular advantage over Aluminum in terms of cost or ease of manufacture into filament form. Copper suffers from corrosion unless treated with inhibitors. Copper plating of large quantities of fine filaments is an expensive process compared with shredding Aluminum foil or Aluminum-coated glass filaments. There are various

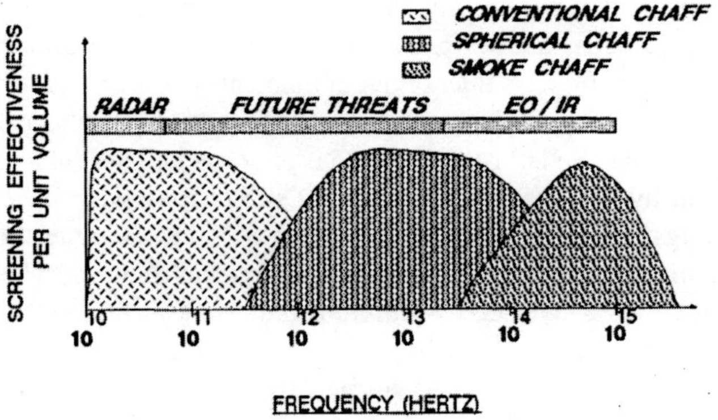

Fig.2: Frequency bands of coverage for various types of chaff material

metals that can be coated on glass fiber but Aluminum is most preferred as it has Low density and same time high electrical conductivity.[4]

Internationally at present Aluminum coated glass fibers are widely used. It is produced by passing glass fibers through molten Al to reach a final diameter of 25 μm (thinner than a human hair). This process is very costly and same time requires precise control of process parameter.

Research is going on to further reduce diameter so that more number of dipoles can be packed in given space, Same time focus is also there to develop non-conventional chaff material such as ellipsoidal and smoke chaff as frequency of radar is increasing and conventional chaff material won't be effective against them. Conventional chaff covers frequencies up to 1011 Hz. Smoke chaff can be effective above about 1014 Hz and ellipsoidal chaff fills the gap between these two regions.[5]

1.2 National Status of Chaff material

There is huge technology gap when it comes to production of Chaff material nationally. Currently Chaff material being produced nationally is Aluminum foil chaff, but Aluminum foil chaff has low packing density and it proves ineffective against high frequency. There is also lack of expertise in producing ultrafine metal coated glass fiber (25-30 μm) which is necessary to end reliance on imports. The available methods for producing metal coated glass fiber in large quantities require huge investment and precise control of process parameters. The challenge there is to produce chaff material with desired properties in limited investment and time. Internationally at present Aluminum coated glass fibers are widely used because it exhibits low density and high electrical conductivity. It can be prepared by passing glass fibers through molten Al to reach a final diameter of 25 μm but it is very costly and same time requires precise control of process parameter. So, normally a fine layer of metal is coated on non-conductive core of glass fiber or nylon filaments in order to reduce density and provide stiffness.[6] There are several different solvents that can be used to etch Al such as Sodium hydroxide, Phosphoric acid, Trisodium phosphate, Potassium hydroxide, etc. After etching slip coating were developed by immersing it in the free palmatic acid and aluminum palmitate as boundary layer lubricant which dispersed within an aqueous medium. The aqueous medium forms a hydrated Aluminum oxide on surface of Aluminum and promotes reaction between the surface oxide and palmatic acid to provide a chemically bonded surface slip coated layer of Aluminum Palmitate.[7,8]

2. Experimental Procedure

In present research work, pure Al fiber (30- 40 μm) were developed from 115 μm diameter fiber by etching with sodium hydroxide at specific concentration and time. It also gives In present research work, pure Al fiber (30- 40 μm) were developed from 115 μm diameter fiber by etching with sodium hydroxide at specific concentration and time. It also gives V-Al_2O_3 and Al_2O_3 as reaction by-product. Fibers produced after Wet etching is subjected to slip coating in different baths of fatty acid at varying dipping time to develop compact, uniform and good corrosion resistance film. The corrosion behaviour of this coating was studied by potentiodynamic test according to ASTM G 5 standard which is Standard Reference Test Method for making Potentiostatic and Potentiodynamic Anodic Polarization Measurements in 0.1 N H_2SO_4 and 3.5 % NaCl solution with the help of potentiostat/ galvanostat Gamry reference 600. The Compactness & uniformity of the film was determined by AC Impedance spectroscopy with the help of potentiostat/ galvanostat Gamry reference 600.[9] SEM analysis was performed to study morphology and micro-structural change due to variation in dipping time & concentration of the bath.

3. Results & Discussions

3.1 Microscopic Analysis of different Fibers by SEM

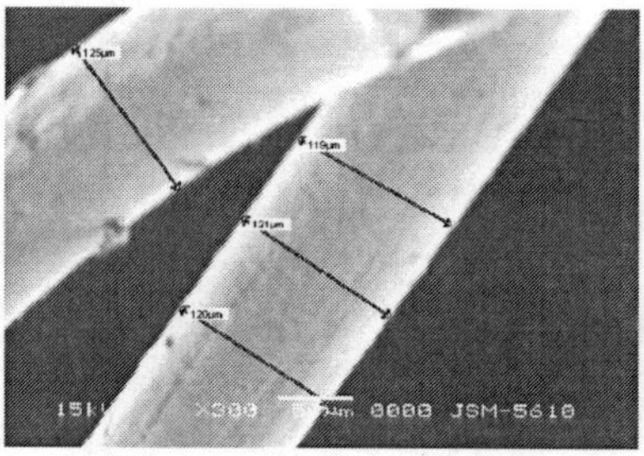

Fig. 3: As received Al fiber

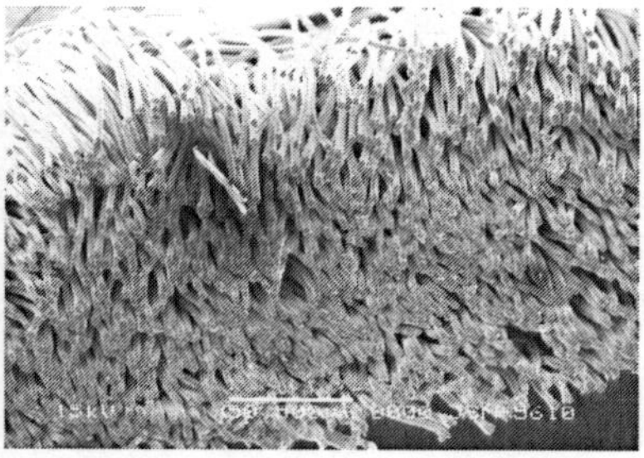

Fig. 4: Al Fibers after Wet Etching

Fig. 3 & 4 shows SEM images of aluminum fiber which reveals that coating is uniform and more compact.

3.2 Coating Thickness measurements by SEM

Fig. 4 & 5 show development of coating after wet etching and slip coating process which indicates that thickness of coating was found to be in the range of 13 to 14 μm.

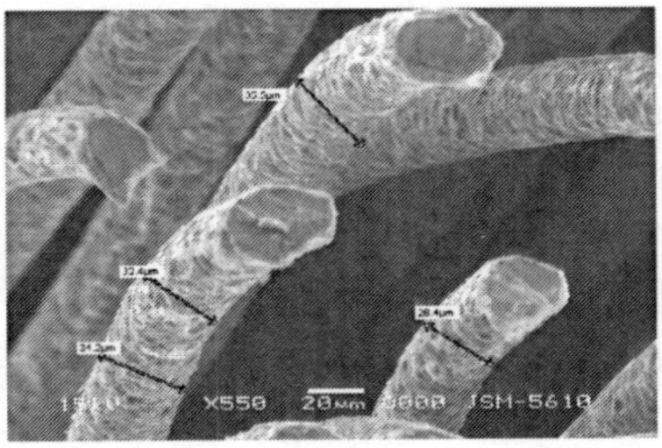

Fig. 4: Al Fibers after wet etching

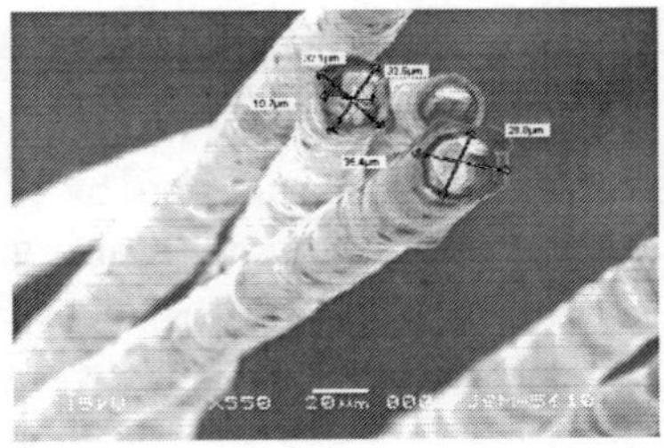

Fig. 5 : Al coated glass fiber

3.3 Results of Electrochemical Impedance Spectroscopy (EIS) scan in 3.5 % NaCl Solution

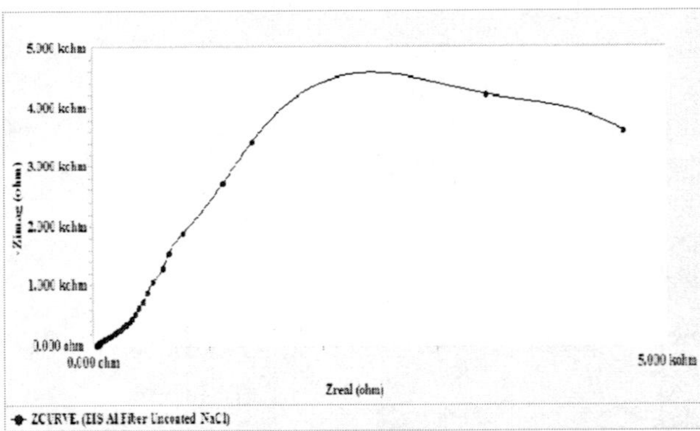

Fig. 6: EIS scan of uncoated pure Al fiber in 3.5 % NaCl solution.

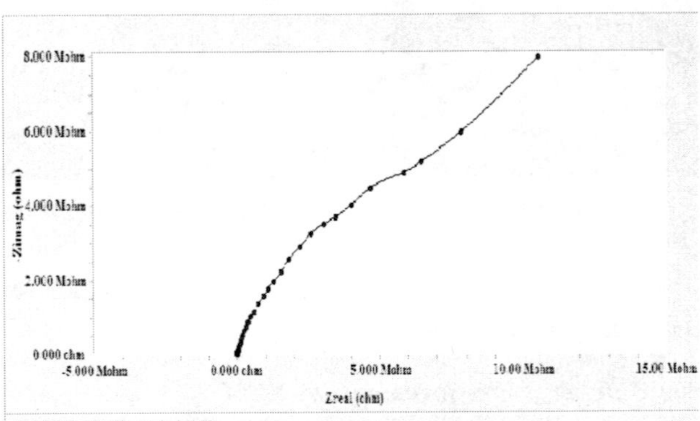

Fig. 7: EIS scan of coated pure Al fiber with Bath No 1 in 3.5 % NaCl solution.

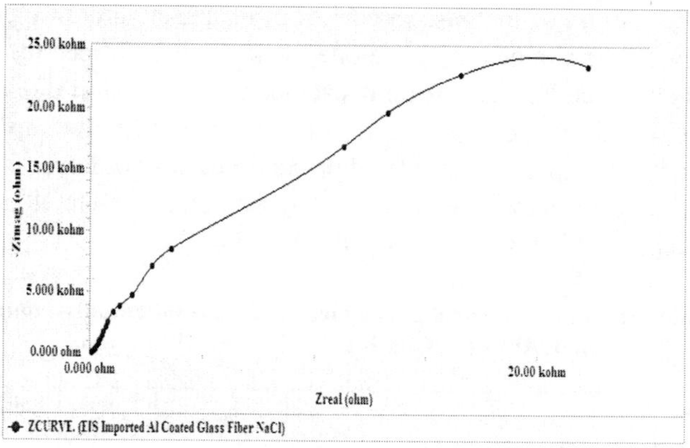

Fig. 8 : EIS scan of coated pure Al fiber with Bath No. 2 in 3.5 % NaCl solution.

Table 1: Capacitance value of EIS scan of fibres in 3.5 % NaCl solution

Sr. No.	Samples	Capacitance value(Ω)
1.	Uncoated Pure Al Fiber	3.4 kΩ
2.	Al Fibre	Coating with Bath-1
3.	Al Fibre	Coating with Bath-2

Fig. 5 to 7 shows the Electrochemical Impedance Spectroscopy scan coated Al fiber in 3.5 % NaCl solution. Coating developed with Bath-2 has lower capacitance value as compared to bath-1 which indicated that coating is slightly porous while coating developed with Bath-1 has higher capacitance value which indicated that coating was uniform, more compact and also has higher value of imaginary part of the impedance in the lower frequency region which indicates that the formation of protective film.

3.4 Corrosion behaviour of Al Fibers slip coated with Bath 1 in 3.5 % NaCl Solution

Fig. 8: Comparison of corrosion behaviours of Coated Al fiber with Uncoated and Imported Al fiber in 3.5 % NaCl solution

Figure 8. shows the various combination of potentiodynamic scans of slip coated Al fibers which were developed with Bath 1(Palmatic Acid, Stearic Acid, Myristic Acid) at different dipping time in 3.5 % NaCl Solution. The corrosion resistance of Al fiber increases due to development of slip coating using various combination of Bath at different process time but it doesn't show trend of increase in corrosion resistance due to increase in process time. The slip coating developed with Bath 1 (5 Seconds dipping time) has exhibited best corrosion resistance with corrosion rate of 0.008 mpy as it reveals exhibits passivation behaviour while the slip coating developed with Bath 1 (15 minutes dipping time) has got lower corrosion resistance with corrosion rate of 0.516 mpy with compared to all other slip coated samples which were developed using Bath 1.

Table 2: Electrochemical parameter of various potentiodynamic Scan of Al fiber of Bath 1 in 3.5 % NaCl solution.

Sr. No	Bath 1	I_{corr}	E_{corr}	Corrosion Rate (mpy)
1.	5 Second Dipping time	4.9 nA	-663.0 mV	0.008
2.	5 Minutes Dipping time	125.0 nA	-675.0 mV	0.214
3.	10 Minutes Dipping time	161.0 nA	-711.0 mV	0.276
4.	15 Minutes Dipping time	30.1 nA	-462.0 mV	0.516
5.	20 Minutes Dipping time	65.9 nA	-767.0 mV	0.113
6.	25 Minutes Dipping time	83.2 nA	-694.0 mV	0.322
7.	Uncoated Al Fiber	4.5 μA	-743.0 mV	7.825
8.	Imported Al Fiber	33.0 nA	-736.0 mV	0.056

3.5 Corrosion behaviour of Al Fibers slip coated with Bath 2 in 3.5 % NaCl Solution

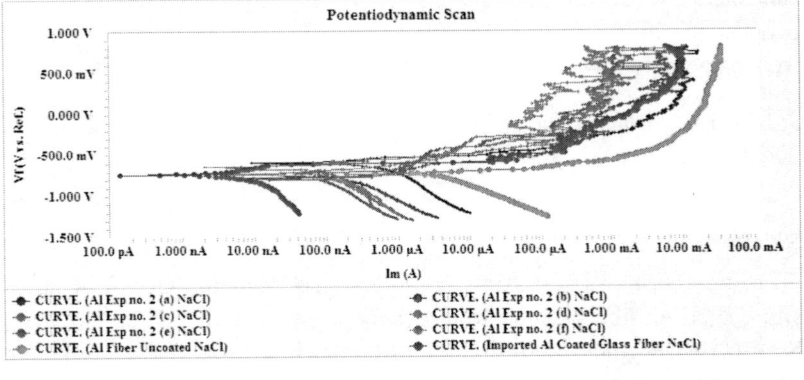

Fig. 9: Comparison of corrosion behaviours of Coated Al fiber with Uncoated and Imported Al fiber in 3.5 % NaCl solution.

Fig. 9 shows the various combination of potentiodynamic scans of slip coated Al fibers which were developed with Bath (Palmatic Acid, Stearic Acid, Lauric Acid) at different dipping time in 3.5 % NaCl Solution.

Table 3: Electrochemical parameter of various potentiodynamic Scan of Al fiber of Bath 2 in 3.5 % NaCl solution.

Sr. No	Bath 2	I_{corr}	E_{corr}	Corrosion Rate (mpy)
1.	5 Second Dipping time	365.0 nA	-600.0 mV	0.625
2.	5 Minutes Dipping time	139.0 nA	-784.0 mV	0.238
3.	10 Minutes Dipping time	104.0 nA	-718.0 mV	0.179
4.	15 Minutes Dipping time	135.0 nA	-734.0 mV	0.173
5.	20 Minutes Dipping time	68.7 nA	-788.0 mV	0.117
6.	25 Minutes Dipping time	11.4 nA	-646.0 mV	0.019
7.	Uncoated Al Fiber	4.5 μA	-743.0 mV	7.825
8.	Imported Al Fiber	33.0 nA	-736.0 mV	0.056

The corrosion resistance of Al fiber increases due to development of slip coating using various combination of Bath 2 at different process time and it shows trend of increase in corrosion resistance due to increase in process time. The slip coating developed with Bath 2 (25 minutes dipping time) has exhibited best corrosion resistance with corrosion rate of 0.019 mpy as it revels passivation behaviour while the slip coating developed with Bath 2 (5 Second dipping time) has got lower corrosion resistance with corrosion rate of 0.625 mpy with compared to all other slip coated samples which were developed using Bath 2.

4. Conclusion

- Al fibers slip coated in Bath 1 with 5 sec dipping time shows best corrosion resistance with corrosion rate of 0.008 mpy in 3.5 % NaCl solution as compared to imported Al fiber.
- Al fibers slip coated in Bath 2 with 25 min dipping time shows best corrosion resistance with corrosion rate of 0.019 mpy in 3.5 % NaCl solution as compared to imported Al fiber.

- different coated specimen developed using Bath-1 shows better corrosion resistance than Bath 2 in 3.5 % NaCl solution .
- Finally it can be concluded that the coating developed on Al fiber using new organic media has got better corrosion resistance, good compactness and uniformity with compared to imported fiber.

References

1. Brian C. F. Butters, "Slip Coating Chaff", US Patents 4,649,076 Pg no. 1.
2. Goebel, Greg. The Wizard War: WW2 & The Origins of Radar v.2.0.2, retrieved 2008-03-18 Jones, R. V. (1978). Most Secret War: British Scientific Intelligence 1939–1945. Hamish Hamilton, London. ISBN 0-241-89746-7.
3. Brian C.F. Butters, "Chaff", I.E.E. PROC. Vol. 129, Part F, No. 3 pg no. 197.]
4. Brian C.F. Butters, "Chaff", I.E.E. PROC. Vol. 129, Part F, No. 3 pg no. 199-200.
5. John A. Konotckick "Ellipsoidal Chaff", US Patents 5,212,488 sheet no. 5.
6. Thomas A Davis "Recovery of Sodium Hydroxide and Aluminium Hydroxide from Etching.
7. waste", US Patents 5,049,233 page 1, [6] [6]. Brian C.F. Butters, "Chaff", I.E.E. PROC. Vol.129, Part F, No.3 pp.199-200.].
8. Brian C F Butters, Ian D Pollicott, "Slip coating Chaff", US Patents 4,649,079, p. 1.
9. A K Sivadasan, Packia Selvam and Sankara Narayanan Potty," Microwave assisted hydrolysis of aluminium metal and preparation of high surface area V-Al_2O_3 powder" Bull. Mater. Sci., Vol. 33, No. 6, December 2010, p. 739].
10. W. Stephen Tait, An Introduction to electrochemical Corrosion Testing For Practicing Engineers and Scientists. Pair ODocs Publications, pp. 18-26.

46

Satellites for the Conduct of Activities in Oceans

—Ajey Lele

During 2008, the Science Magazine has published the findings from the research undertaken by the group of scientists from the School of Life Sciences, Arizona State University, United States titled 'A Global Map of Human Impact on Marine Ecosystems'. This study attempted to determine the ecological impact of human activities like fishing, shipping, pollution, climate change etc on the oceans. Scientists found that almost no areas associated with eco-system of the seas have been left unspoiled and that more than 40% of the world's oceans have been heavily affected. In comparison, the oceans at the poles are found less affected, but melting ice sheets still leaves them vulnerable. At the same time it is also important to note that the lifeline of the world totally depends of the activities humans undertake in the oceans. Maritime transpor-tation is indispensable to global economy as over 90% of the world's trade is carried by sea. Trade through oceans would continue to happen since it is most economical way to do business. Oceans also are at the strategic heartland for many centuries and projection of sea power both during peacetime and combat operations has been vital for projection of state's influence and capabilities. The marine environment has historically been an arena for power struggles at the same time a domain of major global business activities. From geostrategic perspective maritime domain has a pecu-liar character, beyond power struggle it is also a domain for international cooperation and diplomacy. Navies do undertake goodwill visits to other states and ports. Broadly, maritime sphere could be viewed as a unique domain where hard power, economic power and soft power coexist.

The 21st century is witnessing growth in the activities in the oceans. Energy a vital resource for human survival has a direct relationship with the oceans: it being the producer/supplier (oil exploration) of the oil and a medium for energy transporta-tion. Activities from merchant shipping, tourism to fishing happening at island and costal states are known to play an important role for the survival of some of such nation-states, because oceans are the only lifelines for them. Today, various types of machineries and technologies are found getting used to undertake several activities in the oceans. Increasingly, technology is found ominously expanding the extent of interactions between humans and the sea, extending the limits of exploration and exploitation to an extraordinary level, both for better or for worse. Amongst various technologies which are finding an increasing role for managing the affairs in the ocean, one technology stands out specifically for its widespread applicability and that is the space technology. The most important aspect of this technology is that the overall architecture associated with this technology operates not from the seas but, from the outer space and has significant use for conduct of activities in the oceans. All in all, satellites in space are found playing an important role towards managing the affairs in the oceans and for the oceans.

Presently, various maritime agencies have established sophisticated infrastructures depending on their role and requirements both in oceans and inland. The inland establishments are basically the ports and other associated facilities. In the oceans, there are various platforms operating which include luxury ships, merchant ships, oil tankers to various vehicles in the service of cost-guard and navy including underwater vehicles. Navies also have aircrafts/drones which are operated either from the oceanic platforms or costal airfields. In addition, there are some additional robotic (self-driven) vehicles which are operated either on the sea surface or underwater. To organise the activities of all these systems timely information is required and also there is a need to share such information immediately (at times in real time) with various concerned agencies. Basically, such information includes weather conditions, navigational inputs, traffic details, information from the ports and other situational information. Historically, before the advent of satellites, various structures used for undertaking maritime surveillance involved ships and shore based installations, radar units and other observational units. Some such structures, still exist.

In the past, major maritime powers had encountered various difficulties in the conduct of day-to-day operations owing to technological limitations. In the arena of communications, particularly long-haul wireless communications had limitations due to limited availability of the high-frequency (HF) band owing to environmental challenges. Navigation systems also were known to have inaccuracies. Weather forecasting had limitations owing lack of widespread observational base. All this used to impact both civilian and military operations. Particularly, Navies had issues with respect to target identification for beyond-line-of-sight (BLOS) targets and also had problems for correct engagement of the targets with the weapon systems.

Few years back, for collecting information on weather conditions, various ships had assistance only from their on-board observatories and radiosonde balloons which are routinely send in air and are monitored by specific instruments (like theodolites, radars etc) to get knowledge about winds in upper atmosphere. Underwater robots (gliders) are used for collecting data on ocean conditions to know about possibility of development of any hurricanes and their possible movements. All such inputs help to know the current sea-state and also help to forecast the future weather conditions including hurricane intensity forecasts. Today, satellites help to gather such and vari-ous other inputs required in conduct of various maritime activities. Satellites provide accurate navigational inputs and secured communications. Broadly, satellites play a major role towards collecting, processing and disseminating information required for smooth conduct of various activities' in the maritime domain.

From early 1960s, space technologies are being successfully used for various purposes. Over last five decades or so, phenomenal technological developments have taken place in the outer space arena. Particularly, the developments in the sensors arena has made a major impact towards making humans understand the universe better. Satellites have emerged as an incredible tools for observing the planet earth. Actually, when satellite is observing the earth, in reality on most the occasions it is observing the oceans since they occupy more than two third area on the planet earth. Various types of satellites have increased the human knowledge about different oceans, peninsulas, archipelagos and other water bodies. Today, almost every activity in maritime domain has direct or indirect dependence on space technologies. Over the years, countries are launching specific satellites like for meteorology, remote sensing, communication and navigation. These satellites come in all shapes and sizes and are positioned in dif-ferent orbits depending on their character and utility. There are some satellites which have been designed and developed exclusively for specific maritime activities too.

Understanding ocean atmosphere is vital for undertaking any activity in the ocean. Presently, satellites offer information about ocean bathymetry, sea surface temperature, ocean colour, coral reefs, and sea and lake ice conditions. Like information about the sea surface temperature is useful for fish industry because the presence of fish in the sea is related to the zones of warmer water in the sea. Overall, the information about different atmospheric parameters is useful for various purposes from tourism industry to scientific research to disaster management. Space based ocean monitoring systems have greatly enhanced the understanding of the core meteo-marine param-eters and overall marine environment. UNESCO's (United Nations scientific, cultural and educational organization) Intergovernmental Oceanographic Commission (IOC) promotes international cooperation and coordinates programmes in marine research, services, observation systems, hazard mitigation, and capacity development. Such programmes depends heavily on the inputs generated by the satellites. The satellite imagery obtained from the satellites launched with modern sensors like the synthetic aperture radars (SARs) are used for applications such as wave and wind retrievals, ship detection, monitoring of sea ice, and the interpretation of signatures of surface cur-rent gradients over oceanic fronts, internal waves, and shallow-water bathymetry. SAR technology is best suited for oil spill monitoring especially over wide areas.

Maritime surveillance is another domain of great importance both for business purposes as well as strategic purposes, and presently various maritime surveillance initiatives are in place. Surveillance is a key element to exercise national sovereignty at sea. One of the main purposes to carryout surveillance is to identify and deter infringements to regulations. Such infringements could be intentional or non-intentional. There are various surveillance and other reporting systems in place like VMS (Vessel Monitoring Systems), AIS (Automatic Identification System) etc and many of them are known do depend on the inputs from the satellite and they also use satellites for communications purposes.

Using satellites for navigation at seas is happening for many years, particularly since the United States global navigational system commonly known as GPS has been made available to everyone. Today, there are few more satellite based navigational systems in place and they are also used for the purposes for the travel in the seas. Also, a major boost to use of satellites for maritime communications took place when the International Maritime Organisation (IMO) decided to develop international maritime satellite system during 1972. For effective understanding of the challenges associated with the security, safety, economy and environment in the maritime domain there is need to develop Maritime Domain Awareness (MDA) and this has become possible owing the assistance from various satellites systems. Today, human activities' in the seas face various challenges from natural and man-made distracters (like say oil spill) to piracy and hence, it is very essential to have structures like MDA in place.

Overall, the experiences of the state actors and other private agencies undertaking various activities in the seas for last few decades indicate that presence of satellite systems in space is assisting their work significantly and bringing in more timeliness, accuracy and efficiency to their work. At the same time it is important to appreciate that satellite technologies would not be able to give answers to all the challenges in the maritime domain. Almost a decade back it was known that 40% of the world's oceans have been heavily polluted and possibly increase in the activities during the last decade has increased this damage further. For all these years satellites are getting effectively used for the conduct of various activities in the maritime domain and since the modern generation satellites with state-of art sensor technologies are increasingly making the concept of 'transparent seas' tangible, it is important that space technologies are effectively puts in use to help improve the 'health" of the oceans.

47

Cryptocurrencies - Potential Threat to Our National Security

— ***Yogesh Udgire***

What is a Cryptocurrency ?

It is an encrypted data string that denotes a unit of currency. It is monitored and organized by a peer-to-peer network also known as a blockchain, which also serves as a secure ledger of transactions. released in 2009 as open-source code. Blockchain technology made it all work, providing a system where data structures (blocks) are broad-casted, validated, and registered in a public, distributed database through a network of communication endpoints (nodes).

Cryptocurrencies have no borders—anyone can send them anytime anywhere, with-out delays or additional/hidden charges from intermediaries. Given their nature, they are more secure from fraud and identity theft as cryptocurrencies cannot be counter-feited, and personal information is behind a cryptographic wall.

What has Cryptocurrency to do with National Security ?

It enables "transactions which financial authorities can't interdict".

"It's just a more recent and increasingly more common way of transacting that serves anyone looking for alternative payment methods."

There are actually over 700 cryptocurrencies, but only some are readily traded in open market.

Over the past few years, several experts have voiced concerns that the Islamic State and other terrorist groups can use or are using crypto currencies such as Bitcoin as a new funding stream to further their operations. Its proven that the use of digital currencies among terrorists is not widespread—yet. Terrorist financing methods and cryptocurrency technology are both Dynamic, however, and the world could soon see the worst-case scenario unfolding. Greater pressure on existing terrorist finance methods coupled with easier-to-use cryptocurrencies that give users greater anonymity may well lead to a large-scale adoption of the technology by extremists.

At present, cryptocurrencies and not a ready to-go solution for terrorist financiers. Most types afford only limited anonymity and with conducting know-your-customer (KYC) and anti-money laundering (AML) norms its becoming difficult being anonymous.

It is difficult to quickly transfer large amounts of money through these systems currently but the way the prices are skyrocketing days are not far, also there is limited acceptance of digital cash in regions where many terrorist groups are most active i.e. the Middle East and North Africa with digital the terrorists are getting access to international financial system, new cryptocurrency technologies are proving to be an attractive alternative, adopting fast and if so, how quickly, is difficult. The answer depends on a host of unknowns, such as what other technologies are around the corner, how the public uses the new cryptocurrencies, and how useful or safe they prove to be. Digital currencies could be used for general funding; for money laundering; or to pay the personnel, associates, and vendors that keep the terrorist machine running. But there can be barriers to use as well, depending on the type of group and how its operations are financed. to use crypto currency, partly because the latter is difficult to convert into a form that could be readily used most cryptocurrency offers neither sufficient anonymity nor ease of use for would-be donors, and until that changes, it remains unlikely to become a significant source of funds. large network of associates in drug and other illicit markets in Latin Ameri-ca's tri-border area integrate many important cryptocurrency services, such as exchanges where cryptocurrency is bought and sold, into various anti-money-laundering programmes.

The more successful a currency becomes, the greater the pressure from users and other stakeholders to work within the traditional financial system and abide by these laws. Greater scrutiny by authorities will inevitably follow.

Examine how to "scale up" Blockchain technology for faster banking, trading, clearing and settlements. With all the trepidation bitcoin has brought, it's underlying frame-work, the Blockchain, has begun to spread like wildfire as more and more imagineers, developers, scientists, cryptographers, mathematicians etc. begin to build new concepts around the decentralisation of trust itself.

Challenges of Cryptocurrency Evolution to National Security

Deanonymization is currently the largest issue preventing terrorists from using cryptocurrency.

Additionally, sophistication terms of cyber technology, with a wide variety of tools at their disposal. They could attack terrorist groups through vulnerabilities not known to the public. Furthermore, even if the crypto currency itself is secure, the computers used for the transactions are vulnerable to the same types of attacks any computer system is, including social engineering, hacking, and physical destruction. Even without these challenges, some terrorist organizations distrust systems funded by Western governments or researchers.

Despite these limitations, technological progress promises advances that could accelerate the adoption of cryptocurrency for both lawful and illicit uses, including ter-rorist financing. Many of the steps currently required to secure anonymous use of cryptocurrencies are not user-friendly, requiring a moderate degree of sophistication and the cumbersome manual transfer of data from secure offline systems. But these usability challenges are likely to fade.

Best practices for security will become more widespread as they become easier to use and better known, which has been the case with other technologies e.g WhatsApp, traceability of transactions, anonymization, and the ability to hide IP addresses.

For now, cryptocurrencies are unlikely to be stable enough or trusted enough for widespread use—and funding is only one small but critical part of terrorist operations. Although cryptocurrency technologies continue to have significant limitations for terrorist use, those barriers should decline over time and cause the use of digital currency to spread to other groups. Terrorists' embrace of cryptocurrencies is not yet apparent, but it is not likely far off on the horizon.

The research, being conducted by Yaya J Fanusie of the Foundation for the Defence of Democracies, is looking as much at how blockchain can help prevent illicit activity as how it can enable it.

"What is needed is a more informed discussion about what the implications may be, because there's so much defensiveness – there's defensiveness on both sides, and I think we should come a little bit to the center, point out potential threats, but also point out benefits it has."

> bitcoin was being used as part of the 'WannaCry' ransomware attacks, in which an estimated 200,000 victims were asked to pay bitcoin to regain access to encrypted computer files.

While potential threats to national security – such as the raising of funds for terrorism, the circumventing of sanctions and the ransoming of vital infrastructure – remain worth researching, Enumerated an International Expert named Fanusie

"Controlling shouldn't always start with criminal responsibility," she believes:

> President Trump recently signed a foreign sanctions bill into law that included provisions mandating that governments monitor cryptocurrency transactions. The bill was passed by the U.S congress last month and is directed at Russia, Iran, and North Korea.... Lyudmila Bokova (deputy chairwoman at the Federation Council's constitutional committee)

The policy makers have to address a question : "How do Government deal with something that they can't control?"

"Bitcoin is like a rebellious teenager, it wants to do its own thing", he said. "So what do you do? Do you ban it? No, you want to have a good relationship with it and influence how it develops"

The Australian government has just recognized digital currency as a legal payment method.

Since July 1, purchases done using digital currencies such as bitcoin are exempt from the country's Goods and Services Tax to avoid double taxation. As such, traders and investors will not be levied taxes for buying and selling them through legal exchange platforms.

Japan, which legitimized bitcoin as a form of payment last April, already expects more than 20,000 merchants to accept bitcoin payments. Other countries are joining the bandwagon, albeit partially: businesses and some of the public organizations in Switzerland, Norway, and the Netherlands. In a recent study, unique, active users of cryptocurrency wallets are pegged between 2.9 and 5.8 million, most of which are in North America and Europe.

But what does the acceptance and adoption of digital currencies have to do with on-line threats? A lot, actually. As cryptocurrencies like bitcoin gain real-world traction, so will cybercriminal threats that abuse it. But how, exactly? What does this mean to businesses and everyday users?

Unfortunately, the same apparent profitability, convenience, and pseudonymity of cryptocurrencies also made them ideal for cybercriminals, as ransomware operators showed. The increasing popularity of cryptocurrencies coincide with the incidences of malware that infect systems and devices, turning them into armies of cryptocurren-cymining machines.

Cryptocurrency-mining malware use similar attack vectors

Bad guys turn to using malware to skirt around these challenges. There is, however a caveat for cybercriminal miners: internet-connected devices and machines, while fast enough to process network data, don't have extensive number-crunching capabilities. To offset this, cryptocurrency-mining malware are designed to zombify botnets of computers to perform these tasks. Others avoided subtlety altogether—in 2014, Harvard's supercomputer cluster Odyssey was used to illicitly mine dogecoins. During the same year, a similar incident happened to US agency National Science Foundation's own supercomputers. In early February 2017, one of the US Federal Reserve's servers was misused to mine for bitcoins.

Cryptocurrency-mining malware can impair system performance and risk end users and businesses to information theft, hijacking, and a plethora of other malware. And by turning these machines into zombies, cryptocurrency malware can even inadvertently make its victims part of the problem.

Bitcoin was the central currency on Silk Road, the infamous and anonymous market-place that was only accessible over the TOR anonymous browsing network on the deep web, and which was closed by the FBI in October 2013. Silk Road was a haven for drug sales, hitment, dodgy porn and other illegal goods.

This prompted US Senator Charles Schumer to call for the site to be shut down, explicitly linking it to bitcoin, which he called a "surrogate currency" and then the US DEA seized bitcoins from a US resident for purchasing a controlled substance in June 2013.

In August 2013, 22 bitcoin companies involved in bitcoin were subpoenaed by the state of New York, a US judge ruled that bitcoin is a form of money; and the Bitcoin Foundation received a cease and desist letter from the state of California.

> A recent article in Newsweek, Leah McGrath Goodman reports that hundreds of ex-perts inside the nation's defence and intelligence agencies, as well as private-sector researchers in finance, technology and various think tanks across the country—some of them under contract with the U.S. government—are now investigating how virtual currencies could undermine America's long-standing ability to disrupt the financial networks of its foes and even permanently upend parts of the global financial system.

"There is a real danger and a challenge here with respect to virtual currencies," says Juan Zarate, a senior adviser at Washington think tank Center for Strategic and International Studies and on the board of advisers for San Francisco's Coinbase, one of the most popular virtual currency exchanges in the world. "And it runs contrary to the very fundamentals of the transparency and accountability that we've tried to build for the last three de-cades to tackle terrorism, human trafficking, money-laundering and many other types of criminal activity."

This ability to financially disrupt, disable and dismantle nefarious networks, is crucial to national security, The biggest concern about virtual currencies, Zarate says, is that terrorists and other enemies might create one so powerful and so untrackable, that they'll no longer need the global banking system, THE World uses to financially starve them.

> *defence and intelligence agencies are already trying to figure out how they might infiltrate or block such a malicious financial network.*

Computer Sciences has hired hundreds of technologists and experts across the banking, insurance and health care sectors to, which Satoshi Nakamoti, the founder of bitcoin revolutionised.

Bala Venkataraman, global chief technology officer of banking and capital markets for Computer Sciences Corp., a digital information-technology company whose sister firm, CSRA Inc., runs the IT backbone of the National Security Agency (NSA) comments:

> *"In a cryptocurrency world, you know who becomes the bank?" he asks. "You and I. You become not just the bank, but the central bank. And that can have enormous ramifications for things like sovereign authority. By 2040, I think we may be fully transitioned over to cryptocurrency. I don't think anyone can stop it from happening."*

> *"With the introduction of Blockchain, a disruption of the global banking system is inevitable," he added in the article.*

No one can stop it from happening? No one except the Americans perhaps – and very likely under the banner of Homeland Security and the Patriot Act.

One significant terrorist act on US soil, alleged or proven to be funded by Bitcoin or another cryptocurrency is very likely all it will take.

Ransomware called WannaCry used leaked hacking tools stolen from the National Security Agency to attack an estimated 200,000 computers in 150 countries.

48

Ensuring the Sea's Indian Maritime Security Strategy

— Dr. Sachin Pendse

India has somehow overlooked the importance of Indian Ocean and had been pre-occupied by its own continental considerations. The importance of Indian Ocean for India is due to three basic factors. Firstly its central location along the Indian Ocean global trade routes that have gained importance in recent decade as it is connecting the major engines of the international economy in the Northern Atlantic and Asia-Pacific. Secondly the Indian Ocean region (IOR) is home to some two billion people. The region infested with a range of complex socio-economic and political conflicts that pose a threat to peace and stability not only in the IOR but also globally. However, the densely populated littoral is also vulnerable to natural or environmental disasters. Finally, the Indian Ocean is rich in natural resources. Forty per cent of the world's off-shore oil production takes place in the Indian Ocean basin.

Today, the almost 90,000 vessels in the world's commercial fleet transport 9.84 billion tonnes of goods worth 5 trillion USD per year pass through the Sea Lanes of Communications (SLOCs) of Indian Ocean to reach nine major ports. Of the total energy resources some 36 million barrels per day—equivalent to about 40 per cent of the world's oil supply and 64 per cent of oil trade—travel through the entryways into and out of the Indian Ocean. Its 4.2 billion inhabitants speak over 3,000 different languages and constitute 61 per cent of the global population. The 36 regional nations they dwell in constitute two of the three largest economies as well as 10 of the 14 smallest. These nations also have seven of the world's 10 largest standing militaries and five of the world's declared nuclear states. With 66 per cent of global oil, 50 per cent of the global container traffic and

33 per cent of global cargo trade passing through the IOR, which stretches from the Persian Gulf to the west to the Malacca Straits in the east.

Post globalization era saw rapidly changing geo-political and geo-strategic checks and balances in the Indian Ocean Region (IOR). India, in its own way had set on path of economic liberalization and growth that had their imperatives in securing its Seal Lanes of Communications and its own maritime domain. The rise of Asian economies, particularly China and India, increasing importance of SLOC's passing through Indian Ocean and reduced presence of USA in IOR, changed the strategic imperatives for India. India looked upon, as a balancing regional force had to change its policies particularly with its maritime domain. Indian Navy remains the principal expression of India's maritime power playing a central role in her security and national interest in maritime domain. It with these imperatives the Indian Navy formulated a policy document in 2015 known as the "Ensuring Secure Seas", the Indian Maritime Security Strategy.

The Indian Navy in its two policy documents published earlier, articulated the Indian navy's maritime strategic outlook, defined its parameters of its employment, and provided overarching guidance for its evolution as a combat force. With the dynamic strategic dimensions and increasing importance of its maritime domain, the earlier policy documents had to be revised to form the third maritime guidance policy document in 2015, "Ensuring Secure Seas", the Indian Maritime Security Strategy. (IMSS-2015).

The key determinants that shaped the maritime security strategy include:

- Broader maritime strategic imperatives.
- Specific maritime security drivers. The key to development of the strategy is India's dependence on seas for national development and steady shift in global economic and military imperatives. The strategic imperatives look into the unique maritime location of India and its reach across the IOR which is also the hub of global trade and commerce. Another important feature is of India's relations with its maritime neighbours and role in maritime neighbourhood based on mutual respect for international laws and desire for cooperative, inclusive development.

The maritime doctrine has increased focuses on:

1. safety and Security of seaborne trade and energy routes, especially in the IOR

2. Importance of maintaining freedom of navigation and strengthening the international legal regime at sea, and
3. Cooperation and coordination between navies to counter common threats.

The maritime security drivers have shown increased complexity particularly due to traditional and non-traditional threats, with continuing increased challenges across the regional maritime security environments. This called for increased focus on these threats. The increased role of Navy to address to both these forms of threats needed structural and organizational changes to strengthen mechanisms for interagency coordination for maritime security.

The dedicated focus in on:

(a) Combating persisting nature of threats emanating from sea
(b) Strengthening mechanisms for interagency coordination and cooperation and
(c) Developing seamless cohesive maritime security framework.

The National Maritime Interests in strategy:

1. Protecting India's sovereignty and territorial integrity in maritime environment.
2. Promote safety and security of Indian citizens, shipping, fishing, energy supply, and resources in maritime domain.
3. Pursue peace and stability and security in India's maritime zones, neighbourhood, and other areas of maritime interest.
4. Preserve and protect other national interests in maritime domain

India's Maritime Security- Its Aim and Objectives:

1. To deter conflict and coercion against India.
2. To conduct maritime military operations in a manner that enables early termination of conflict on terms favourable to India.
3. To shape favourable and positive maritime environment, for enhancing net security in India's areas of maritime interests.
4. To protect Indian coastal and offshore assets against attacks and threats emanating from sea.
5. To develop requisite maritime force levels and maintain the capability for meeting India's maritime security requirements.

"Ensuring the Secure Seas: Indian Maritime Security Strategy", is an outcome of comprehensive review of India's maritime environment, including prevailing threats, challenges, and future trends. Comprising of five constituent strategies, each with its multiple doctrinal roles and associated objectives, Ensuring Secure Seas, provides a holistic perspective. The Indian Navy will continue to grow in its force levels and capabilities for undertaking the range of missions, tasks and responsibilities to provide overall maritime security and safeguard national interests. The efforts to develop the three elements of naval combat power i.e conceptual, human, and physical will be progressed. The focus will remain on developing and maintaining the navy as a formidable force, multi-dimensional, balanced, and networked force, capable of countering the full range of maritime threats and challenges.

As stated earlier, "Ensuring the Secure Seas" has evolved out of changing global geo-political situations. Though futuristic, it will probably have to realign itself as the checks and balances will change in the highly volatile scenarios keeping in mind the China, North Korea and Pakistan factors and the rapidly spreading intensity of Low Intensity Conflicts (LIC), maritime terrorism etc. Prime Minister Shri 'Narendra Modi' unveiled a four-part framework for the Indian Ocean which focuses on: defending India's maritime territory and interests; deepening economic and security cooperation with maritime neighbours and island states; promoting collective action for peace and security; and seeking a more integrated and cooperative future for sustainable development. This framework was more or less in tandem with the naval policy, though published a bit later. The focus remains on India's core strategic arena of the Indian Ocean. It is now that the Indian Navy has a greater role to play.

Statutory Disclaimer

- Published by Adv. Shrihari Narayan Desai, 30/1 Parekh Mahal Lady Jamshetji Road, Mahim, Mumbai – 400 16, Email snd4950@gmail.com
- Views expressed by the Authors in this Compendium are their individual views and not the views of FINS.
- FINS has received declaration that the Articles written by the Authors are their original creation and it does not infringe any Copyright of any other person.
- FINS has no intention of hurting sentiments, values of any Caste, Creed, Religion and the published material is a part of platform for freedom of expression for the writers, thinkers, scholars, academician, policy makers and such intellect.
-

Index

M